Woodrow Wilson and American Internationalism

In this new work, one of the world's leading historians of U.S. foreign relations, Lloyd E. Ambrosius, addresses enduring questions about American political culture and statecraft by focusing on President Woodrow Wilson and the United States in international relations during and after World War I. Updated to include recent historiography as well as an original introduction and conclusion, *Woodrow Wilson and American Internationalism* features nine different essays closely linked together by the themes of Wilson's understanding of Americanism, his diplomacy to create a new world order in the wake of World War I, and the legacy of his foreign policy. Examining the exclusive as well as universal dimensions of Wilsonianism, Ambrosius assesses not only Wilson's role during his presidency but also his legacy in defining America's place in world history. Speaking to the transnational turn in American history, Ambrosius shows how Wilson's liberal internationalist vision of a new world order would shape U.S. foreign relations for the next century.

Lloyd E. Ambrosius is Emeritus Professor of History and Samuel Clark Waugh Distinguished Professor of International Relations at the University of Nebraska–Lincoln, which honored him with the Louise Pound-George Howard Distinguished Career Award in 2015. He is the author of *Woodrow Wilson and the American Diplomatic Tradition: The Treaty Fight in Perspective* (Cambridge University Press, 1987), *Wilsonian Statecraft: Theory and Practice of Liberal Internationalism during World War I* (1991), and *Wilsonianism: Woodrow Wilson and His Legacy in American Foreign Relations* (2002).

Cambridge Studies in U.S. Foreign Relations

Edited by

Paul Thomas Chamberlin, *Columbia University*
Lien-Hang T. Nguyen, *Columbia University*

This series showcases cutting-edge scholarship in U.S. foreign relations that employs dynamic new methodological approaches and archives from the colonial era to the present. The series is guided by the ethos of transnationalism, focusing on the history of American foreign relations in a global context rather than privileging the United States as the dominant actor on the world stage.

Also in the Series

Renata Keller, *Mexico's Cold War: Cuba, the United States, and the Legacy of the Mexican Revolution*

Elisabeth Leake, *The Defiant Border: The Afghan-Pakistan Borderlands in the Era of Decolonization, 1936–1965*

Tuong Vu, *Vietnam's Communist Revolution: The Power of Limits and Ideology*

Michael Neagle, *America's Forgotten Colony: Cuba's Isle of Pines*

Geoffrey Stewart, *Vietnam's Lost Revolution: Ngô Đình Diệm's Failure to Build an Independent Nation, 1955–1963*

Woodrow Wilson and American Internationalism

LLOYD E. AMBROSIUS

University of Nebraska–Lincoln

CAMBRIDGE
UNIVERSITY PRESS

CAMBRIDGE
UNIVERSITY PRESS

One Liberty Plaza, 20th Floor, New York, NY 10006, USA

Cambridge University Press is part of the University of Cambridge.

It furthers the University's mission by disseminating knowledge in the pursuit of
education, learning, and research at the highest international levels of excellence.

www.cambridge.org
Information on this title: www.cambridge.org/9781316615065
DOI: 10.1017/9781316678602

© Lloyd E. Ambrosius 2017

First published 2017

Printed in the United States of America by Sheridan Books, Inc.

A catalogue record for this publication is available from the British Library.

Library of Congress Cataloging-in-Publication Data
Names: Ambrosius, Lloyd E., author.
Title: Woodrow Wilson and American internationalism /
Lloyd E. Ambrosius, University of Nebraska–Lincoln.
Description: New York, NY: Cambridge University Press, 2017. |
Series: Cambridge studies in U.S. foreign relations |
Includes bibliographical references and index.
Identifiers: LCCN 2017008235 | ISBN 9781107163065 (hardback) |
ISBN 9781316615065 (pbk.)
Subjects: LCSH: United States – Foreign relations – 1913–1921. |
Wilson, Woodrow, 1856–1924 – Influence. | Internationalism – History – 20th century.
Classification: LCC E768.A443 2017 | DDC 327.73009/041–dc23
LC record available at https://lccn.loc.gov/2017008235

ISBN 978-1-107-16306-5 Hardback
ISBN 978-1-316-61506-5 Paperback

To my wife
Margery M. Ambrosius
and our sons
Walter T. Ambrosius
and Paul W. Ambrosius

Contents

Acknowledgments

The chapters in this book first appeared as articles in journals and chapters in edited books.

Chapter 1 originally appeared as Lloyd E. Ambrosius, "U.S. Military and Diplomatic Affairs during the Gilded Age and Progressive Era," *The Oxford Encyclopedia of American Military and Diplomatic History*, ed. Timothy J. Lynch (New York: Oxford University Press, 2013), Vol. 1, 420–32.

Chapter 2 originally appeared as Lloyd E. Ambrosius, "Making the World Safe for Democracy," *The Guide to U.S. Foreign Policy: A Diplomatic History*, eds. Thomas W. Zeiler and Robert J. McMahon (Sag Harbor, NY: DWJ Books, 2012), Vol. I, 129–41.

Chapter 3 originally appeared as Lloyd E. Ambrosius, "Woodrow Wilson and *The Birth of a Nation*: American Democracy and International Relations," *Diplomacy and Statecraft* 18 (December 2007): 689–718.

Chapter 4 originally appeared as Lloyd E. Ambrosius, "The Others in Wilsonianism," *U.S. Foreign Policy and the Other*, eds. Michael Patrick Cullinane and David Ryan (Oxford and New York: Berghahn Books, 2014), 124–41.

Chapter 5 originally appeared as Lloyd E. Ambrosius, "The Great War, Americanism Reconsidered, and the Anti-Wilson Crusade," *A Companion to Theodore Roosevelt*, ed. Serge Ricard (Malden, MA: Wiley-Blackwell, 2011), 468–84.

Chapter 6 originally appeared as Lloyd E. Ambrosius, "Woodrow Wilson, Alliances, and the League of Nations," *The Journal of the Gilded Age and Progressive Era* 5 (April 2006): 139–65.

Chapter 7 originally appeared as Lloyd E. Ambrosius, "Wilsonian Diplomacy and Armenia: The Limits of Power and Ideology," *The American Response to the Armenian Genocide*, ed. Jay Winter (Cambridge: Cambridge University Press, 2003), 113–45.

Chapter 8 originally appeared as Lloyd E. Ambrosius, "Woodrow Wilson and George W. Bush: Historical Comparisons of Ends and Means in Their Foreign Policies," *Diplomatic History* 30 (June 2006): 509–43.

Chapter 9 originally appeared as Lloyd E. Ambrosius, "Legacy and Reputation," *A Companion to Woodrow Wilson*, ed. Ross A Kennedy (Malden, MA: Wiley-Blackwell, 2013), 569–87.

I wish to thank the original publishers for permission to include them in this book. I also want to express my gratitude to Deborah Gershenowitz, Senior Editor at Cambridge University Press, and to Lien-Hang Nguyen and Paul T. Chamberlin, General Editors of the Cambridge Studies in U.S. Foreign Relations series, for welcoming my proposal for this book and accepting it for the series. I also appreciate the two anonymous readers, who recommended its publication.

Introduction

Focusing on President Woodrow Wilson and the United States in international relations, this collection of essays addresses enduring questions about American political culture and statecraft. His liberal internationalist vision of a new world order, which he articulated during World War I and which expressed his version of Americanism, would shape U.S. foreign policy for the next century. The following chapters thus assess not only his role during his presidency but also his legacy in defining the United States' place in world history. They explore the nexus between American culture and international relations, between ideas and diplomacy, between ideology and power, and between humanitarian promises and self-interests. My critique of Wilson's leadership in international relations highlights the limits of his definition of a new world order, notably with respect to religion and race. His belief in God's providential mission for the United States in world history and his racial/ethnic identity profoundly limited the president's international vision and statecraft, which expressed a Eurocentric, particularly Anglo-American, bias and drew a global color line. This book thus examines the exclusive as well as the universal dimensions of Wilsonianism.

Modern Anglo-American liberalism furnished the ideological foundation for Wilson's new foreign policy in the early twentieth-century Progressive Era, an era in world history of imperialism and both nationalism and internationalism. When he called for making the world safe for democracy through American intervention in the European war, he envisaged a new world order that projected his understanding of U.S. national identity. He affirmed the tenets of collective security through a new League of Nations, national self-determination as the rationale for drawing new borders, and an "open door" for international commerce and finance as well as travel and cultural exchange. This vision required the freedom of the seas and the removal of barriers to trade and investment across borders. Hoping the Great War would culminate in the creation of a global community of liberal democracies with capitalist economies, he saw nation-states as the building blocks of this new world order.

Paradoxically, Wilson's American vision of a new world order followed an old European intellectual tradition with biblical and classical roots. As Jan Willem Schulte Nordholt observed in *The Myth of the West* (1995), the idea of America came from the old world, not from the frontier in the American West as Wilson as well as Frederick Jackson Turner affirmed. This worldview depicted the United States as the culmination of world history, and gave Americans confidence in their future. Their new land represented a "city on a hill" or "last frontier" or "end of history."[1] Their incomparable empire was not really like those of other great powers that had risen and fallen. The myth promised the United States a happier destiny with unending progress. Wilson embraced this mythic American exceptionalism in his understanding of world history.

Wilson applied this nationalist perspective to international relations during and after World War I. Within the framework of American exceptionalism, the president claimed to offer the postwar world its best hope for lasting peace. The League, which he saw as the centerpiece of the Versailles Treaty with Weimar Germany, promised a new era of international relations. It would protect modern civilization against barbarism. It would replace old rivalries with "the united power of free nations" to keep the peace. He sought to establish the United States as the world's preeminent leader in pursuit of "international social control" or, actually, of U.S. hegemony. The League, he believed, would enable Americans to provide worldwide leadership largely through their moral influence over public opinion, and thus fulfill their God-given destiny. "America shall in truth show the way," he affirmed as he presented the peace treaty to the Senate.[2] At stake was nothing less than the defense of civilization against the barbarism of another world war.

---

[1] Jan Willem Schulte Nordholt, *The Myth of the West: America as the Last Empire* (Grand Rapids, MI, 1995).

[2] Address to Senate, July 10, 1919, Woodrow Wilson, *The Public Papers of Woodrow Wilson: War and Peace*, eds. Ray Stannard Baker and William E. Dodd (New York, 1927), 1: 537–54; Woodrow Wilson, *The Papers of Woodrow Wilson*, ed. Arthur S. Link (Princeton, NJ, 1989), 61: 426–36.

Wilson's belief in America's God-given destiny and its progressive history blinded him from seeing what Wolfgang Schivelbusch called "the culture of defeat" in other countries. Born and raised in the American South, the president had experienced the trauma of defeat after the Civil War. This experience profoundly influenced him. Yet he found it difficult to empathize with foreigners who also suffered from military defeat. In *The Culture of Defeat* (2004), Schivelbusch compared the American South after the Civil War, France after the Franco-Prussian War of 1870–71, and Germany after World War I. The losers in all three wars claimed moral superiority over their conquerors. They regarded themselves as true defenders of civilization against barbaric victors.[3] Wilson's claim to have created a new world order of "civilized men" at the Paris Peace Conference of 1919 did not appear that way to most Germans in the Weimar Republic. Nor did it look that way to French premier Georges Clemenceau, who had experienced military defeat in the Franco-Prussian War. Wilson shared the white South's trauma after the American Civil War, but he did not understand either Clemenceau's fixation on French security or Weimar Germany's almost universal rejection of the Versailles Treaty. Wilson's new world order fell short of French and German expectations, and those of other nations that had anticipated more from the peacemakers in 1919. Widespread disillusionment fed belligerent nationalism, which manifested the culture of defeat and contributed to the failure of democracy and peace after World War I. Wilson's concept of a global community of nations offered no solution to the postwar conflicts in Europe. Nor did it fulfill the hopes of anticolonial nationalists on the other side of the color line elsewhere in the world.

Wilson's biographers and historians of his role in international relations have typically applauded the positive qualities of Wilsonianism. So too have political scientists. Emphasizing supposedly universal principles of his liberal internationalism, they have tended to downplay his religious and racial prejudices. In contrast, Joyce Carol Oates, in her novel *The Accursed* (2013), depicted his as well as Princeton's provincialism in 1905–06, although, as the university's president, he was one of the most cosmopolitan residents in this predominantly white Protestant community. He embraced its "Anglo-Saxon Christianity." In the novel Wilson asserted, "the United States is charged by God with spreading Christian democracy throughout the world, and opening the markets of the East as

[3] Wolfgang Schivelbusch, *The Culture of Defeat: On National Trauma, Mourning, and Recovery* (New York, 2004).

well – by diplomacy if possible, by power otherwise." His Calvinist faith required both local and global engagement on "a battleground between the forces of Good and the forces of Evil."[4] Oates portrayed the demonic consequences in Princeton of this racial and religious mission, and by implication, potentially elsewhere in the world whenever provincial Americans encountered foreign peoples and ideas. Essays in this book explore such encounters in Wilson's diplomacy and statecraft during and after World War I and in his legacy of Wilsonianism.

This book provides my historical perspective on fundamental issues in the ongoing debates over the role of the United States in the world. Other historians such as David Reynolds[5] and political scientists such as G. John Ikenberry[6] have recognized the importance of the Wilsonian legacy. As they observed, the history of World War I and of Wilson's role in it has continued to influence international relations throughout the twentieth century and into the twenty-first. My book on Wilson and his definition of America's place in world history will offer insights not only on his diplomacy and statecraft and on American political culture during the World War I era but also on his legacy in current international relations.

Since the end of the Cold War, two major trends in historiography have provided new perspectives on America's place in the world. In this new era of globalization after the opening of the Berlin Wall in 1989 and the collapse of the Soviet Union in 1991, historians have sought to escape the limits of Cold War scholarship that emphasized the global division among the First, Second, and Third Worlds. In that framework, the United States and its allies had defended their freedom, democracy, and capitalism against the threat of dictatorial communism from the Soviet Union and other communist countries in a rivalry that had often played out in the Third World. With the apparent triumph of liberal democracy and capitalism over communism and the new era of globalization, historians looked for better ways to understand not only the present but also the past. One major historiographical trend was the emergence of the field of world history. No longer restricted by Cold War categories, scholars in this field sought to understand the history of various peoples and regions of the world by comparing them and identifying their transnational and international connections. Their focus was global, typically not adopting

---

[4] Joyce Carol Oates, *The Accursed: A Novel* (New York, 2013), 57, 212, 351.
[5] David Reynolds, *The Long Shadow: The Legacies of the Great War in the Twentieth Century* (New York, 2014).
[6] G. John Ikenberry, *Liberal Leviathan: The Origins, Crisis, and Transformation of the American World Order* (Princeton, NJ, 2011).

an America-centric or Eurocentric viewpoint like the one that privileged the First World during the Cold War. The second new historiographical trend was the internationalizing of American history. Scholars in this field also looked for transnational connections between developments in the United States and comparable ones elsewhere in the world. Historians of U.S. foreign relations, including myself, have contributed to and bene-fited from these two trends in contemporary historiography.

CONCEPTUALIZING WORLD HISTORY

In *Navigating World History* (2003), Patrick Manning described how his-torians have created a global past by developing the field of world history and making it a significant part of historical studies. It has become an important subject for courses at colleges and universities and for research. He found the modern roots of Western ideas about world history in early modern Europe's Renaissance and Enlightenment. Nineteenth-century Europeans further developed a philosophy of history that placed Western civilization at its core. "In the emerging hierarchy of empires, nations, and colonies," Manning explained, "the term *civilization* became part of the vocabulary of every philosophical camp. The term served as a double-edged weapon for confirming the primacy of European (and later, North American) nations in the world order. For premodern times, *civilization* referred to the succession of leading empires and societies, in contrast to each other and to the timeless barbarians beyond their limits. For mod-ern times, *civilization* meant *the civilized world*, including the leading nations and imperial homelands but not the colonies."[7] World War I, he noted, expanded global awareness. Thus, Manning observed, "Woodrow Wilson, who as a historian participated actively in the nationalistic style of writing about American history, became a theorist for a new world order once he became president and a leader of the Allied war effort.... Wilson's vision of the League of Nations contributed, in the minds of some, to the notion of world government."[8] He proceeded from nation-alism to internationalism.

Manning recognized that scholars in the new field of world history studied primarily the subjects that had characterized diplomatic his-tory. "World historians have worked in most detail on the social sphere,

[7] Patrick Manning, *Navigating World History: Historians Create a Global Past* (New York, 2003), 31.
[8] Manning, *Navigating World History*, 43–44. See also Mark Mazower, *Governing the World: The History of an Idea* (New York, 2012), 116–88.

focusing especially on politics, warfare, commerce, and the rise and fall of states." But they no longer interpreted these subjects within the nineteenth-century framework that continued to shape the thinking of twentieth-century leaders such as Wilson. Instead, they recognized greater diversity and relativity among the historical actors and their viewpoints. Manning emphasized that

the logic of world history, while reliant on the facts as they are known, leads inevitably instead to a multiplicity of interpretations. Thus, writers a century ago chose to focus on "civilization" as the basic concept in world history, and attempted to write master narratives focused on this concept.... By the opening of the twenty-first century, civilization had ceased to be an absolute standard. It maintained its significance, but, like everything else in world history, civilization had to be relativized.[9]

Recent historical scholarship on World War I has increasingly embraced the perspective of world history. Rather than adopting a single national viewpoint, historians have placed the war in the broader framework of international and transnational history. Although the assassinations of Austria's archduke and his wife by a Serbian terrorist in Sarajevo precipitated the July 1914 crisis in Europe, the resulting war quickly became global. It involved not only European empires around the world but also independent nations in Asia and the Western Hemisphere. It soon led to conflict between Japan and China and eventually to intervention by the United States and other nations in the Western Hemisphere. Not only did the war become global; it also became total, affecting all aspects of the state and civil society. In *The Cambridge History of the First World War* (2014), edited by Jay Winter, the authors interpreted it as both global and total.[10] Other historians also framed their studies of the war and postwar peacemaking as world history. This perspective characterized Hew Strachan's *The First World War* (2001), Margaret MacMillan's *Paris 1919* (2001), Niall Ferguson's *The War of the World* (2006), Erez Manela's *The Wilsonian Moment* (2007), and Adam Tooze's *The Deluge* (2014).[11]

Emily S. Rosenberg and her coauthors in *A World Connecting* (2012) examined the period from 1870 to 1945 as an era of major transition

[9] Manning, *Navigating World History*, 117–18.
[10] Jay Winter, ed., *The Cambridge History of the First World War*, Vol. I: *Global War*, Vol. II: *The State*, and Vol. III: *Civil Society* (Cambridge, 2014).
[11] Hew Strachan, *The First World War*, Vol. I: *To Arms* (Oxford, 2001); Margaret MacMillan, *Paris 1919: Six Months that Changed the World* (New York, 2001); Niall Ferguson, *The War of the World: Twentieth-Century Conflict and the Descent of the West* (New York, 2006); Erez Manela, *The Wilsonian Moment: Self-Determination and the International Origins of Anticolonial Nationalism* (New York, 2007); Adam Tooze,

in world history. They analyzed the invention of modern statehood, examined the global reach of empires, studied the migrations of peoples around the world, traced commodity chains in the global economy, and focused on transnational and international currents in the shrinking world. The contributions of this book demonstrated the paradoxical experience of the world becoming more interdependent and yet apparently more diverse as different peoples increasingly interacted with each other. "Over the period from 1870 to 1945," Rosenberg observed in the introduction, "the world became both a more familiar and a stranger place. Fast ships, railroads, telegraph lines, inexpensive publications, and film all reached into hinterlands and erased distances. The exchange of people and products accelerated, while the fascination with traveling around and describing foreign areas–long evident in human history– reached new heights." This interaction created not only a greater sense of familiarity but also of strange differences. "New connections highlighted all kinds of regional differences," Rosenberg noted, "and the awareness of difference could promote suspicion and repulsion perhaps even more easily than it facilitated understanding and communication." In this modern era of interdependence and fragmentation, the world was increasingly characterized by both "the intensifying global interconnectedness" and "the multiple processes of disintegration and reintegration."[12] For better or worse, in the late nineteenth and early twentieth centuries, what happened in one place vitally impacted people in other countries or regions of the world, increasingly connecting the local and the global.

INTERNATIONALIZING AMERICAN HISTORY

As the field of world history was emerging, the Organization of American Historians launched its Project on Internationalizing the Study of American History. Directed by Thomas Bender, its *La Pietra Report* (2000) called for "new understandings of the American nation's relation to a world that is at once self-consciously global and highly pluralized."[13] In *Rethinking American History in a Global Age* (2002), which Bender

---

The Deluge: The Great War, America and the Remaking of the Global Order, 1916–1931 (New York, 2014).

[12] Emily S. Rosenberg, ed., *A World Connecting, 1870–1945* (Cambridge, MA, 2012), 3–4. See also C. A. Bayly, *The Birth of the Modern World, 1780–1914* (Malden, MA, 2004), 1–3.

[13] Thomas Bender, *La Pietra Report* (Organization of American Historians and New York University, 2000), 5.

edited, he explained the purpose of this new direction in historiography. "My argument and that of this book," he wrote, "is not for increasing the study of American foreign relations, although that is important. The point is that we must understand every dimension of American life as entangled in other histories. Other histories are implicated in American history, and the United States is implicated in other histories. This is not only true of this present age of globalization; it has been since the fifteenth century, when the world for the first time became self-consciously singular."[14] Bender offered his own understanding of "America's place in world history" in *A Nation Among Nations* (2006).[15]

As historians of the United States increasingly transcended national borders in their scholarship, they also crossed the artificial boundaries between subfields of American history. Historians of U.S. foreign relations often pioneered in this new direction but they were soon joined by others, especially as they too sought to internationalize the study of their particular specialties. Outstanding examples of this recent scholarship combined American diplomacy, culture, and economics,[16] gender and international history,[17] race and U.S. foreign relations,[18] U.S. diplomatic and American western history,[19] labor and U.S. foreign relations,[20] American intellectual and diplomatic history,[21] immigration and U.S. foreign relations,[22] and religion in American war and

---

[14] Thomas Bender, ed., *Rethinking American History in a Global Age* (Berkeley, CA, 2002), 6.

[15] Thomas Bender, *A Nation Among Nations: America's Place in World History* (New York, 2006).

[16] Emily S. Rosenberg, *Spreading the American Dream: American Economic and Cultural Expansion, 1890–1945* (New York, 1982); Emily S. Rosenberg, *Financial Missionaries to the World: The Politics of Culture and Dollar Diplomacy, 1900–1930* (Cambridge, MA, 1999).

[17] Gail Bederman, *Manliness & Civilization: A Cultural History of Gender and Race in the United States, 1880–1917* (Chicago, 1995); Kristin L. Hoganson, *Fighting for American Manhood: How Gender Politics Provoked the Spanish-American and Philippine-American Wars* (New Haven, CT, 1998).

[18] Paul A. Kramer, *The Blood of Government: Race, Empire, the United States, & the Philippines* (Chapel Hill, NC, 2006).

[19] Walter Nugent, *Habits of Empire: A History of American Expansion* (New York, 2008).

[20] Julie Greene, *The Canal Builders: Making America's Empire at the Panama Canal* (New York, 2009); Elizabeth McKillen, *Making the World Safe for Workers: Labor, the Left, and Wilsonian Internationalism* (Urbana, IL, 2013).

[21] Christopher McKnight Nichols, *Promise and Peril: America at the Dawn of a Global Age* (Cambridge, MA, 2011).

[22] Donna R. Gabaccia, *Foreign Relations: American Immigration in Global Perspective* (Princeton, NJ, 2012).

diplomacy.²³ These historical studies provided new perspectives on America's place in the world by transcending national borders and disciplinary boundaries that divided scholarship into fields and subfields.

Placing the United States in the global context of world history involved comparisons between American values and institutions and those of others. It required scholars to study the popular and scholarly claims of American exceptionalism, which affirmed that the United States was a providential nation with a unique history and mission. President Ronald Reagan expressed his belief in American exceptionalism in his farewell address on January 11, 1989. He saw the United States as still a "shining city upon a hill," misquoting Puritan leader John Winthrop's sermon to English settlers upon their arrival in the new world in 1630, to describe the "God-blessed" America he imagined as a land of "freedom."²⁴ In the new era of globalization after Reagan's presidency, his widely shared belief in American exceptionalism continued to shape how the United States defined its place in the world. This nationalist mythology still influenced American historiography as well. Among others, Australian historian Ian Tyrrell challenged this perspective that had characterized the way Americans had typically interpreted their history for the past century. He heralded a new framework to escape this exceptionalist perspective. "The internationalization of scholarship itself," he noted, "is steadily eroding the boundaries that at the turn of the [twentieth] century created strong national historiographical traditions, including American exceptionalism."²⁵

Within this new framework, which the OAH Project on Internationalizing the Study of American History promoted, historians placed the United States in a global context but without regarding it as an exceptional nation. Yet they understood that Americans, such as Wilson and Reagan, affirmed American exceptionalism. For example, Daniel T. Rodgers examined the transatlantic connections of social politics in the "progressive age" of the early twentieth century in *Atlantic Crossings* (1998). He noted that American progressives initially derived many of their ideas from European reformers, but this changed when the United States intervened in World War I. "Into the heart of guidebook Europe the American expeditionary army

²³ Andrew Preston, *Sword of the Spirit, Shield of Faith: Religion in American War and Diplomacy* (New York, 2012).
²⁴ Ronald Reagan, Farewell Address to the Nation, January 11, 1989, <https://reaganlibrary.archives.gov/archives/speeches/1989/011189i.htm>.
²⁵ Ian Tyrrell, "American Exceptionalism in an Age of International History," *American Historical Review* 96 (October 1991): 1031–55.

had rushed in the summer of 1918, not as a junior partner in an entangling foreign alliance but, as the American progressives preferred to see it, in a crusade to rescue civilization itself." Leadership shifted to the United States.

"America had the infinite privilege of fulfilling her destiny and saving the world," Woodrow Wilson put the war's moral in a nutshell in late 1919, in the messianic rhetoric that American war propaganda agencies had disseminated wholesale on both sides of the Atlantic. With Wilson mapping out the future of democracy in liberated Europe, with cheering crowds lining his procession through Dover, Paris, and Rome, it was not hard to imagine that the torch of world progress had indeed passed, once more, to the United States.[26]

For Wilson, but not Rodgers, the emergence of the United States as the top progressive global leader during World War I seemed to vindicate America's exceptionalist role in world history.

Ian Tyrrell also offered a transnational interpretation of American history that eschewed the framework of American exceptionalism that Wilson, both as historian and president, had embraced. In *Reforming the World* (2010), he examined "the creation of America's moral empire" during the Gilded Age and Progressive Era.

The new internationalism that moral reformers supported turned on the exchange of ideas, norms, and values among like-minded individuals in voluntary organizations across national boundaries. Ordinary people would work together in non-state relationships to enhance international understanding, to foster ethical conduct, and to promote moral reform. Peace between nations would flow from the activities of clubs and reform organizations.

This transnational culture of moral reform, he noted, usually exerted only an indirect influence on U.S. foreign policy. "While moral reform networks and missionaries did contribute at times to specific policy outcomes," Tyrrell observed, "these were usually determined by realpolitik. Rather than determine statecraft, the Christian coalition contributed to a missionary and reformist *Weltanschauung* within the higher echelons of American politics."[27] Within that cultural milieu, Wilson defined his vision of a new world order during World War I.

---

[26] Daniel T. Rodgers, *Atlantic Crossings: Social Politics in a Progressive Age* (Cambridge, MA, 1998), 368. See also James T. Kloppenberg, *Uncertain Victory: Social Democracy and Progressivism in European and American Thought, 1870–1920* (New York, 1986) and Axel R. Schäfer, *American Progressives and German Social Reform, 1875–1920* (Stuttgart, 2000).

[27] Ian Tyrrell, *Reforming the World: The Creation of America's Moral Empire* (Princeton, NJ, 2010), 192, 232–33. See also Ian Tyrrell, *Transnational Nation: United States History in Global Perspective Since 1789* (New York, 2007), 134–69.

In *American Exceptionalism* (2015), Finnish political scientist Hilde Eliassen Restad argued persuasively that the national identity of the United States profoundly influenced its approach to international relations. Its British heritage, including Puritanism, persisted in ideas about race and religion that characterized America's national identity, shaping both its nationalism and its internationalism. Rejecting the false dichotomy between isolationism and internationalism, she observed that throughout their history Americans had instead alternated between "exemplary" and "missionary" internationalism. The United States had never tried to isolate itself from the world, although it sought to control its own involvement. In accordance with American exceptionalism, which combined both universalism and uniqueness, it pursued "unilateral internationalism." Restad observed that this tradition characterized U.S. foreign relations from the American Revolution to George W. Bush's global war on terrorism after 9/11. In agreement with my scholarship, she affirmed that "President Wilson ... applied a nationalist perspective to America's new world role. Specifically, he utilized the rhetorical framework of American exceptionalism, arguing that the United States and its system offered the world the best hope for enduring peace." Restad challenged many of the restrictive categories that other political scientists used. But she lapsed back into the more traditional dichotomy when she identified Wilson only with "multilateral internationalism" and Senator Henry Cabot Lodge, his opponent in the fight over the League of Nations, with "unilateral internationalism." She did not recognize that Wilson's liberal internationalism combined both unilateralism and multilateralism. Like most political scientists, she equated Wilsonianism with multilateralism, thus removing Wilson from the American diplomatic tradition of "unilateral internationalism," although she viewed him as "American exceptionalism personified."[28]

RECENT SCHOLARSHIP ON WOODROW WILSON AND AMERICAN INTERNATIONALISM

In contrast to Rodgers, Tyrrell, and Restad, Frank Ninkovich argued in *The Global Republic* (2014) that American exceptionalism did not shape U.S. foreign relations. Instead, he emphasized

[28] Hilde Eliassen Restad, *American Exceptionalism: An Idea That Made a Nation and Remade the World* (London, 2015), 37, 130–37.

the historical singularity of [U.S.] policies whose formulation, implementation, and consequences were prompted by an unprecedented commitment to maintaining an international society that had developed independently of American initiative. American exceptionalism, by contrast, suggests a redemptive compulsion to export American views and values to an unreformed world.

He noted that American exceptionalism was not unique to the United States because it had originated in the political ideology inherited from Great Britain. It came from British exceptionalism, which John Winthrop had expressed in his Puritan vision of "a city upon a hill" for "the eyes of all people." The lineage of this ideological perspective, moreover, went back to classical Greece and Rome and to the Renaissance and Enlightenment in Europe. During the American Revolution, the new nation drew on this European, particularly British, heritage to launch its unique experiment in republican government, which was exceptional in the late eighteenth-century era of monarchs and empires. However, Ninkovich argued, despite the founding fathers' desire for the United States to serve as a model for the old world, they did not use their liberal republicanism to define an exceptionalist foreign policy to redeem the world. Thus, he concluded, "America's uniqueness as a geopolitically isolated republic was not matched by a corresponding exceptionalism in its approach to foreign relations."[29]

In Ninkovich's view, the United States became even less exceptional after the Civil War as it experienced the transnational process of civilization, later called globalization. "Civilization was a convenient abstraction for powerful forces of history that had altered seemingly everything concrete: how people lived and died, governed, worked, loved, worshipped, proselytized, traveled, and understood themselves and the world." This structural transformation created an international society beyond the political control of any nation: "it just happened." Although this process originated in the West, initially in Great Britain, it produced "a new global civilization." "Thanks to globalization," Ninkovich argued, "the old world was no longer old and the new world no longer distinctively new. Instead, both were caught up in the process of becoming modern."[30] Cosmopolitan Americans embraced the ideas of British liberals such as John Bright, Walter Bagehot, and William Gladstone to explain this transformation and define America's place in the changing world. Transatlantic

---

[29] Frank Ninkovich, *The Global Republic: America's Inadvertent Rise to World Power* (Chicago, 2014), 5–6, 16, 38.
[30] Ninkovich, *Global Republic*, 41, 46, 48.

Anglo-American liberalism provided the cultural foundation of American internationalism, as Ninkovich perceptively explained in *Global Dawn* (2009). "The issue was not the Americanization of England or the Anglicization of America, but rather the globalization of both." He noted, moreover, that "one of the principal legatees of nineteenth-century liberalism" was Woodrow Wilson, who believed its universalism would allow the United States to escape European power politics even after it entered World War I. Accordingly, when the president asserted America's interest in world peace, not just Europe's, Ninkovich concluded, "Wilson's declaration was a reaffirmation of the nineteenth-century liberal belief in the primacy of the globalizing process."[31]

At the turn of twentieth century, as Ninkovich observed in *The Global Republic*, the United States had joined the international club of European empires, creating its own new empire with its "civilizing mission." This departure from the nation's non-imperial westward expansion across North America provoked a debate over imperialism. "Though both sides of the debate on empire sought to package their ideas in exceptional rhetoric," he emphasized, "the global frame of reference had little to do with national ideals." After its "aberration" of empire-building, the United States soon looked for a different relationship with Europe's great powers. "It was the pursuit of cooperation among the so-called civilized powers, and not empire, that would leave a deeper and more lasting imprint on American policy," Ninkovich claimed. U.S. presidents during the Progressive Era – Theodore Roosevelt, William Howard Taft, and then Wilson – imagined and pursued new ways of relating to the international society.[32]

Wilson's liberal internationalism seemed to provide the answer during World War I. "Among a host of other important consequences," Ninkovich observed, "the war also launched the career of Wilsonianism as the ideological embodiment of America's ingrained belief that it was the world's redeemer nation. Despite its fall from grace, for both its diehard supporters and its critics Wilsonianism would remain the supreme expression of the nation's exceptionalist spirit." Ninkovich offered a different interpretation, arguing that it was really an anomaly. Its central feature, the League of Nations, was actually "far more British and European than American." Moreover, the president was not a crusader for democracy. "For Wilson, making the world safe for democracy did

---

[31] Frank Ninkovich, *Global Dawn: The Cultural Foundation of American Internationalism, 1865–1890* (Cambridge, MA, 2009), 90, 322.
[32] Ninkovich, *Global Republic*, 75, 78.

not mean democratizing the world. As John Milton Cooper Jr. has noted, the phrase was crafted in the passive voice that did not envision an American jihad against nondemocratic infidels." Although Wilson advocated anti-imperialism and national self-determination, Ninkovich noted, he restricted the application of this vision. "For the foreseeable future, democratization and national self-determination for most peoples was a pipe dream." In the peacemaking after World War I, Wilson's ideals failed to materialize in a new world order. "The story of the League fight," Ninkovich concluded, "suggests that Wilsonianism was not the paradigmatic example of American idealism at work, but an anomaly in the history of US foreign relations – an exceptionalist exception whose guiding ideas were short-lived in practice."[33]

This interpretation of Wilsonianism departed in some basic respects from Ninkovich's earlier versions. Rather than viewing it as an anomaly, he had seen it as the core ideology of U.S. foreign policy in *The Wilsonian Century* (1999). In that book, he argued, "the Wilsonian century was the product of an imaginative interpretation of history that survived not only because it seemed to make sense of a confusing modern world, but also because it successfully passed the test of experience." "It was Wilson's gift for historical interpretation rather than empirical observation that enabled him to give such a compelling reading of a chaotic world scene," Ninkovich added. He applauded the president for positing the concept of a nonexistent "world opinion" and for rejecting the realist tradition of power politics in international relations.

It would have been a remarkable story if the United States had gone from isolationism to world politics by following the traditional path of power politics. But the nation took a different and altogether more extraordinary course by radically redefining what it meant to be a world power. American internationalism in the 20th century *was* truly exceptional because it abandoned the idea of interest as traditionally understood over thousands of years, opting instead to identify its national security with global needs.[34]

Ninkovich still defined America's foreign threat in the same way he did in *Modernity and Power* (1994), when he credited Wilson with originating the Domino Theory.[35] Yet that metaphor, which influenced U.S. foreign

---

[33] Ninkovich, *Global Republic*, 96–97, 99, 108–09, 118.
[34] Frank Ninkovich, *The Wilsonian Century: U.S. Foreign Policy Since 1900* (Chicago, 1999), 11, 13–14, 16.
[35] Frank Ninkovich, *Modernity and Power: A History of the Domino Theory in the Twentieth Century* (Chicago, 1994).

policy throughout the Cold War, obscured real cultural distinctions among diverse nations or peoples in a globalized world.

In *The Global Republic* Ninkovich stressed the external environment of the international society rather than the internal origins of U.S. foreign policy. Instead of any particular ideology such as American exceptionalism or its manifestation in Wilsonianism, he emphasized the universal and progressive historical process of globalization toward modern civilization. Like Wilson, who projected presumably universal principles of modern Anglo-American liberalism onto the world, Ninkovich emphasized interdependence between the local and the global. Unlike realists who recognized the diversity of interests and cultures in the modern world, he focused on the homogeneity of the emerging international society. He still applauded Wilson's rejection of traditional power politics. Like him, Ninkovich conflated Western civilization with global civilization and identified American nationalism with internationalism, which blinded them from seeing or understanding the world's diversity of peoples and nations. This profound failure to recognize pluralism in the modern world was the fundamental flaw in Wilsonianism and in Ninkovich's various interpretations of it. Neither Wilson nor Ninkovich was alone in this common limitation. As Glenda Sluga revealed in *Internationalism in the Age of Nationalism* (2013), even "the international turn" in the modern Western world did not enable self-identified internationalists to escape their own nationalism.[36] They projected their own visions of an international society onto the world and called it global.

In *Woodrow Wilson* (2009), John Milton Cooper, Jr. offered an affirmative biography, yet acknowledged some flaws. He noted the president's poor record on race and civil liberties but did not allow it to tarnish the story of his remarkably successful career as an academic leader and statesman. Cooper downplayed Wilson's racism, while other recent scholarship emphasized that he drew the color line at home by introducing Jim Crow segregation in the federal government and abroad by rejecting racial equality in the League of Nations and national self-determination for peoples of color. His racism coincided with his liberalism, fundamentally influencing his foreign policy.[37] Recent scholarship, moreover, highlighted

[36] Glenda Sluga, *Internationalism in the Age of Nationalism* (Philadelphia, 2013).
[37] Stephen Skowronek, "The Reassociation of Ideas and Purposes: Racism, Liberalism, and the American Political Tradition," *American Political Science Review* 100 (August 2006): 385–401; Lloyd E. Ambrosius, "Woodrow Wilson and *The Birth of a Nation*: American Democracy and International Relations," *Diplomacy and Statecraft* 18 (December 2007): 689–718. See also Andrew Zimmerman, *Alabama in Africa: Booker T. Washington, the German Empire, and the Globalization of the New South* (Princeton,

religion as another key factor in Wilson's statecraft. The Social Gospel in American Christianity profoundly influenced his worldview.[38] Cooper, however, argued that "Wilson practiced a severe separation not only between church and state but also between religion and society," claiming that he was not "a secular messiah or a naïve, wooly-headed idealist." Cooper saw him as "one of the most careful, hardheaded, and sophisticated idealists of his time." The president led the United States into the Great War as a shrewd statesman, not as a crusader for democracy. "Wilson spoke the language of exalted idealism, but he did it in a humble, circumspect way.... He did not say that Americans must make the world safe for democracy; he did not believe that they could. They could only do their part, join with other like-minded nations, and take steps toward that promised land."[39] Under Wilson's leadership, in Cooper's view, the United States sought to reach the "promised land" through progressive reform of the world, but not as an exceptionalist redeemer nation.

Cooper saw Theodore Roosevelt, in contrast to Wilson, as more of a crusader, and in some ways he was. TR criticized Wilson for his failure to condemn Germany's invasion of Belgium and France in 1914 and for his weak response to its sinking of the *Lusitania* in 1915. He thought the United States should have entered the war sooner than 1917 and denounced Wilson for his belated and insufficient efforts to protect the democratic nations of Western Europe and for his failure to demand Germany's unconditional surrender in 1918. Despite later perceptions to the contrary, Roosevelt's internationalism, more than Wilson's, affirmed the British (and French) liberal tradition of humanitarian intervention to protect human rights.[40]

NJ, 2010) and Jens-Uwe Guettel, *German Expansionism, Imperial Liberalism, and the United States, 1776–1945* (Cambridge, 2012).

[38] Lloyd E. Ambrosius, *Woodrow Wilson and the American Diplomatic Tradition: The Treaty Fight in Perspective* (Cambridge, 1987), 12–13; Malcolm D. Magee, *What the World Should Be: Woodrow Wilson and the Crafting of a Faith-Based Foreign Policy* (Waco, TX, 2008); Mark Benbow, *Leading Them to the Promised Land: Woodrow Wilson, Covenant Theology, and the Mexican Revolution, 1913–1915* (Kent, OH, 2010); Milan Babik, *Statecraft and Salvation: Wilsonian Liberal Internationalism as Secularized Eschatology* (Waco, TX, 2013); Cara L. Burnidge, "The Business of Church of State: Social Christianity in Woodrow Wilson's White House," *Church History* 82 (September 2013): 659–66; Preston, *Sword of the Spirit, Shield of Faith*, 233–90.

[39] John Milton Cooper, Jr., *Woodrow Wilson: A Biography* (New York, 2009), 4–5, 10–11, 397.

[40] Gary J. Bass, *Freedom's Battle: The Origins of Humaniatarian Intervention* (New York, 2008). See also H. W. Brands, *T.R.: The Last Romantic* (New York, 1997), 747–816, and Patricia O'Toole, *When Trumpets Called: Theodore Roosevelt after the White House* (New York, 2005), 317–405.

In fundamental disagreement with Cooper, A. Scott Berg emphasized the centrality of Wilson's Christian faith in all aspects of his life. He used religious terms for all chapter titles in *Wilson* (2013). In this biography Berg observed that

the Wilson Cabinet of 1913 was a ten-way mirror, each panel of which reflected a different aspect of the man at the center. This was mostly a team of Rebels – lawyers from the South who had pursued other professions and never shed their Confederate biases, Anglo-Saxon Protestants all, mostly newcomers to Washington, if not politics altogether.... For the most part, the President would delegate power to his Secretaries ... to run their own departments, as he seldom found reason to countermand any of them. Every decision from this administration, noted one close observer, would contain a moral component, inspired by "the breath of God."

After the United States entered the Great War, moreover, Wilson hoped "to carry the 'Gospel of Americanism' to every corner of the globe."[41]

Richard Striner as well rejected Cooper's interpretation in a sharply critical account of *Woodrow Wilson and World War I* (2014). He argued that "the religious heart of Wilson's sensibility cannot be denied" and that "Wilson's brand of Christianity was heavily (and perhaps unusually) *millennial*." Perhaps Georges Clemenceau went too far when he sneered that the president thought of himself as another Jesus Christ. "And yet," Striner stressed, "since the very beginning of the war, he had felt that he himself might be destined by God to play the central role in putting an end to the horror: he himself would find a way to create the new dispensation." However, by the time of the armistice, Wilson had alienated the Republicans to such an extent that there was no prospect for successful bipartisan peacemaking. "With Wilson being the stubborn and delusional man he had become by the final months of 1918," Striner concluded, "what good would the presence of leading Republicans in the American delegation have done? Wilson, being Wilson, was his own worst enemy in ways that were far beyond retrieval. Any blunders he committed were the latest missteps in a very long series that were leading him, his country, and the world to disaster."[42] Unlike Cooper's Wilson, who was taking the United States toward the promised land of a world safe for democracy, Striner's Wilson was heading it toward global disaster.

---

[41] A. Scott Berg, *Wilson* (New York, 2013), 266–67, 449.
[42] Richard Striner, *Woodrow Wilson and World War I: A Burden Too Great to Bear* (Lanham, MD, 2014), 171, 229.

Like Cooper, Charles E. Neu offered a generally positive view of Wilson and his close friend, Edward M. House, in his biography of *Colonel House* (2015). In assessing House, Neu concluded that

in foreign affairs he was the most cosmopolitan of Wilson's advisers, having traveled extensively in Western Europe in the years before the outbreak of the war. House followed great power politics closely, and during his wartime trips to Europe he tried to assess the complex currents of the struggle. He understood, earlier than most Americans, that the United States could not stand apart from events in Europe, that it must find a way to end the war and to rebuild international community.

Despite this praise, Neu inadvertently supported Striner's critique of Wilson with his devastating criticism of House's incompetence during his trips to Europe in 1914, 1915, and 1916 in search of peace. Referring to the 1916 peace mission, Neu observed, "House's curious performance in Paris revealed once again his uneven skills as a diplomat. He had exaggerated his own accomplishments, misunderstood French leaders, and conveyed to Wilson an inaccurate assessment of the possibilities for peace." When House then returned to London, he once more showed his inability to comprehend European international relations. "Instead," Neu argued, "he continued to pursue his illusion of peace."[43] This damning critique of House begged the question as to why the president persisted in relying on House's judgment and gave him important diplomatic assignments until 1919, when Wilson finally lost confidence in his close friend during the peace conference.

Wilson exiled House to London to represent the United States on the Commission on Mandates during the summer of 1919. That commission laid the foundation for dividing former Ottoman territories and German colonies into League of Nations mandates based on a racial hierarchy but, presumably, on the level of development toward civilization of the different peoples of color. Not only Wilson but also Jan Smuts of South Africa, both of whom were dedicated to white supremacy, collaborated during the peace conference to create this alternative to traditional empires. "Everywhere," Susan Pedersen observed in *The Guardians* (2015), "mandatory administrations deployed the language of civilization to justify their presence. Occasionally, however, the realities of race and power shone through."[44] Neu barely mentioned House's

---

[43] Charles E. Neu, *Colonel House: A Biography of Woodrow Wilson's Silent Partner* (New York, 2015), 232, 235, 510.
[44] Susan Pedersen, *The Guardians: The League of Nations and the Crisis of Empire* (New York, 2015), 74; Mark Mazower, *No Enchanted Palace: The End of Empire and the Ideological Origins of the United Nations* (Princeton, NJ, 2009), 28–65; Jörg Fisch,

part in the Commission on Mandates and remained silent on the racial factor in U.S. policy toward the League mandates or in any other aspect of Wilson's and House's diplomacy. Nor did Neu recognize the religious factor in Wilsonianism. These were serious omissions from his biography of House.

What Cooper could not see in Wilson, Cara Lea Burnidge brought into sharp focus in *A Peaceful Conquest* (2016). She recognized the centrality of religion in Wilson's statecraft and in his paternalistic and racist ideas about American nationalism and internationalism. "Southern evangelicalism and social Christianity shaped Wilson's conception of democracy," she observed.

For Wilson, democracy was a form of government based in a Calvinist notion of God's order that regulated citizens according to social divisions he understood to be natural and inherently good, particularly whites' racial superiority and patriarchy. He also regarded democracy as a national way of life, an ideal society reflecting the ethos of the social gospel and, therefore, worth spreading around the world. Successful evangelization of this democracy unified America's domestic politics and foreign policy with the telos of humanity.

Religion and politics merged in the president's vision of a new world order. While Burnidge agreed with Cooper that "Wilson supported the separation of church and state," she emphasized, in contrast, that "his ideas of separating his religion and his politics were another matter entirely." Wilson's worldview prevented him from understanding that his particular Christian American perspective was not universally relevant as the foundation for a new world order. "Following the tradition of social Christians before him," Burnidge noted, "Wilson conflated his particular, and peculiarly, white American Protestant view of equality with a universally applicable truth. The distance between his specific religious ideologies and universal truisms was lost on Wilson as he associated them with 'American' values." She explained that "Wilson's Presbyterian childhood taught him that all people were equal in the eyes of God, but it also taught him that God created both masters and slaves who were equal in their sin, salvation, and access to God's grace but not equals in society on earth." What appeared as hypocritical to others seemed inherently natural as an "integral part" of "providential design" to the president. He did not see the disparity between his advocacy of democracy and

The Right of Self-Determination: The Domestication of an Illusion (Cambridge, 2015), 91–159; Eric D. Weitz, "Self-Determination: How a German Enlightenment Idea Became the Slogan of National Liberation and a Human Right," *American Historical Review* 120 (April 2015): 462–96.

his commitment to racial inequality. "His effort to spread democracy, then, was an enterprise qualified by a particular *type* of democracy, born in America and made more perfect through the 'civilizing' force of his Christianity."[45]

Burnidge observed that Wilson's religion shaped his understanding of America's place in the modern world. "Drawing upon white Protestant moralisms," she wrote, "he based his version of American exceptionalism upon a teleological interpretation of U.S. and world history in which the U.S. government, formed by the consent of the people, served as the culmination of Christian progress. In this way, Wilson believed, American democracy stood as a testament to God's order and represented the progressive unfolding of God's will. It was not perfect, but citizens could adapt and improve it over time. Democracy in the United States, then, continually developed through the will of the people, a will he firmly believed flowed naturally from the well-spring of providential design." Having incorporated modern British liberalism into his vision of a new world order, the president saw the British Empire as a partner in establishing it at the Paris Peace Conference. Like him, the British sought to preserve global leadership for white men who presumably represented the best of Western civilization, including Protestant Christianity. They too drew a global color line. Burnidge noted, "Wilson's particular understanding of democracy, like the British delegation's view of world order, assumed the superiority and authority of white Protestants to *properly* lead. White male leadership, especially by Protestants, was the fundamental assumption at the heart of the informal moral establishment that had made America exceptional and social Christianity a unique social justice enterprise."[46] For the president, this exceptionalist American vision seemed universally relevant as the foundation for a new, predominantly Anglo-American, world order. His American nationalism and internationalism expressed his fundamental religious beliefs.

ABSTRACTS OF CHAPTERS

Major trends in recent historiography toward "navigating world history" and "rethinking American history in a global age" have provided new perspectives on America's place in the world. My scholarship on

---

[45] Cara Lea Burnidge, *A Peaceful Conquest: Woodrow Wilson, Religion, and the New World Order* (Chicago, 2016), 16, 26, 65, 74.
[46] Burnidge, *Peaceful Conquest*, 79, 99.

Woodrow Wilson and American internationalism has both contributed to and benefited from these two historiographical trends, as shown by the chapters in this book.

Chapter 1 focuses on "U.S. Military and Diplomatic Affairs during the Gilded Age and Progressive Era."[47] Between 1877 and 1920, the United States emerged as one of the world's great powers. It made the historic transition from so-called American isolationism to President Wilson's liberal internationalism during World War I. Leaders in all countries, whether global empires or small states, regarded him as the preeminent statesman at the Paris Peace Conference of 1919. Anticolonial nationalists looked to him as the potential champion of their aspirations against their imperial masters. That global status, which Wilson enjoyed briefly, was quite different from the minimal role the United States had played in world affairs in 1877. This transition resulted from major developments in the United States and throughout the world.

Chapter 2 analyzes "Making the World Safe for Democracy."[48] By April 1917, Wilson decided to take the United States into the European war against Imperial Germany on the side of the Allies. The war had started in the summer of 1914 and then continued year after year with no end in sight. It expanded beyond Europe to become a world war and did not end until November 1918. Except for large-scale fighting by the great powers in Western Europe, it did not totally halt even then. When Wilson had finally decided in 1917 to recommend that the U.S. Congress declare war against Germany, he hoped to guide Europe and other nations into a new world order. As he proclaimed in his war message, he wanted to make the world safe for democracy. That vision proved far easier for the president to articulate in theory than to accomplish in practice in a world that was deeply divided by competing ideologies as well as imperial, national, racial/ethnic, and economic claims and interests. A new liberal democratic world order eluded the peacemakers after the Great War.

Chapter 3 examines "Woodrow Wilson and *The Birth of a Nation*: American Democracy and International Relations."[49] Wilson led the

---

[47] Lloyd E. Ambrosius, "U.S. Military and Diplomatic Affairs during the Gilded Age and Progressive Era," *The Oxford Encyclopedia of American Military and Diplomatic History*, ed. Timothy J. Lynch (New York, 2013), Vol. 1, 420–32.

[48] Lloyd E. Ambrosius, "Making the World Safe for Democracy," *The Guide to U.S. Foreign Policy: A Diplomatic History*, eds. Thomas W. Zeiler and Robert J. McMahon (Sag Harbor, NY, 2012), Vol. I, 129–41.

[49] Lloyd E. Ambrosius, "Woodrow Wilson and *The Birth of a Nation*: American Democracy and International Relations," *Diplomacy and Statecraft* 18 (December 2007): 689–718.

United States into World War I, promising to make the world safe for democracy. Advocating liberal internationalism, he called for collective security and national self-determination. He wanted democratic states to create the League of Nations as a partnership for peace in a new world order. But in his thinking and statecraft, the text of modern liberalism was intertwined with the subtext of white racism. His friendship with Thomas Dixon, Jr., and his contributions to David W. Griffith's 1915 film *The Birth of a Nation* revealed this nexus between modern liberalism and white racism. His liberal civic ideals appeared quite different from the ultra-racism of the film, which was based on Dixon's novels. He seemed to advocate inclusive nationalism, in contrast to its exclusive Americanism. The president's apparently universal principles, however, were still influenced by the white South's Lost Cause. His diplomacy and his legacy of Wilsonianism combined racism with liberalism. He adhered to the color line at home by promoting Jim Crow segregation in the federal government and abroad by limiting his liberal internationalism in practice. Historians and political scientists have typically identified Wilsonian diplomacy only with liberalism. To see him and his legacy in international history from a different perspective, which brings into focus the experience of people of color, it is necessary to recognize the subtext of racism in the text of Wilson's liberalism. Racism shaped his understanding of America's national identity and global mission, and thus his vision of liberal democracy and peace.

Chapter 4 highlights "The Others in Wilsonianism."[50] Wilson affirmed modern liberalism as the foundation for America's foreign policy when he led the United States into World War I. Liberal democratic ideals, which he proclaimed as potentially applicable throughout the world, should define America's wartime purposes and guide its postwar peacemaking. In his war message he called for making the world safe for democracy. In subsequent speeches he outlined his vision of a new world order that, he hoped, would replace the old, discredited European order, which had collapsed in 1914. The president's liberal vision, later known as Wilsonianism, was apparently universal. His rhetoric suggested that it could apply to all nations. Yet in practice he did not believe in the universality of his modern liberal principles and did not plan to implement them for the benefit of all peoples. Although apparently universal, Wilson's vision left some peoples on the outside at least in the foreseeable

---

[50] Lloyd E. Ambrosius, "The Others in Wilsonianism," *U.S. Foreign Policy and the Other*, eds. Michael Patrick Cullinane and David Ryan (Oxford and New York, 2014), 124–41.

future. He saw real or potential enemies, whether at home or abroad, as disqualified in some way from full participation in his new world order. Unless or until they conformed to his vision, if they could, these others would be kept out. Thus, a fundamental paradox of apparent universality and actual exclusivity characterized Wilsonianism.

Chapter 5 deals with "The Great War, Americanism Revisited, and the Anti-Wilson Crusade."[51] From the beginning of the Great War in 1914 to his death in 1919, Theodore Roosevelt identified the national interests of the United States with the European Allies. He blamed the Central Powers for starting the war, and especially Imperial Germany for its brutal aggression against neutral Belgium. The former president soon directed sharp criticism against President Wilson, who called on the American people to remain neutral in thought as well as deed. Never neutral in his attitude toward the two sides, TR expressed his views in private letters and public speeches as well as published articles and books. He sharply criticized the Wilson administration for its aloofness from the global conflict and for its lack of military preparedness in anticipation of America's entry into the war. Even after the United States declared war against Germany on April 6, 1917, Roosevelt persisted in his anti-Wilson crusade. He advocated Allied military victory over the Central Powers. He blamed Wilson for failing to mobilize U.S. military force more quickly and for favoring a negotiated peace with the Central Powers that would not require their unconditional surrender. Identifying Americanism and patriotism with the all-out pursuit of total victory, TR attacked the Wilson administration for its continuing weakness and ineptitude in the Great War.

Chapter 6 focuses on "Woodrow Wilson, Alliances, and the League of Nations."[52] Wilson's vision of the League of Nations and its place in a new world order after World War I evoked both praise and criticism. Looking back on his leadership during the Paris Peace Conference of 1919, scholars have variously lauded or condemned his statecraft, including his role in drafting the League Covenant. His responsibility for the U.S. Senate's rejection of the Versailles Treaty, which contained the Covenant as an integral part of the peace settlement with Germany, has likewise remained a subject of debate. What was Wilson's own understanding of the postwar League of Nations? Why did he make its creation

---

[51] Lloyd E. Ambrosius, "The Great War, Americanism Reconsidered, and the Anti-Wilson Crusade," *A Companion to Theodore Roosevelt*, ed. Serge Ricard (Malden, MA, 2011), 468–84.

[52] Lloyd E. Ambrosius, "Woodrow Wilson, Alliances, and the League of Nations," *The Journal of the Gilded Age and Progressive Era* 5 (April 2006): 139–65.

his top priority at the Paris Peace Conference? How did he conceive of the League and its potential role in a new era of international relations? What limits did he place on the new League's functions and thus on American obligations under the Covenant? Answers to these questions can help clarify the ongoing debates among scholars and in public discourse over Wilson's historical record and over his legacy for future generations after World War I.

Chapter 7 evaluates "Wilsonian Diplomacy and Armenia: The Limits of Power and Ideology."[53] Armenia emerged as a new nation during World War I, joining the world order that was taking shape in the wake of collapsing empires. President Wilson, in his wartime addresses, proclaimed the principles that should guide the peacemaking. His decision to attend the Paris Peace Conference of 1919 increased the expectations that all peoples, including the Armenians, would have a better future in a new world order, which would feature national self-determination guaranteed by the League of Nations. Wilsonian ideology promised peace and justice for all nations, both old and new. American power would presumably enable the United States to help others fulfill Wilson's ideals in the postwar world. Contrary to these hopes, however, Armenia failed as a new nation, revealing not only its own limits but also those of Wilsonianism. The realities of international politics prevented the Armenian people, who had suffered so much in the past, from achieving the Wilsonian promise after the Great War. The limits of American power and ideology resulted in an outcome very different from what the Armenians wanted and what the U.S. president had heralded.

Chapter 8 on "Woodrow Wilson and George W. Bush: Historical Comparisons of Ends and Means in Their Foreign Policies" contrasts the ideology and statecraft of these two presidents.[54] After 9/11 Bush used the Wilsonian promise to justify America's global war on terrorism. Affirming triumphal Americanism in response to the terrorist attacks, he retaliated in Afghanistan and then launched a preventive war in Iraq, ostensibly to create a new world order of freedom and democracy. He rallied the nation with Wilsonian rhetoric, as noted by historians and other pundits. But his unilateralism and his approval for abusive methods, including torture that violated U.S. and international law, marked a

---

[53] Lloyd E. Ambrosius, "Wilsonian Diplomacy and Armenia: The Limits of Power and Ideology," *The American Response to the Armenian Genocide*, ed. Jay Winter (Cambridge, 2003), 113–45.

[54] Lloyd E. Ambrosius, "Woodrow Wilson and George W. Bush: Historical Comparisons of Ends and Means in Their Foreign Policies," *Diplomatic History* 30 (June 2006): 509–43.

radical departure from Wilson's legacy, despite some commonality. Bush's goals were similar, but his means were more extreme.

Chapter 9 evaluates Woodrow Wilson's "Legacy and Reputation."[55] The president left an enduring legacy, which enhanced his lasting reputation, in both American and world history. Although the Republicans triumphed over the Democrats in the elections of 1920, they did not overturn all the progressive reforms he had achieved with his New Freedom at home. Nor did they succeed in killing his vision of America's new mission in international relations. With Republicans in charge of the White House and Congress during the 1920s, the nation turned away from Wilson's style of presidential leadership and his progressive domestic and foreign policies. But that reversal ended with the Great Depression in the 1930s and World War II in the 1940s. These new crises created the context for President Franklin D. Roosevelt to revive and expand Wilson's progressive agenda at home and abroad. In its continuously revised forms, Wilson's legacy influenced American and world history throughout the remainder of the twentieth and into the twenty-first century. The Cold War consensus affirmed his modern liberalism. In the aftermath of the Cold War and of 9/11, Americans still avowed many of his beliefs and policies. The ideological framework of Wilsonianism helped them explain America's place in contemporary history. His legacy and reputation were thus enduring.

---

[55] Lloyd E. Ambrosius, "Legacy and Reputation," *A Companion to Woodrow Wilson*, ed. Ross A Kennedy (Malden, MA, 2013), 569–87.

I

U.S. Military and Diplomatic Affairs during
the Gilded Age and Progressive Era

During the Gilded Age and Progressive Era (1877–1920), the United States emerged as one of the world's great powers. It made the historic transition from so-called American isolationism of the nineteenth century to President Woodrow Wilson's liberal internationalism during World War I. Leaders in all countries, whether global empires or small states, regarded him as the preeminent statesman at the Paris Peace Conference of 1919. Anticolonial nationalists looked to him as the potential champion of their aspirations against their imperial masters. That global status, which Wilson enjoyed briefly, was quite different from the minimal role the United States had played in world affairs in 1877. This transition resulted from major developments both in the United States and throughout the world.

AGE OF EMPIRES AND NATIONALISM

America's emergence as a great power occurred during the age of empires and nationalism in world history. Its success abroad depended on its strength at home. After the bitter divisions between the North and the South during its Civil War, the United States began to restore national unity with its military triumph over the southern Confederacy. This process continued during the era of postwar Reconstruction (1865–77). Most white southerners, although still remembering their Lost Cause with nostalgia, accepted the Union's restoration and the abolition of slavery. They welcomed reunion of the nation-state on the condition that northerners acquiesced in white supremacy, which manifested itself in the South's Jim Crow laws of racial discrimination. A new generation of white southerners and northerners reunited not only at home but also in fighting Spain in 1898 to liberate Cuba and acquire new colonies for the United States. They now shared a common sense of American nationalism.[1]

The United States was not alone in unifying itself and expanding its empire. Nor was it alone is using war as the means to achieve these goals. Thanks to Chancellor Otto von Bismarck, Prussia consolidated most German states in the middle of Europe, outside the Austro-Hungarian Empire, under its jurisdiction. Its military victory over France in the Franco-Prussian War of 1870–71 enabled Prussia to establish the German Empire. At the same time, Italians unified their country into a new nation-state and prepared for imperial expansion. They too wanted an empire. With the Meiji Restoration in 1868, Japan consolidated its power at home and began to extend it abroad, particularly against Korea and China. While Germany, Italy, and Japan created nation-states and new empires, old European empires also expanded their domains. Russia under the Romanov czars and Austria-Hungary under their Habsburg kaiser/king annexed territories that had once belonged to the ailing Ottoman Empire. Like Turkish leaders in the Ottoman Empire, rulers in the Spanish, Portuguese, and Dutch empires endeavored to retain their earlier global conquests. Other Western European empires, however, continued to seek more colonies. British, French, and Belgian leaders entered into the scramble for Africa, dividing most of that continent into new colonies for themselves. Germans belatedly seized some lands in Africa too. Western imperialists also expanded into Asia. In competition with Japan, the British, French, Russian, and German governments sought concessions in China, the one large country they had not yet divided among their empires.

Empires involved dominance by some people over others. Even if the subjects in an empire were of the same nationality and religion as the ruler who exercised state sovereignty over them, the hierarchical relationship denied democratic rights to them. When the government and its subjects were of different nationalities and religions, the empires typically limited the cultural autonomy of ethnic and religious minorities. Romanov czars restricted freedom for Jews in Russia and Muslims in Central Asia, whom

[1] Walter LaFeber, *The American Search for Opportunity, 1865–1913*, Vol. II in *The Cambridge History of American Foreign Relations*, ed. Warren I. Cohen (Cambridge, 1993); Warren Zimmermann, *First Great Triumph: How Five Americans Made Their Country a World Power* (New York, 2002); Fareed Zakaria, *From Wealth to Power: The Origins of America's World Role* (Princeton, NJ, 1998).

they more recently added to their empire. Jews also increasingly experienced anti-Semitism in the Austro-Hungarian Empire. The Habsburg kaiser favored German-speaking Austrians over Hungarians, Bohemians, or Poles, although most of them were also Catholic. The Hungarians forced him to recognize their special status as a kingdom, but they too dominated other nationalities. Turkish rulers discriminated against Armenian Christians, Jews, and other minorities in the Ottoman Empire. The Poles, who had once lived in their own state before its partition in the late eighteenth century, were still divided among the German, Russian, and Austro-Hungarian empires. These patterns of dominance were typical of the great empires in Europe and elsewhere in the world at the turn of the twentieth century.

Unifying their states at home by appeals to nationalism, rulers in both old and new empires sought to protect and expand their territories and colonies. Their imperial rivalries defined international relations in the late nineteenth and early twentieth centuries, when the United States was making its historic transition from a regional to a global power.

THE GLOBAL COLOR LINE

Beyond the familiar pattern of dominance in empires, the new imperialism of this era involved the drawing of a global color line. As the great powers of Europe carved up much of sub-Saharan Africa and Asia, claiming these foreign lands for their empires, they often justified their control in the name of what was now known as scientific racism. They asserted the superiority of white Europeans over the peoples of color in Africa and Asia. So too did Americans as they acquired colonies for the United States during the Spanish-American War. Racism was not new at this time, but a modern consciousness of race and color in the United States as well as Europe during this era of nationalism led to more rigid divisions between white and nonwhite peoples, in contrast, for example, to the earlier Spanish and Portuguese empires, which witnessed much greater mixing among Europeans, Native Americans, and Africans. In race relations, Americans drew a global color line in their overseas empire comparable to Jim Crow segregation in the American South.[2]

White Europeans and Americans expected to control their new protectorates and colonies. Even if these imperialists anticipated eventual

---

[2] Marilyn Lake and Henry Reynolds, *Drawing the Global Colour Line: White Men's Countries and the International Challenge of Racial Equality* (Cambridge, 2008).

self-rule for the people living in newly acquired territories, as U.S. leaders did for Cuba and the Philippines, they did not think this would happen anytime soon. Presidents from William McKinley to Woodrow Wilson asserted that the United States needed to teach "backward" or "underdeveloped" people in these countries how to govern themselves before they might eventually enjoy the benefits of modern civilization with their own freedom and democracy. By promising self-determination to the colonial people in the future, Americans might deny even to themselves that they had become imperialists like the Europeans. Meanwhile, the United States could justify its new conquests while affirming the ideals of liberal democracy.[3]

Drawing the global color line made white Americans more distrustful of Japan's rising empire than of the old or new European empires. Unlike black Americans, they feared a "yellow peril," as did Europeans. After Japan's victory in the Sino-Japanese War of 1894–95, European statesmen forced the Japanese to surrender some of their gains in China. During the Russo-Japanese War of 1904–05, President Theodore Roosevelt likewise intervened diplomatically to prevent Japan from profiting too much at Russia's expense or threatening Western interests in China. The Treaty of Portsmouth, which he mediated to end the war, accomplished his goals. It also signaled that the United States had emerged as a great power. This treaty did not originate at a conference in London, Paris, Rome, Vienna, or Berlin, but at an American naval base in New Hampshire. While limiting Japan's victory, Roosevelt hoped to accommodate its legitimate interests in East Asia. He did not want to confront the Japanese over their expansion into Korea and northeastern China. It was more important to restrict their immigration into the United States, which he accomplished by negotiating the 1907 Gentleman's Agreement. In contrast to Roosevelt's efforts to balance American and Japanese interests, President William H. Taft challenged Japan's position in East Asia. Wilson too resisted Japan's ambitions in China, especially its seizure of Germany's concessions in Shandong during World War I. At the Paris Peace Conference, Wilson also rejected the idea of racial equality, which the Japanese delegates sought to affirm in the Covenant of the new League of Nations. In collaboration with the British delegation, he drew the global color line in international relations.

[3] Paul A. Kramer, *The Blood of Government: Race, Empire, the United States, & the Philippines* (Chapel Hill, NC, 2006).

Both the British and the Americans feared that affirming racial equality in the Covenant might open their empires to Asians after World War I. The United States had restricted Chinese immigration as early as 1882 and did not intend to open its borders to either Chinese or Japanese workers. Wilson believed that "new immigrants" from Southern and Eastern Europe, mostly Catholic and Orthodox Christians or Jews, could become Americans. He opposed immigration restrictions against them, affirming the possibility of their assimilation. But he did not want to risk opening the nation's borders to Asians. He doubted that most of them could ever become true Americans even if they lived in the United States. Like Roosevelt, Wilson held a racialized view of the nation, which privileged white Anglo-Saxon Protestants. Despite his belief in liberal assimilation for Europeans, he doubted that the American "melting-pot" could ever make Asians into equal citizens. In his racial hierarchy, they were lower than Europeans, although higher than Africans. Like black people, however, they were on the other side of the global color line.[4]

AMERICA'S RISE AS A GREAT POWER

Internal developments enabled America's emergence as a great power during the late nineteenth and early twentieth centuries. Reunion after the Civil War provided political stability for the United States to extend its global influence. Moreover, the Gilded Age and Progressive Era witnessed phenomenal growth in the American economy, which provided the means as well as the incentives for greater involvement abroad.

During the Civil War, President Abraham Lincoln and the Republican Congress enacted several laws to promote agriculture and industry, thereby laying the foundation for the nation's economic development. Thereafter, the federal government subsidized the construction of transcontinental railroads, granted homesteads to farmers, established land-grant universities, erected higher tariffs on imports to protect U.S. factories from foreign competition, chartered national banks, and created a national currency. Its soldiers also cleared the American West for settlement by forcing Native Americans off their ancestral lands and onto reservations. Given the country's abundant natural resources and availability of labor from its large families and foreign immigrants, these measures stimulated

---

[4] Gail Bederman, *Manliness & Civilization: A Cultural History of Gender and Race in the United States, 1880–1917* (Chicago, 1995).

very rapid economic development. After 1877, the New South joined the North and West in the expanding American marketplace.

Other countries too were experiencing economic growth but not nearly as rapidly as the United States. It accounted for only 14.7 percent of the world's manufacturing output in 1880, but reached 32.0 percent in 1913. America's industrial potential grew more than six times during this era, while the other great powers – Great Britain, Germany, France, Russia, Austria-Hungary, Italy, and Japan – expanded their combined production just over four times. Great Britain ranked first in 1880, but the United States surpassed it by 1913, while Germany moved into second place. On the eve of the Great War, the United States produced more than four-fifths as much iron and steel as the total of the other industrial nations. Even with the rapid increase in its population as a consequence of natural growth and immigration, America's per capita level of industrialization expanded faster than that of any other country. This rapid industrialization required an increase in energy consumption of 3.7 times. Fortunately, the availability of coal, oil, natural gas, and hydroelectricity in the United States made it self-sufficient in energy. Its rising agricultural productivity also allowed the nation not only to feed and clothe its expanding urban population but also to sell food and fiber products abroad. These internal developments enabled the United States to emerge as a great power.[5]

External conditions also contributed to America's rise. None of its neighbors posed a serious obstacle. Neither Canada nor Mexico could match its potential military power, which the Civil War had recently demonstrated. Great Britain, which possessed the world's leading navy and a global empire, might have attempted to curb the United States, but instead adopted a long-term policy of appeasement. In 1895, Great Britain accepted arbitration as proposed by the United States to determine the boundary between British Guyana and Venezuela. During this border dispute, President Grover Cleveland accused the British government of violating the Monroe Doctrine. That doctrine, which had developed since President James Monroe had unilaterally proclaimed it in 1823, denied the right of Europeans to acquire new colonies or interfere with independent nation-states in the Western Hemisphere. Although the British government denied the Monroe Doctrine's validity under international law, it chose not to challenge American hegemony in this region.

---

[5] Paul Kennedy, *The Rise and Fall of the Great Powers: Economic Change and Military Conflict from 1500 to 2000* (New York, 1987).

In 1898, the British declined to join other European great powers to support Spain against the United States. As a consequence, none of them challenged America's intervention in Cuba. On April 21, 1898, Congress authorized U.S. military action against Spain to liberate this island. Four days later, after Spain declared war, the United States did too. Americans easily triumphed, asserting manliness in war.[6] Spain conceded McKinley's demands in an armistice on August 12 and a peace treaty in Paris on December 10, 1898. Other great powers did not try to prevent the United States from acquiring the Spanish colonies of Puerto Rico, Guam, and the Philippines, nor from also annexing Hawaii. Great Britain also abstained from the subsequent Philippine-American War of 1899–1902, when the Filipinos continued to fight for their independence against foreign masters.

Presidents McKinley and Roosevelt appreciated British restraint during America's imperial wars at the turn of the century. They reciprocated by showing comparable deference toward the British Empire elsewhere in the world. This Anglo-American rapprochement shaped international relations in the early twentieth century. Great Britain might have supported Canada in the dispute over the Canadian-Alaskan border, but instead favored the United States. After the British persuaded the Canadians to settle the conflict by arbitration, they sided with the United States to award the disputed area to Alaska. The British government also deferred to the rising great power in the new world on other occasions. During the Venezuelan crisis in 1902, which resulted from Venezuela's default on payments of European loans, the British, German, and Italian governments decided to blockade Venezuela's ports to force repayment. When Roosevelt began to see a potential threat to the Monroe Doctrine, the British showed greater deference toward the United States than the Germans did. This pattern of British appeasement later paid dividends. During World War I, Roosevelt became an early advocate of U.S. intervention on Great Britain's side against Germany. President Wilson, although more reluctant to enter the war, also favored Britain over Germany in his interpretation of U.S. neutrality, and he eventually took the United States into the war to help Britain and its allies defeat Germany.[7]

---

[6] Kristin L. Hoganson, *Fighting for American Manhood: How Gender Politics Provoked the Spanish-American and Philippine-American Wars* (New Haven, CT, 1998).
[7] William N. Tilchin, *Theodore Roosevelt and the British Empire: A Study of Presidential Statecraft* (New York, 1997); Nancy Mitchell, *The Danger of Dreams: German and American Imperialism in Latin America* (Chapel Hill, NC, 1999).

AMERICAN EXCEPTIONALISM

The rise of the United States as a great power in a world of empires appeared exceptional within the framework of American nationalism. Most Americans, including U.S. presidents, regarded their country as a providential nation. The Civil War had challenged that interpretation of history, but the postwar reunion and rapid economic growth seemed once more to confirm that God had blessed America. With the justification of "manifest destiny," the United States had expanded across the North American continent and then acquired Alaska and islands in the Pacific Ocean. Despite the phenomenal success of their westward expansion, Americans often denied the similarities between their territorial conquests and those of European empires. They saw their nation, unlike Europe's empires, as the champion of liberty and democracy. The new world, in their perspective, was still different from the old.[8]

American exceptionalism shaped the debate over imperialism at the turn of the twentieth century. After the Spanish-American War, anti-imperialists condemned McKinley's acquisition of colonies, particularly the Philippines. Imperialists and anti-imperialists agreed that the United States should not incorporate these islands as new states in the American Union. Because so many people of color lived there, the prospect that white settlement could overwhelm the existing population did not look promising, unlike the pattern in territories previously acquired in North America. Anti-imperialists feared the negative impact on republican government at home from imperial rule abroad. William Jennings Bryan, the Democratic candidate against McKinley in 1900, sought to turn the election into a referendum on imperialism. Both sides focused on the question of possessing colonies. Bryan's defeat indicated that American voters welcomed the rise of the United States as a great power, even as a new colonial empire. Imperialists and anti-imperialists mutually overlooked that the United States had already created an empire in the new world. Equating imperialism with colonialism enabled them to view America's earlier westward movement as nation-building, not as imperial expansion. Imperialists and anti-imperialists restricted their debate to overseas colonies, which the United States acquired with its new imperialism – the so-called aberration in American history.

Even imperialists soon recognized the problems of a colonial empire. The Philippine-American War showed the costs of imperial rule over

[8] Alan Dawley, *Changing the World: American Progressives in War and Revolution* (Princeton, NJ, 2005).

another people. Granting independence to the Philippines in the future became an increasingly popular idea. Roosevelt shifted his stance during his presidency after McKinley's assassination. As McKinley's running mate in 1900, he had defended the new imperialism and denounced Bryan. But as president, he began to anticipate Philippine independence. Wilson likewise favored the new imperialism at the turn of the century, but later changed his mind. As president, he called for eventual Philippine self-government. In 1916, Congress approved and he signed the Jones Act, promising independence in the future. During World War I, however, Wilson delayed the end of American colonialism for an indefinite time. He still did not think the Filipinos were ready to govern themselves as a free and democratic nation. They needed more tutelage by the United States. His preference for delaying Philippine independence revealed the same reservations about self-determination for people of color that led him after World War I to advocate a new system of mandates under the League of Nations. He touted the League mandates as an alternative to imperialism, although only for colonies and territories of the former German and Ottoman empires. Yet by condemning their imperialism, Wilson reaffirmed the ostensibly substantial contrast between the new and old worlds. He still believed in American exceptionalism.

ISOLATIONISM AND INTERNATIONALISM

As a rising great power during the Gilded Age and Progressive Era, the United States shifted from isolationism to internationalism. Yet these apparently opposite definitions of America's place in the world expressed the same conception of nationalism. Isolationist and internationalist foreign policies, as these alternatives were called after World War I, manifested a common view. Wanting to protect or project their national identity, Americans sought either to remain aloof from Europe's wars and diplomacy or to reform the old world in accordance with their own values and institutions. The transition in America's role in international relations thus occurred within the ideological framework of its exceptionalism.[9]

Historians interpreted America's involvement in the world as the continuation of its own national experience. Noting the closing of the

[9] Christopher McKnight Nichols, *Promise and Peril: America at the Dawn of a Global Age* (Cambridge, MA, 2011).

western frontier by 1890, Frederick Jackson Turner offered his famous thesis to explain the significance of westward expansion. In his 1893 paper "The Significance of the Frontier in American History," delivered to the American Historical Association in Chicago, he attributed the growth of freedom and democracy in the United States to the experience of settling the American West. Because the frontier had nurtured free and democratic values and institutions, however, its closing presented a challenge. Imperialists responded by creating new frontiers overseas. Wilson, as a historian, offered his own frontier thesis and used it as an explanation for America's new imperialism. He regarded the nation's involvement in the Spanish-American War and subsequent acquisition of colonies as the progressive development abroad of its nation-building at home. Later as president, he offered his internationalism as the ultimate culmination of this historical progression. He linked American and world history. His vision of a new world order promised other nations what Americans had already accomplished at home.

In a similar fashion, Americans changed the definition of the Monroe Doctrine. In 1823, while admonishing Europeans to keep out of the new world, Monroe promised that the United States would not entangle itself in the old world's politics and wars. As it made the transition from a regional to a global power, the United States transformed the Monroe Doctrine. In 1904–05, Roosevelt worried that European governments might intervene in the Dominican Republic to collect customs at the ports for the purpose of repaying loans to European creditors. To prevent this intervention, he decided that the United States, at the invitation of the Dominican Republic, should take over the collection of customs, use the revenue to repay creditors, and reform that nation's finances. He articulated the Roosevelt Corollary to justify U.S. involvement in internal Dominican affairs as a defensive measure. This new corollary converted the Monroe Doctrine from a warning against European intervention into a rationale for U.S. intervention.

Presidents in the Progressive Era expanded America's involvement in Latin America and the Caribbean. In 1903, Roosevelt recognized Panama's independence and gained its permission for the United States to construct a canal between the Atlantic and Pacific oceans. To maintain orderly government and impose financial reforms, Taft and Wilson deployed U.S. marines and soldiers to establish long-term protectorates over Nicaragua in 1912, Haiti in 1915, and the Dominican Republic in 1916. Wilson also intervened in the Mexican Revolution, authorizing the U.S. navy to seize Veracruz in 1914 and sending General John J. Pershing's military expedition into northern Mexico in 1916–17. In response to provocative incidents, he tried to teach the Mexicans how to behave toward the United States.

By 1917, Wilson began to project the Monroe Doctrine onto the entire world. He promised that, if European belligerents would conclude a "peace without victory" to end the Great War, the United States would join them in a League for Peace to preserve it. He likened this proposed league to the global extension of the Monroe Doctrine. Thus he offered American principles and policies as the basis for ending the war and reforming the old world. He used the traditional doctrine of nonintervention as the rationale for U.S. involvement overseas, thereby transforming isolationism into internationalism.

GLOBALIZATION AND THE OPEN DOOR

Throughout the Gilded Age and Progressive Era, isolationist and internationalist foreign policies promoted the interests of capitalism. Since Americans had won their independence from the British Empire, they asserted their rights to trade with foreign countries, ship goods across the oceans, and travel wherever they desired. In contrast to European mercantile empires, they advocated an open world with fewer barriers to commerce and shipping. During European wars, they expected the belligerents to respect U.S. neutral rights as defined by their liberal vision of international relations. Throughout the nineteenth century, when Europeans fought only limited wars among themselves, succeeding generations of Americans championed the rights or policies that would open the world to greater commerce and other forms of exchange such as the sending of U.S. missionaries to foreign countries. In the late nineteenth century, they focused this vision on China. They wanted to open the China market to U.S. products and also to convert the Chinese people to Christianity. In China as elsewhere, Americans fostered what would later be called globalization.

In 1899 and 1900, John Hay, McKinley's secretary of state, summarized the traditional U.S. policies toward China in his Open Door Notes. As the British, French, Russians, Germans, and Japanese aggressively acquired concessions from China, Hay affirmed the Open Door policy, asserting that foreign governments should not use their concessions to exclude equal access by others, including Americans, to the China market. Hay also asserted the American commitment to China's territorial integrity and political independence, thus opposing the carving up of this country into colonies like the Europeans had done in Africa.

Presidents during the Progressive Era upheld and expanded the Open Door policy in China. Roosevelt sought to protect the China market for Americans, but without alienating the Japanese. Taft took a more aggressive stance. His "dollar diplomacy" asserted the right of American banks and other firms to make loans and invest in enterprises in China, not just the right of merchants to trade with this country or missionaries to live there. Although nominally denouncing "dollar diplomacy," Wilson actually pursued the same larger definition of the Open Door policy, which likewise contributed to Japanese-American tensions. In 1915, he resisted Japan's Twenty-One Demands against China, but at Paris in 1919, he acquiesced in Japan's acquisition of Germany's former concessions in Shandong, thereby alienating first the Japanese and then the Chinese.[10]

During World War I, Wilson endeavored to protect U.S. neutral rights until 1917. In a sense, he expanded the Open Door policy beyond China to the entire world. He expected the European belligerents to respect the rights of Americans to trade with foreign markets, ship their commodities across the oceans, and travel even through the war zone. He asserted the rights of U.S. passengers on the *Lusitania*, a British ship that a German submarine sank off the Irish coast in 1915. Both the Allies and the Central Powers jeopardized Wilson's liberal definition of neutral rights. But Germany's submarines posed a greater threat than Great Britain's offshore blockade of Europe. In 1917, after Germany resorted to unrestricted submarine warfare, the sinking of three U.S. ships led Wilson to call Congress into special session and recommend a declaration of war. Wilson's efforts to protect neutral rights thus culminated in America's entry into the European war against Germany.[11]

NATIONALISM AND SELF-DETERMINATION

In his war message to Congress on April 2, 1917, Wilson announced an even larger mission for the United States. He called for making the world safe for democracy. He described Germany's submarine warfare as an attack on the rights of all nations. He aligned the United States with the Allies, although only as an Associated Power. Instead of joining a

[10] Emily S. Rosenberg, *Financial Missionaries to the World: The Politics and Culture of Dollar Diplomacy, 1900–1930* (Cambridge, MA, 1999).
[11] Justus D. Doenecke, *Nothing Less Than War: A New History of America's Entry into World War I* (Lexington, KY, 2011).

military alliance to restore the European balance of power, he intended to transform the old world, beginning with Germany. He blamed its military masters, not its people, for sinking U.S. ships and, more generally, for the Great War itself. He promised to liberate the Germans from their dictatorial masters. All nations, including Germany, should enjoy the benefits of peace and democracy. Four days later, after Congress voted, the president announced America's entry into the war.[12]

In this age of empires and nationalism, Wilson regarded nation-states as the building blocks of a new world order. With the Union's restoration after the Civil War, the American government epitomized the combination of state sovereignty and democracy that he identified with national self-determination. Since the 1648 Peace of Westphalia, Western rulers had accepted state sovereignty as the norm in international relations. But not until the American Revolution did sovereign states begin to embrace democracy too. The French Revolution also promoted the new concept of popular sovereignty. By the time Wilson took the United States into World War I, the Western Allies – Great Britain, France, and Italy – had all established liberal democratic states. With the Russian czar's abdication in March 1917, Russia also seemed to be progressing toward democratic government. Wilson wanted these and other democratic nations to join the United States in a global mission not only to defeat Germany but also to make the world safe for democracy.[13]

Wilson elaborated his vision of peace in his famous Fourteen Points address on January 8, 1918. In Russia, the Bolsheviks had seized power in November 1917 and opened negotiations with the Germans for a separate peace on the eastern front. To counter their appeal for peace without annexations or indemnities, the American president outlined the conditions for a new world order. He devoted most of his points to the application of national self-determination in the future peace settlement, although he also reaffirmed the Open Door policy and his commitment to a league of nations. At the core of his thinking was the idea of nation-states, which should exercise self-determination, engage in trade and other forms of open exchange with each other, and join a partnership of democracies to prevent future wars and thus

---

[12] Robert W. Tucker, *Woodrow Wilson and the Great War: Reconsidering America's Neutrality, 1914–1917* (Charlottesville, VA, 2007).

[13] Tony Smith, *America's Mission: The United States and the Worldwide Struggle for Democracy in the Twentieth Century* (Princeton, NJ, 1994).

avoid the need for military alliances or large armies and navies. Such a liberal peace settlement, Wilson anticipated, could transform international relations.[14]

Creating this new world order, however, required the United States and the Allies to defeat of the Central Powers. In 1917, Wilson named General Pershing as commander of the American Expeditionary Force (AEF), which did not yet exist. Before the AEF could contribute to victory, the United States needed to recruit, train, organize, and transport the troops to France, where they would eventually join the Allies on the western front. With appeals to patriotism, the Wilson administration mobilized the nation-state for war. Although Pershing and a small contingent of the AEF soon arrived in France, it took more than a year before they were ready to make a major military contribution on the western front. The greatest American fighting came only during the final weeks of the war.[15]

By the summer and fall of 1918, the Allies, with growing American assistance, began to defeat the Central Powers. They had stopped Germany's spring offensive. The German generals, recognizing that their prospects for victory would diminish in 1919, urged their government to open negotiations for an armistice on the basis of Wilson's Fourteen Points. They hoped to avoid the consequences of defeat by securing peace conditions that appeared more lenient than those of the Allies. Rather then rushing into an armistice at Germany's request, Wilson wanted to know whether the German government spoke for the German people or only for their military masters. He also wanted to commit the Allies to the Fourteen Points. Two days before the armistice finally ended the war on November 11, 1918, a revolution in Berlin replaced the Hohenzollern kaiser with a new republican government. Meanwhile, the Allies had accepted the Fourteen Points with two reservations, and the other Central Powers were disintegrating in defeat. The collapse of the German, Austro-Hungarian, and Ottoman empires allowed the emergence of new nation-states. Thus it appeared that conditions in the old world were progressing toward the new world order that Wilson had heralded.[16]

---

[14] Glenda Sluga, *The Nation, Psychology, and International Politics, 1870–1919* (New York, 2006); David S. Fogelsong, *The American Mission and the "Evil Empire": The Crusade for a "Free Russia" since 1881* (Cambridge, 2007).

[15] David F. Trask, *The AEF and Coalition Warmaking, 1917–1918* (Lawrence, KS, 1993).

[16] Ross A. Kennedy, *The Will to Believe: Woodrow Wilson, World War I, and America's Strategy for Peace and Security* (Kent, OH, 2009).

AMERICA AND THE GLOBAL COMMUNITY

At the Paris Peace Conference, Wilson endeavored to create the global community that he envisaged. He focused primarily on creating the League of Nations, which promised what a later generation called collective security. He chaired the commission that drafted the Covenant for the League. Article 10, which he regarded as the key to its success, committed the nation-states in the League to protect the territorial integrity and political independence of each other against external aggression. Wilson viewed this as a moral obligation. He ensured that the victorious great powers – the United States, Great Britain, France, Italy, and Japan – would dominate the League as permanent members of the Council, while other nation-states would only have seats in the Assembly and serve temporarily on the Council. Wilson and the Allies excluded Germany from the League until it could demonstrate its commitment to peace and democracy during a period of probation. They also kept Bolshevik Russia out of the peace conference and the new global community.[17]

Wilson expected the United States to play the preeminent role in the League. It would exercise hegemony – although he never used this word – over the other nations. For this reason, he saw no conflict between his new internationalism and American nationalism. The United States would unilaterally decide whether to respond under Article 10 with its troops to defend other League members against aggression, just as it had done under the Monroe Doctrine in the Western Hemisphere. In any case, he thought that the mobilization of world public opinion through the League would settle most disputes without the use of military force.

Wilson negotiated with the Allied leaders to implement his Fourteen Points in drawing the postwar borders for Germany and the new nation-states in Eastern and Central Europe. This proved more complicated than he had anticipated. Nationalism fostered competing claims to the same lands. In accordance with his understanding of national self-determination, the president sought to make the fewest possible changes in historical borders. The Allied leaders agreed with him to keep the same boundary between Germany and the Habsburg successor states that had divided the German and Austro-Hungarian empires, thus denying Germany's right to annex Austria or any of Czechoslovakia. The restoration of Poland and the return of Alsace-Lorraine to France, which the Fourteen Points promised, required some border changes. When the

---

[17] Lloyd C. Gardner, *Safe for Democracy: The Anglo-American Response to Revolution, 1913–1923* (New York, 1984).

Germans finally received the peace treaty at Versailles, they protested the loss of territory in Europe and of their overseas colonies. Their interpretation of national self-determination, which affirmed the right of all Germans to live in Germany, was quite different from Wilson's. These differences created enduring conflicts after the war.[18]

Making only a few concessions, Wilson and the Allies forced the Germans to sign the peace treaty at Versailles on June 28, 1919. By then it was apparent that he had failed to create a global community. The Germans hated the treaty. Italy and Japan approved it, but both were disappointed. Chinese delegates left Paris in protest. Great Britain and France made substantial gains, but both distrusted each other and feared the future. Anticolonial nationalists were alienated from Wilson because he had not supported them. New nation-states in Europe fought over their borders. And Bolshevik Russia remained as a pariah on the periphery. Although Wilson had succeeded in creating the League of Nations, this was not the new world order he had promised.[19]

WILSONIANISM

After returning home, Wilson continued to tout his vision of liberal internationalism. When he submitted the Versailles Treaty to the Senate, he claimed that it fulfilled the tenets of what would later be called Wilsonianism. It included the Covenant of the League of Nations, which would facilitate the resolution of disputes still facing the global community. In accordance with the Fourteen Points, the treaty applied the ideal of national self-determination and incorporated the larger Open Door policy. Thus the peace settlement, Wilson affirmed, represented progress toward the creation of a new world order – the work of God's hand.

Henry Cabot Lodge and his Republican colleagues in the Senate thought otherwise. They refused to approve the treaty without amendments or reservations, which Wilson vigorously resisted. As a consequence of the stalemate between them, which focused on the League, the United States rejected the treaty in November 1919 and again in March 1920. It would not join the League. Wilson lost the treaty fight, but he succeeded in framing the issue. It subsequently appeared that the only

---

[18] Klaus Schwabe, *Woodrow Wilson, Revolutionary Germany, and Peacemaking, 1918–1919: Missionary Diplomacy and the Realities of Power* (Chapel Hill, NC, 1985).

[19] Margaret MacMillan, *Paris 1919: Six Months That Changed the World* (New York, 2001); Erez Manela, *The Wilsonian Moment: Self-Determination and the International Origins of Anticolonial Nationalism* (New York, 2007).

alternatives were Wilsonian internationalism or Republican isolationism. This narrowing of the debate obscured other internationalist conceptions of America's role in the world.

Republicans preferred other options. They had looked to international law and arbitration as ways to minimize the risk of war and maintain peace. McKinley and Roosevelt sent U.S. delegations to the 1899 and 1907 Hague Peace Conferences, which established the Permanent Court of Arbitration and revised the definition of its role. Elihu Root, Roosevelt's secretary of state, negotiated bilateral treaties of arbitration, which exempted issues of national honor or independence. Taft attempted to expand the scope of arbitration by omitting these exemptions from new treaties with Great Britain and France in 1911, but never won approval from the Senate. Lodge opposed him as he later did Wilson. After the Great War, Root participated in creating the Permanent Court of International Justice. Wilson showed little interest in this world court. Key Republican leaders, including Lodge and Root, favored the Franco-American security treaty, which promised U.S. protection for France against German aggression. At Paris, Wilson approved this treaty in a compromise to prevent France from separating the Rhineland from Germany, while the British prime minister, who had proposed the compromise, extended the same guarantee. Some of the leading Republicans preferred this specific Anglo-American commitment to France rather than the League's universal obligations. But since Wilson focused on the League, other options received little attention in postwar peacemaking.[20]

Wilson left an enduring legacy in world history.[21] Wilsonianism shaped the ongoing debate over America's global role long after the Gilded Age and Progressive Era.

---

[20] Lloyd E. Ambrosius, *Woodrow Wilson and the American Diplomatic Tradition: The Treaty Fight in Perspective* (Cambridge, 1987).
[21] Cooper, John Milton, Jr., *Woodrow Wilson: A Biography* (New York, 2009).

2

Making the World Safe for Democracy

By April 1917, President Woodrow Wilson decided to take the United States into the war in Europe against Imperial Germany on the side of the Allies. The Great War had started in the summer of 1914 and then continued year after year with no end in sight. It had quickly expanded beyond Europe to become a world war. Known as the First World War after the Second World War a generation later, it did not end until November 1918. Except for the cessation of large-scale fighting by the great powers in Western Europe, it did not totally halt even then. Many wartime conflicts continued or resumed as small wars in the postwar era. These involved the great powers on the periphery, where they sought to preserve or extend their empires, and also many peoples who were struggling to establish their national identities in new states. The Great War continued to influence domestic politics and international relations in the coming years.

When Wilson had finally decided in 1917 to recommend that the U.S. Congress declare war against Germany, he hoped to guide Europe and other nations into a new world order. He wanted, as he proclaimed in his war message, to make the world safe for democracy. That vision proved far easier for the president to articulate in theory than to accomplish in practice in a world that was deeply divided by competing ideologies as well as imperial, national, racial/ethnic, and economic claims and interests. A new democratic world order eluded the peacemakers after the Great War.

WOODROW WILSON'S MODERN LIBERALISM

Wilson's vision of a new world order expressed his understanding of modern liberalism. He had developed his political philosophy long before he was elected as New Jersey's new progressive Democratic governor in 1910 and as U.S. president in 1912. As an undergraduate student at Princeton, he began to read and articulate the ideas that would later characterize his statecraft. He continued his education with the study of law at the University of Virginia. After passing the bar exam, a dismal career as an attorney in Atlanta, Georgia, convinced him to abandon the legal profession and enter the new graduate program in history at Johns Hopkins University in Baltimore. While there, he wrote his first book, *Congressional Government* (1885). Johns Hopkins accepted it as his doctoral dissertation and awarded him a PhD. He then taught various courses in history and political science at other institutions of higher education before returning to Princeton as a professor in the 1890s. During the first decade of the twentieth century, he became Princeton's first president not to be an ordained clergyman. As its new leader, he sought to modernize the small Presbyterian college with his progressive ideas before he later endeavored to reform New Jersey and the United States. In every instance, he applied strong, even arbitrary, executive leadership to achieve what he regarded as liberal or democratic goals.

Wilson devoted much of his academic study to the democratic state, its institutions, and its style of leadership. Although he focused particularly on his own nation, he also examined the origins of governments from ancient Greece and Rome through medieval and modern Europe to the United States. *The State* (1889), his second major book, offered a comparative analysis of statecraft. He traced the development of governance or nation-building in the history of the West, which was, for him, the essence of world history. He saw an evolutionary pattern of development that culminated in the liberal democratic state. He attributed this final triumph of democracy in the United States to both historical experience and racial origins. The Americans had inherited not only their liberal politics and constitutional traditions from the British Empire but also their primordial Anglo-Saxon origins. Thus, Anglo-Americans, like himself, were best qualified to preserve democracy in the United States and promote it abroad.

In his next major book, *Division and Reunion* (1893), Wilson emphasized the unique historical experience on the western frontier of the United States. In his own frontier thesis, which anticipated Frederick Jackson Turner's, he stressed that the westward movement of America's frontier had contributed to the emergence of its democracy, which President Andrew Jackson had epitomized. Wilson's interpretation thus shifted from his previous emphasis on primordial Anglo-Saxon origins to the historical experience on the frontier. The new democratic nation had emerged by 1829. It divided, however, by 1861, giving rise to the tragic civil war between the states. After the war and especially after the bitter postwar experience of southern Reconstruction, the South and the North had begun to overcome their differences and achieve national reunion. Although he had come from the South, having been born in Virginia and raised in Georgia, South Carolina, and North Carolina during the Civil War and Reconstruction, he favored the northern Union's triumph over the southern Confederacy. He identified President Abraham Lincoln as a great national leader during the war. He was far more critical of the postwar experience. Deploring the brief era of "radical" Republican interracial governments in the South, he applauded the reconciliation between white southerners and northerners that ended Reconstruction in 1877. From his perspective of white supremacy, the Democratic Party's triumph against the "radical" governments had restored democracy in the South. With America's ever expanding westward movement, the democratic nation was not only reuniting the North and the South but also extending its frontier into the West. Thus, while joining Turner to focus on the historical experience of the frontier's contribution to American democracy, Wilson did not fully abandon his belief in Anglo-American racial superiority or primordial Anglo-Saxonism.

Wilson's modern liberalism emphasized freedom of the individual within a democratic community. He valued liberty more than equality. He understood liberty in the United States within the framework of law under the U.S. Constitution. Based on British traditions of liberty, freedom for Americans had emerged from their colonial experience. The British had taught the colonists about self-government for nearly two centuries before they had revolted against the mother country in the late eighteenth century to create their own new nation. The American Revolution had allowed them to preserve their British heritage as free people – Wilson would have stated it as free men – while they embarked on self-government as a new nation. This heritage enabled the Americans to create a liberal and increasingly democratic state, which President Jackson's style of frontier politics epitomized. For Wilson, as for most Americans, freedom and democracy were deeply intertwined. His belief in constitutional liberalism as the framework for freedom and democracy was typical among white Americans in the nineteenth and early twentieth centuries, despite the long history of slavery in the colonies and in the United States, especially in the South, and its legacy of racial inequality under the Jim Crow laws.

In Wilson's modern liberalism, freedom for the individual not only guaranteed civil rights under the law but also economic opportunities. Capitalism coincided with democracy as the dual achievements of free people. Wilson's progressive reforms in New Jersey did not threaten that state's reputation as a favorable location for corporations. He did not want to destroy them but at most to regulate them so that new entrepreneurs would have access to the market. He wanted to promote industrial development. His idea of progress affirmed the expansion of America's liberal democracy and its capitalism into new frontiers.

As the Democratic candidate for the presidency in 1912, Wilson offered his program of New Freedom to address the major problems that he saw in the political economy. After winning the election, the new president advocated three reforms to improve the working of American capitalism. First, he called on Congress to adopt a lower tariff, which would reduce prices for consumers and force U.S. industries to become more efficient by facing foreign competition. This would hopefully also help control the tendency of corporations to become both larger and monopolistic. Congress responded by passing the Underwood-Simmons Tariff, which Wilson signed in October 1913. Second, Wilson called on Congress to create a new banking system. Like most bankers, businessmen, and farmers, he saw the need for reforms to stabilize the flow of capital to industry and agriculture. Democrats and Republicans disagreed over the particular solutions, but they shared a general consensus that fundamental changes in the banking system were required. As finally adopted in December 1913, the Federal Reserve Act created a new Federal Reserve Board and twelve regional or federal reserve banks. These new central and regional banks, which combined the public and private sectors, strengthened the banking system at home and also placed the United States in a stronger position in the international financial world during the Great War. Third, Wilson called on Congress to revise and strengthen the nation's antitrust laws. He wanted to prevent monopolies from dominating the marketplace, thereby excluding competitors. He sought to preserve opportunities for new entrepreneurs to engage in free enterprise. Congress complied by passing the Clayton Antitrust Act in October 1914. Meanwhile, in September, it also voted to create the Federal Trade Commission to regulate commerce. Wilson signed both laws to ensure the better functioning of capitalism. These three reforms – tariff, banking, and antitrust – were the essence of Wilson's New Freedom, which focused on freedom for individual producers in industry and agriculture. He wanted to protect their economic opportunities.

Wilson's progressive vision of New Freedom did not call for expanding democracy to include more Americans as participants. He did not advocate any new law or constitutional amendment to grant the right to vote to women. He had no qualms about excluding African Americans and other people of color from political participation and economic opportunities that white citizens enjoyed. To the contrary, the Wilson administration brought the Jim Crow system of racial segregation, which southern states had written into their constitutions and laws in the late nineteenth and early twentieth centuries, into the federal government. The president encouraged and permitted southerners whom he had appointed to his cabinet to draw the color line in their departments. He did not champion civil liberties for all Americans. He wanted to expand freedom for white Americans, not equality for people of color. While seeking the support of working-class Americans within the Democratic Party, Wilson abhorred socialism and hesitated to recognize the rights of labor unions. He sought primarily to expand economic opportunities for producers in industry and agriculture. His modern liberalism did not challenge the existing gender, race, and class divisions in the American nation. His vision of American democracy and capitalism focused on the rights of white men.

WILSONIANISM AND AMERICAN EXCEPTIONALISM

Wilson's modern liberalism furnished the ideological foundation for his new foreign policy, which historians have labeled as liberal internationalism or Wilsonianism. When he called for making the world safe for democracy, he envisaged a new world order that embraced four fundamental tenets that he identified with America's national identity. He hoped the Great War would culminate in the creation of an international community of liberal democracies with capitalist economies. He saw nation-states as the building blocks of this new world order.

During the war, Wilson developed the idea for a postwar international organization that would preserve the peace by preventing future aggression across national borders. He gave top priority to the creation of a new League of Nations at the Paris Peace Conference of 1919. It promised what would later be called collective security, the first tenet of Wilsonianism. As the president conceived it, the League would consist of democratic nation-states that joined together to guarantee their mutual defense against external aggression, and thereby enforce international peace. As a global community of nations, it would replace the old world order that had relied on balances of power and military alliances. It would provide national security for the League's members without their having to maintain large armies or navies.

As Wilsonianism's second tenet, the president advocated the idea of national self-determination. It affirmed both state sovereignty and democracy. Ideally, he thought, all nations should enjoy the right of self-government. Just as Americans had claimed this right during their revolution against the British Empire, some new nations might emerge from the dissolution of the old Russian, German, Austro-Hungarian, and Ottoman empires in Europe and the Middle East. While proclaiming the idea of national self-determination as a universal principle, Wilson hesitated to promote it for all peoples throughout the world. Only nations that had achieved a mature level of political development could be entrusted to govern themselves.

As its third tenet, Wilson's vision of a liberal democratic world order favored the Open Door in international commerce and finance as well as in travel and cultural exchange. He wanted to guarantee the freedom of the seas and to remove barriers to trade and investment across borders. He called as well for open diplomacy to make international transactions more transparent. This kind of liberal world order would facilitate the operations of international capitalism, just as his New Freedom promoted it at home.

As the fourth, undergirding tenet of Wilsonianism, the president believed in progressive history. In his view, world history revealed a progressive pattern of development in all aspects of life as primitive peoples moved toward greater maturity over the generations. This pattern was most apparent in the West, the region of the world where he focused his attention as a scholar and later as president. The idea of progress in human history seemed as self-evident to him as the theory of evolution in science. Because the United States represented the apogee of progressive historical development, it furnished the best model for other nations.

Wilson espoused the ideology that scholars have called American exceptionalism. He believed that making the world safe for democracy required the global triumph of Wilsonianism. The president's modern liberalism defined its key tenets. His Americanism provided the vision for his new world order. Ironically, while he offered the United States as the ideal model for the world, he avowed its own uniqueness. As the global fulfillment of America's own providential history and destiny, Wilson affirmed that the United States would help other nations achieve the same blessings of liberty for themselves. On Memorial Day in 1917, he proclaimed that "we are saying to all mankind, 'We did not set this Government up in order that we might have a selfish and separate liberty, for we are now ready to come to your assistance and fight out upon the field of the world the cause of human liberty.' ...Such a time has come, and in the providence of God America will once more have an opportunity to show to the world that she was born to serve mankind."[1]

After the war, despite the many difficulties Wilson encountered at the peace conference in seeking to establish his new world order, he continued to interpret international relations within the ideological framework of American exceptionalism. On his western tour in September 1919, he reaffirmed his belief that the United States should fulfill its God-given mission by joining the new League of Nations. He thought it would "make every nation a nobler instrument of Divine Providence – that is world politics." In his view, America's providential mission had now become the world's. Thus he saw no contradiction between nationalism and internationalism. "I have sometimes heard gentlemen discussing the questions that are now before us with a distinction drawn between nationalism and internationalism in these matters," he said in St. Louis.

It is very difficult for me to follow their distinction. The greatest nationalist is the man who wants his nation to be the greatest nation, and the greatest nation is the nation which penetrates to the heart of its duty and mission among the nations of the world. With every flash of insight into the great politics of mankind, the nation that has that vision is elevated to a place of influence and power which it cannot get by arms, which it cannot get by commercial rivalry, which it can get only by no other way than by that spiritual leadership which comes from a profound understanding of the problems of humanity.[2]

Wilson claimed to have offered that understanding to the peacemakers at Paris and expected his fellow Americans to accept it as well by supporting the Versailles Treaty with Germany, and especially the Covenant that made the new League of Nations an integral part of the peace settlement.

THE GREAT WAR, 1914–1918

Wilson's vision of America's providential mission to reform the world, which he heralded during the Great War and sought to implement at the

---

[1] Memorial Day Address, May 30, 1917, Woodrow Wilson, *The Public Papers of Woodrow Wilson: War and Peace* [hereafter *PPWW: War & Peace*], eds. Ray Stannard Baker and William E. Dodd (New York, 1927), 1: 53; Woodrow Wilson, *The Papers of Woodrow Wilson* [hereafter *PWW*], ed. Arthur S. Link (Princeton, NJ, 1983), 42: 422–23.

[2] Address, St. Louis, Sept. 5, 1919, *PPWW: War & Peace*, 1: 621; *PWW* (1990), 63: 43–51.

Paris Peace Conference, challenged his fellow Americans to undertake an unprecedented role in international affairs. At the beginning of the war, he had not yet developed his plans.

In August 1914, after the Allies and the Central Powers resorted to war, the president proclaimed American neutrality. He wanted to protect the nation's neutral rights but without entangling it in the European war. Like all presidents since George Washington, he did not want the United States to join either side as a belligerent. The difficulty for Wilson, however, lay in the contradiction between isolating the United States from the war and protecting its neutral rights vis-à-vis the competing alliances. Both Great Britain, the preeminent naval power among the Allies, and Imperial Germany, the dominant Central Power, threatened U.S. neutral rights and interests. The president refused to surrender America's stakes in shipping and travel on the high seas or its opportunities for investment and commerce with the belligerents. Non-entanglement in the old world and preservation of traditional neutral rights proved to be mutually exclusive. The British established an off-shore blockade that curtailed American trade with Germany, while the Germans retaliated with submarine attacks on Allied ships.

The sinking on May 7, 1915, of the British passenger liner *Lusitania*, which carried Allied munitions as well as American and European passengers, highlighted the dilemma. Wilson vigorously protested to Germany over the deaths of 128 Americans but refused, contrary to Secretary of State William Jennings Bryan's advice, to make an equivalent protest against British violations of U.S. neutral rights. Only when the Germans halted their submarine warfare to avoid a confrontation with the United States that might provoke it into joining the Allies did Wilson have the opportunity to keep the nation out of the war and also protect its neutral rights on the high seas and in commerce and investment, particularly with the Allies. As Bryan foresaw when he resigned in the midst of the *Lusitania* crisis, Wilson's ability to keep the United States out of the war and also protect all the neutral rights he claimed for American passengers, shippers, merchants, and bankers depended on Germany's restraint in the use of its submarines. Wilson too recognized the potential contradiction between keeping out of the war and asserting U.S. neutral rights. He might be, as he announced during the *Lusitania* crisis, "too proud to fight" at this time, but he could not resolve the dilemma so easily over the long run. If Germany resorted to submarine warfare in the future, he could no longer avoid war without surrendering rights that he vigorously claimed for Americans.

Ending the war though American diplomatic intervention or mediation offered one potential solution to the dilemma. Toward that end, he sent his close friend Edward M. House to Europe in pursuit of a compromise. House had been in Europe as the president's envoy during the summer of 1914 at the time of the July crisis that eventually led to war. When he returned home just before the Great War erupted, he thought he had helped diminish the Anglo-German naval rivalry. He had clearly failed to comprehend what was happening. House was no more successful on his subsequent trips to Europe during the early months of 1915 and again in 1916. Because of the immense power of the United States and the desire of the belligerents to avoid alienating Wilson, the governments in London, Paris, and Berlin welcomed House but never allowed him to interfere with the pursuit of their own war aims. His efforts at mediation were essentially irrelevant to the wartime diplomacy, leaving Wilson with the dilemma.

In December 1916, after Wilson won reelection as president with the campaign slogan that he had kept the United States out of war, he made one final effort to end the fighting. In a peace note to the Allies and the Central Powers, he asked both sides to disclose their war aims. Professing indifference toward the political and territorial settlement in the old world, he wanted the Europeans to conclude a "peace without victory." "There must be," he told the Senate on January 22, 1917, "not a balance of power, but a community of power; not organized rivalries, but an organized common peace." If the belligerents would conclude that kind of peace, the president promised that the United States would help guarantee it with a new League for Peace. He further asserted that "no nation should seek to extend its polity over any other nation or people, but that every people should be left free to determine its own polity, its own way of development, unhindered, unthreatened, unafraid, the little along with the great and powerful." He proposed "government by consent of the governed" along with freedom of the seas and moderation in the size of armies and navies, which would keep them from being used for future aggression. Offering these American principles and policies as those of "forward looking men and women everywhere," he avowed that all nations should adopt them in a new postwar world order. Otherwise the United States would isolate itself from the old world rather than join what he now called a League for Peace.[3]

[3] Address to Senate, Jan. 22, 1917, Woodrow Wilson, *The Public Papers of Woodrow Wilson: The New Democracy*, eds. Ray Stannard Baker and William E. Dodd (New York, 1926), 2: 410, 414; *PWW* (1982), 40: 533–39.

Wilson's hope for a "peace without victory" that would enable the United States to escape the dilemma that had plagued him during the period of American neutrality soon collapsed. Germany announced that it would resort to unrestricted submarine warfare against neutral as well as Allied shipping in the war zone around the British Isles. The president broke diplomatic relations with Germany. Once German submarines sank three U.S. ships in mid-March, he saw no option but war. To protect neutral rights, he abandoned official neutrality. Germany's submarine warfare led to his decision for war, thereby resolving the dilemma.

Yet in his war message to Congress on April 2, 1917, Wilson offered a much larger purpose for American intervention into the Great War than upholding U.S. neutral rights. "The present German submarine warfare against commerce is a war against mankind," he proclaimed. "It is a war against all nations." In this global struggle, the president heralded a new world order. With the United States now entering the war, he wanted democratic nations to join together not only to defeat Imperial Germany and its allies but to create a new era of international relations. He hoped to reform the world. "A steadfast concert for peace can never be maintained except by a partnership of democratic nations," he explained. "No autocratic government could be trusted to keep faith within it or observe its covenants." In this new world order, peace among nations would depend on democratic governance within them. "We are glad, now that we see the facts with no veil of false pretense about them," Wilson avowed, "to fight thus for the ultimate peace of the world and for the liberation of its peoples, the German peoples included: for the rights of nations great and small and the privilege of men everywhere to choose their way of life and of obedience. The world must be made safe for democracy. Its peace must be planted upon the tested foundation of political liberty."[4]

Responding to Wilson's call, both the House of Representatives and the Senate voted to declare war against Germany, which he announced on April 6, 1917. The United States joined the Allies but only as an Associated Power, thereby reaffirming America's separate national identity and its traditional isolation from Europe. He wanted the United States, rather than entangling itself in the politics and wars of the old world, to transform it by creating a new liberal world order. This vision expressed American exceptionalism.

[4] Address to Congress, April 2, 1917, *PPWW: War & Peace*, 1: 8, 12, 14; *PWW* (1983), 41: 519–27.

It seemed to Wilson that history was progressing in the direction he desired. In March 1917, the Russian czar had abdicated and a provisional liberal democratic government had replaced him. This Russian Revolution apparently allowed the Russian people to exercise their right of national self-determination. In his war message, the president rejoiced:

Russia was known by those who knew it best to have been always in fact democratic at heart, in all the vital habits of her thought, in all the intimate relationships of her people that spoke their natural instinct, their habitual attitude towards life. The autocracy that crowned the summit of her political structure, long as it had stood and terrible as was the reality of its power, was not in fact Russian in origins, character, or purpose; and now it has been shaken off and the great, generous Russian people have been added in all their naive majesty and might to the forces that are fighting for freedom in the world, for justice, and for peace.[5]

Now that the major European Allies – Russia as well as Great Britain, France, and Italy – all had democratic governments, Wilson thought the United States could associate itself with them in pursuit not just of a military victory and a new balance of power but of a new world order. Defeating the Central Powers, all of which still had autocratic governments, would advance the cause of freedom. It would, as he said, make the world safe for democracy.

Wilson blamed Imperial Germany's government under Kaiser Wilhelm II, not its people, for the war. "The war was begun by the military masters of Germany, who proved to be also the masters of Austria-Hungary," he asserted on June 14, 1917. "Their plan was to throw a broad belt of German military power and political control across the very center of Europe and beyond the Mediterranean into the heart of Asia; and Austria-Hungary was to be as much their tool and pawn as Serbia or Bulgaria or Turkey or the ponderous states of the East." With their resort to unrestricted submarine warfare, they denied the right of the United States to remain neutral. So Wilson now called for a war to liberate not only the German people from their rulers but also the other nations under German military dominance. He said, "[T]his is a People's War, a war for freedom and justice and self-government amongst all the nations of the world." Defeating Germany would vindicate American principles and secure "the salvation of the nations."[6]

---

[5] Address to Congress, April 2, 1917, *PPWW: War & Peace*, 1: 12–13; *PWW*, 41: 519–27.
[6] Flag Day Address, June 14, 1917, *PPWW: War & Peace*, 1: 62–63, 66–67; *PWW*, 42: 498–504.

To achieve that end, the president had appointed General John J. Pershing to command the American Expeditionary Force in Europe. Before it could join the Allied armies on the western front and contribute to victory, however, the United States needed to recruit, train, equip, and ship the soldiers to France. At the time Congress voted for war, the Wilson administration was just beginning to mobilize. Only with the passage of military and naval laws in 1916 to expand the nation's armed forces did it begin to prepare for possible participation in the war. It was still far from ready. Consequently, the Allies faced large-scale offensives by the Central Powers on the eastern front in 1917 and on the western front in 1918 without much American military assistance. Except for token troops on the western front, the United States contributed indirectly by loaning money to the Allies and supplying them with agricultural and industrial goods.

Germany's eastward advance into Russia in the summer of 1917 further weakened that country's provisional government, which also faced serious internal challenges. Wilson sent a diplomatic mission under the leadership of Republican elder statesman Elihu Root to encourage the Russians to remain in the war against Germany and proceed with drafting a new constitution for a liberal democratic government. Various socialists called for the end of war and for more radical reform in the new government than Wilson anticipated. Led by Vladimir I. Lenin, the Bolsheviks posed the most serious threat. In November 1917, they seized power in Petrograd and began to extend their control over what remained of the Russian Empire. Early in the new year, they stopped the recently elected constituent assembly from drafting a liberal democratic constitution. Meanwhile, the Bolsheviks called for peace without annexations or indemnities and challenged the Allies to join them in ending the war with the Central Powers. Wilson and the Allies rejected their appeal and continued to fight, while the Bolsheviks quickly concluded an armistice with Germany. The ensuing negotiations between the Bolsheviks and the Germans culminated on March 3, 1918, in the Treaty of Brest-Litovsk, which ended the war on the eastern front. This separate peace threatened the Allies with the prospect that Germany might win the war on the western front before the United States could mobilize the American Expeditionary Force to rescue them.

Wilson appealed to both Russians and Americans to support the war and his liberal goals, in contrast to the radical socialist agenda of the Bolsheviks. "We are fighting for the liberty, the self-government, and the undictated development of all peoples," he had proclaimed in a message to Russia on May 26, 1917.[7] After the Bolshevik Revolution, he continued to hope that the Russian people would remain in the war. He denounced Lenin and his associates as dreamers and urged American workers not to heed their appeal for peace. At the American Federation of Labor convention on November 12, 1917, he warned, "Any body of free men that compounds with the present German Government is compounding for its own destruction. But that is not the whole of the story. Any man in America or anywhere else that supposes that the free industry and enterprise of the world can continue if the Pan-German plan is achieved and German power fastened upon the world is as fatuous as the dreamers in Russia." Loyalty by all classes during the war was, for Wilson, "the meaning of democracy."[8] After Lenin's government nevertheless concluded the separate peace with Germany, Wilson still appealed to the Russian people. He hoped they would eventually prevail against both the Germans and the Bolsheviks, who were now collaborating in their resistance to his liberal vision of a new world order. "The whole heart of the people of the United States," he told them on March 11, 1918, "is with the people of Russia in the attempt to free themselves forever from autocratic government and become the masters of their own life."[9]

As a counter to the Bolshevik appeal for peace, Wilson outlined his own vision of peace in his famous Fourteen Points address to Congress on January 8, 1918. He summarized the four tenets of Wilsonianism. He called for a new era of open diplomacy and arms reduction by states and for equality of commercial and financial opportunities across national or imperial borders; for self-determination by nations that had reached the maturity that qualified them for self-rule and for good governance of colonial peoples who had not reached that level of development; for a new League of Nations that would guarantee mutual security for democratic states; and, in general, for historical progress toward a new world order. "An evident principle runs through the whole program I have outlined," he concluded. "It is the principle of justice to all peoples and nationalities, and their right to live on equal terms of liberty and safety with one another, whether they be strong or weak."[10]

Although Wilson's Fourteen Points did not prevent the Bolsheviks from negotiating a separate peace with Germany and consolidating their

---

[7] Message to Russia, May 26, 1917, *PPWW: War & Peace*, 1: 50.
[8] Address to American Federation of Labor, Nov. 12, 1917, *PPWW: War & Peace*, 1: 120, 122; *PWW* (1984), 45: 11–17.
[9] Message to Russia, March 11, 1918, *PPWW: War & Peace*, 1: 191; *PWW* (1984), 46: 598.
[10] Address to Congress, Jan. 8, 1918, *PPWW: War & Peace*, 1: 162; *PWW*, 45: 534–39.

power in what remained of the former Russian Empire, they did raise expectations elsewhere about the future peace settlement. Even German military leaders, after the Allies halted their spring offensive in 1918 and the American Expeditionary Force began to take over a sector on the western front later that summer, saw in the Fourteen Points a possible escape from total defeat. In contrast to Allied war aims, Wilson's principles might allow Germany to minimize its losses. At the insistence of its generals, the German government appealed to the president for an armistice on the basis of his Fourteen Points. Wilson responded favorably but cautiously, seeking to ascertain whether the German government spoke on behalf of the German people. He endeavored to commit the Allies as well to his Fourteen Points by sending House to Europe on another diplomatic mission. They agreed with qualifications. A revolution in Germany on November 9 replaced the emperor with a republic and thus seemed to fulfill Wilson's requirement for regime change. The new German government sent a civilian delegation to sign the armistice, which ended the war on November 11, 1918, with the promise of a liberal peace based on the Fourteen Points.

THE PARIS PEACE CONFERENCE OF 1919

Believing that he could achieve his goals better than anyone else, Wilson decided to attend the Paris Peace Conference of 1919. Before it opened, he toured Allied countries, which welcomed him as a triumphal world leader. "There is a great wind of moral force moving through the world," he told his Paris audience on December 21, 1918, "and every man who opposes himself to that wind will go down in disgrace." In his view, history was progressing toward the new world order he had heralded during the war. Explaining his vision, he said,

My conception of the League of Nations is just this, that it shall operate as the organized moral force of men throughout the world, and that whenever or wherever wrong and aggression are planned or contemplated, this searching light of conscience will be turned upon them and men everywhere will ask, "What are the purposes that you hold in your heart against the fortunes of the world?" Just a little exposure will settle most questions.[11]

In Carlisle, England, on December 29, he affirmed, "I believe that as this war has drawn the nations temporarily together in a combination of

---

[11] Address at University of Paris, Dec. 21, 1918, *PPWW: War & Peace*, 1: 330; *PWW* (1986), 53: 461–63.

physical force we shall now be drawn together in a combination of moral force that will be irresistible."[12]

Wilson gave top priority in Paris to creating the League of Nations. He collaborated with the British delegates in drafting the Covenant for this new international organization. He chaired the League commission that undertook this task. Article 10, which he regarded as the key to the League's success, committed all its members to guarantee each other's territorial integrity and political independence from external aggression. This form of collective security promised to defend democratic states against their aggressive neighbors. He reported the commission's first draft of the Covenant to a plenary session of the peace conference on February 14 before returning to the United States for a brief time. After returning to Paris, the president sought to revise the Covenant to meet the criticism of Republican senators. He wanted to exempt the Monroe Doctrine from the League's jurisdiction, thereby assuring U.S. hegemony in the Western Hemisphere. Japanese delegates seized this moment to propose their own amendment to affirm the racial equality of all nations in the League. Along with the British delegates, Wilson drew the color line. He defeated the Japanese amendment in the commission, while winning approval of his own Monroe Doctrine amendment. The Japanese persisted in the final plenary session on April 28, but again failed. On this occasion, the president emphasized "the capital significance of this Covenant, the hopes which are entertained as to the effect it will have upon steadying the affairs of the world, and the obvious necessity that there should be a concert of the free nations of the world to maintain justice in international relations, the relations between people and between the nations of the world."[13] Wilson's liberal rhetoric sounded universal, but he still drew the color line. Yet despite his racial prejudices, he anticipated that the League would guarantee a new world order that originated from the global ideology of modern Anglo-American liberalism.

Wilson agreed with the Allied leaders at the peace conference to exclude Germany from membership in the League of Nations but resisted some of their other proposals for postwar security. He wanted Germany to prove that it had become a peaceful democratic state during a period of probation before it joined the new partnership. Doubting that Germany could ever pass this test, French premier Georges Clemenceau viewed the

[12] Address at Carlisle, England, Dec. 29, 1918, *PPWW: War & Peace*, 1: 347–48; *PWW*, 53: 541.
[13] Address at Fifth Plenary Session of Peace Conference, April 28, 1919, *PPWW: War & Peace*, 1: 472; *PWW* (1988), 58: 199–202.

League as a postwar alliance to protect his country against future German aggression. He also advocated other measures to enforce the peace. He wanted to disarm Germany so that it would not have the military capacity to attack its neighbors, and to annex the entire left bank of the Rhine, not just Alsace-Lorraine, to France. Wilson and British prime minister David Lloyd George shared Clemenceau's desire for German disarmament but resisted his efforts to separate the Rhineland from Germany, which they saw as a gross violation of the principle of national self-determination. Lloyd George proposed a compromise that eventually resolved this conflict. He and Wilson offered to sign Anglo-French and Franco-American security treaties, which would commit Great Britain and the United States to defend France in the event of German aggression, while requiring France to abandon its plans to separate the Rhineland from Germany. The British and American leaders approved only the temporary occupation of the Rhineland for a maximum of fifteen years. Wilson acquiesced in the French security treaty by interpreting it as a particular instance of what the United States might do under Article 10, although he never liked this military alliance and later ignored it.

Negotiating Germany's postwar borders revealed differences among the peacemakers over the meaning of national self-determination. They agreed that France could annex Alsace-Lorraine, which Wilson had promised in his Fourteen Points, but not the Saar Valley, although the French would continue to administer this region and benefit from its coal mines. They also gave small slices of territory to Belgium and Denmark and readily agreed to prevent Germany from annexing what remained of Austria. Germany's new eastern borders caused the most serious problems. Clemenceau supported Poland's claims to a land corridor to the Baltic, which would transfer substantial portions of East Prussia from Germany to the new nation. He foresaw Poland and Czechoslovakia as future allies on the eastern front, replacing Russia as a deterrent against Germany. Wilson did not share Clemenceau's strategic concerns but strongly supported the emergence of Poland, as he had promised in his Fourteen Points. He also welcomed other new nations, notably Czechoslovakia and Yugoslavia, arising from the collapse of the Habsburg or Austro-Hungarian Empire. In his Fourteen Points he had called only for autonomy for the nationalities within that empire, but now he recognized their claims to self-determination as new states. In his liberal view, these new nations – Poland, Czechoslovakia, and Yugoslavia – would comprise several different nationalities as citizens, as did the United States. He favored the assimilation of various peoples in the new democratic nation-states, not their separation along ethnic lines. Lloyd George, who saw Britain's primary interests outside continental Europe, was more indifferent than either Clemenceau or Wilson toward the new nations in Central and Eastern Europe. Only when the British prime minister became increasingly concerned that Germany might not accept the peace treaty did he take a keen interest in trying to minimize Germany's territorial losses.

Various peoples outside as well as inside Europe had understood Wilson's advocacy of national self-determination as a promise to them. But he drew the color line. Anticolonial nationalists, who sent delegates to Paris to present their cases, claimed this apparently universal right. He disappointed them. He did not think that most peoples outside Europe had reached the level of political development to qualify them for self-government. His attitude toward such claims against the Allies was similar to his view of the Philippines, which he thought was not yet ready for independence. Just as the United States still needed to keep the Philippines as a colony, so too did the European Allies need to keep their empires. The only exceptions were the defeated Central Powers. To provide governance for Germany's former colonies, which were stripped from it under the peace treaty, and for most of the lands of the former Ottoman Empire, Wilson sought to create a new system of mandates under the League of Nations. With these mandates, the Allies would acquire control over peoples of color in Africa and Asia as well as the Middle East. Although the League would provide some international supervision, the victorious Allies essentially expanded their colonial empires with Wilson's blessing.

Wilson championed the Open Door principle with mixed results at Paris. He wanted to ensure equal opportunities for commerce and investment throughout the world. He applied this principle to the countries under the League mandates as well as to Germany. He also sought to uphold the Open Door in China by requiring Japan to renounce its claims to Germany's former concessions in the Shandong province. In 1914 Japan had declared war against Germany and joined the Allies to seize its possessions in China and some of its Pacific islands. After Wilson killed Japan's racial equality amendment, its delegates adamantly resisted his insistence that Japan restore its claims in Shandong to China. To ensure that Japan would remain at the peace conference and join the League of Nations, he finally capitulated on Shandong. This violation of China's sovereignty over its province deeply disillusioned the Chinese with Wilson, whom they had regarded as their friend, and provoked a strong anticolonial nationalist uprising in the form of the May Fourth

Movement. He was more successful in writing the Open Door principle into the treaty's provisions that prohibited Germany from postwar economic discrimination against the United States or the Allies. But he also agreed with the Allies to require Germany to pay more reparations, although not total war costs, than the Germans regarded as consistent with his Fourteen Points. Almost everyone was disappointed with some aspect of the new economic conditions in the peace settlement.

After Wilson and the Allied leaders finished negotiating the peace treaty among themselves, they presented it to the German delegation at Versailles on May 7, 1919. The Germans vigorously protested against its conditions, denouncing it as a gross violation of the Fourteen Points. They criticized Germany's exclusion from the League of Nations and its disarmament while the Allies retained their armies and navies. They objected to the loss of their territory on Germany's western and eastern borders, especially to Poland, and of their colonies overseas. They opposed the continuation of American and Allied occupation of the Rhineland and the demand for substantial reparations, especially because these payments were justified by the allegation of Germany's war guilt. They demanded extensive revisions of the treaty. Lloyd George inclined to appease the Germans, especially at the expense of France, but Wilson stood firm with Clemenceau. They finally forced the Germans to sign the peace treaty on June 28, 1919.

THE LIMITS OF WILSONIANISM IN THE
POSTWAR WORLD

Wilson returned to the United States and submitted the Versailles Treaty to the Senate on July 10. He acknowledged, "It was not easy to graft the new order of ideas on the old, and some of the fruits of the grafting may, I fear, for a time be bitter." He stressed the League as the key to world peace. "A league of free nations had become a practical necessity. Examine the treaty of peace and you will find that everywhere throughout its manifold provisions its framers have felt obliged to turn to the League of Nations as an indispensable instrumentality for the maintenance of the new order ... in ... the world of civilized men." Affirming American exceptionalism and his progressive vision, Wilson concluded,

The stage is set, the destiny disclosed. It has come about by no plan of our own conceiving, but by the hand of God who led us into this way. We cannot turn back. We can only go forward, with lifted eyes and freshened spirit, to follow the vision. It was of this that we dreamed at our birth. America shall in truth show the way. The light streams on the path ahead, and nowhere else.[14]

Although the president still touted his vision of a new world order, the peace treaty had not reformed the world as he had promised. At Paris foreign leaders had resisted or rejected his ideas, forcing him to compromise. The real world did not match his vision of a community of nations based on modern liberalism. The Allies pursued their own national or imperial interests, although they agreed sufficiently with the president to allow them to draft the Versailles Treaty. Germany challenged the peace settlement in a more fundamental way. Even after formally ratifying the treaty, the Germans evaded its requirements and sought its revision. The peace conference represented only the victors. It had excluded Lenin's Bolshevik regime, which Wilson and the Allies did not regard as Russia's legitimate government. The Russian civil war continued throughout the peacemaking. After the Bolsheviks consolidated their power, the new Soviet Union also became a revisionist power, sometimes collaborating with Germany. It rejected both liberal democracy and capitalism. Most delegations that came to Paris from beyond Europe were also outsiders, allowed to present their cases only unofficially. The United States, Great Britain, and France dominated the proceedings. Although Italy and Japan were present among the top five great powers at the peace conference, their contributions were minimal. They signed the treaty but were alienated by their failures to achieve more of their demands. China refused to accept the treaty, departing from Paris in protest. In short, Wilsonianism had failed to furnish the foundation for a new world order.

At home Wilson also experienced rejection of his liberal vision. The U.S. Senate, now controlled by the Republicans under Henry Cabot Lodge's leadership, refused to approve the peace treaty, especially the League Covenant, without attaching amendments or reservations to the resolution of ratification. The president resisted any changes. In September 1919, he went on a speaking tour of western states to win public support for the League, defending it as the best way to ensure peace by stopping aggression and containing the spread of Bolshevism into Western Europe. Highlighting the Bolshevik threat even to the United States, he contributed to the Red Scare that coincided with the treaty fight. Wilson's western tour not only failed; it also led to the collapse of his health. In early October, he suffered a massive stroke, which left him with limited

[14] Address to Senate, July 10, 1919, *PPWW: War & Peace*, 1: 541, 542, 551–52; *PWW* (1989), 61: 426–36.

capacity to fulfill his presidential duties. After adopting Republican reservations, the Senate voted against the treaty in November and again in March 1920. Democratic senators voted against the treaty with the reservations, while their Republican colleagues voted against it without them. Irreconcilable senators voted against it both ways to ensure its defeat. Because the treaty lacked a two-thirds majority, the United States declined to join the League of Nations that Wilson regarded as his principal contribution to a new world order. His vision, having failed after the Great War, nevertheless persisted in the minds of his followers. Although he had not made the world safe for democracy, they maintained the hope and promise of Wilsonianism.

3

Woodrow Wilson and *The Birth of a Nation*

American Democracy and International Relations

What was President Woodrow Wilson's concept of democracy when he led the United States into World War I, promising to make the world safe for democracy? In his thinking, the text of modern liberalism was intertwined with the subtext of white racism. His friendship with Thomas Dixon, Jr. and his contributions to David W. Griffith's 1915 film *The Birth of a Nation* revealed this connection, which marked his statecraft during the Progressive Era. Wilson's liberalism might appear quite different from the film's ultra-racism. His liberal civic ideals seemed to offer inclusive nationalism, in contrast to its exclusive Americanism. The president's apparently universal principles promised a new world order. Yet the white South's Lost Cause still influenced his racist understanding of America's national identity and its global mission, as it did Dixon's. Both liberalism and racism characterized Wilson's vision of democracy and peace.

MODERN LIBERALISM AND RACISM

Wilson's liberal internationalism, or Wilsonianism, expressing his belief in God and progressive history, heralded world peace.[1] In apparent

[1] Lloyd E. Ambrosius, *Woodrow Wilson and the American Diplomatic Tradition: The Treaty Fight in Perspective* (Cambridge, 1987); Thomas J. Knock, *To End All Wars: Woodrow Wilson and the Quest for a New World Order* (New York, 1992); Amos Perlmutter, *Making the World Safe for Democracy: A Century of Wilsonianism and Its Totalitarian Challengers* (Chapel Hill, NC, 1997); Frank Ninkovich, *The Wilsonian Century: U.S. Foreign Policy since 1900* (Chicago, 1999); John Milton Cooper, Jr., *Breaking the Heart of the World: Woodrow Wilson and the Fight for the League of Nations* (Cambridge, 2001); Lloyd E. Ambrosius, *Wilsonianism: Woodrow Wilson and His Legacy in American*

contrast to his modern liberalism, the film epitomized America's most extreme racism. Based on Dixon's novels *The Leopard's Spots* (1902) and *The Clansman* (1905), it glorified the Ku Klux Klan's violent role in restoring white supremacy in the American South after the Civil War. Its racist interpretation of Reconstruction praised the KKK for saving southern states from the era's interracial governments.[2] Mythology turned into history in the New South, which memorialized the Lost Cause as it created a modern future. In the late nineteenth century, reconciliation between white southerners and northerners gave birth to a new nation, still at the expense of African Americans.[3] By Wilson's presidency, the white South redefined the national agenda in race relations. Its Jim Crow system became public policy throughout the United States, and white supremacy shaped America's international relations.

The Birth of a Nation reaffirmed Wilson's historical interpretation of the American Civil War and Reconstruction. It quoted from his fifth volume of *A History of the American People* (1902). Wilson was clearly identified as the author. His words were slightly altered, but not his meaning. Using his quotations, the film blamed northern carpetbaggers for exploiting both black and white southerners. It elaborated the consequences of this northern invasion as "a veritable overthrow of civilization in the South ... in their determination to '*put the white South under the heel of the black South.*' " Against this threat to civilization, white men organized the Ku Klux Klan to redeem the South. "The white men were roused by the mere instinct of self-preservation ... until at last there had sprung into existence a great Ku Klux Klan, a veritable empire of the South, to

Foreign Relations (New York, 2002); Robert W. Tucker, *Woodrow Wilson and the Great War: Reconsidering America's Neutrality, 1914–1917* (Charlottesville, VA, 2007); Erez Manela, *The Wilsonian Moment: Self-Determination and the International Origins of Anticolonial Nationalism* (New York, 2007).
[2] Thomas Dixon, Jr., *Leopard's Spots: A Romance of the White Man's Burden* (New York, 1902), and *The Clansman: An Historical Romance of the Ku Klux Klan* (New York, 1905); Robert Lang, ed., *The Birth of a Nation: D. W. Griffith, director* (New Brunswick, NJ, 1994); Anthony Slide, *American Racist: The Life and Films of Thomas Dixon* (Lexington, KY, 2004); Michele K. Gillespie and Randall L. Hall, eds., *Thomas Dixon Jr. and the Birth of Modern America* (Baton Rouge, LA, 2006).
[3] Gaines M. Foster, *Ghosts of the Confederacy: Defeat, the Lost Cause, and the Emergence of the New South* (New York, 1987); Anthony Gaughan, "Woodrow Wilson and the Legacy of the Civil War," *Civil War History* 43 (September 1997): 225–42; Alessandra Lorini, *Rituals of Race: American Public Culture and the Search for Racial Democracy* (Charlottesville, VA, 1999); David W. Blight, *Race and Reunion: The Civil War in American Memory* (Cambridge, MA, 2001); Michael Dennis, "Looking Backward: Woodrow Wilson, the New South, and the Question of Race," *American Nineteenth Century History* 3 (Spring 2002): 77–104; W. Fitzhugh Brundage, *The Southern Past: A Clash*

protect the southern country." The film used the president's words to validate its claim that "this is an historical presentation of the Civil War and Reconstruction," disingenuously adding that it "is not meant to reflect on any race or people of today."[4]

Born and raised in the South, Wilson had experienced the trauma of the Civil War and Reconstruction firsthand. He witnessed profound changes in race relations that followed the Confederacy's defeat. His memory shaped his history. Wilson blamed the Republican Congress for overthrowing President Abraham Lincoln's moderate policy for restoring the Union. Lincoln, he claimed, would have left former slaves under the tutelage of white southerners, requiring their emancipation by the Thirteenth Amendment but not their equality or self-rule. President Andrew Johnson also followed this moderate approach. Radical Republicans, however, had rejected the presidential policy. They intervened in the South to create interracial state governments that gave "privilege and protection" to former slaves. Congress overturned the black codes that southern states had adopted to control freedmen. "It was a menace to society itself that the negroes should thus of a sudden be set free and left without tutelage or restraint," Wilson asserted. He justified the black codes as normal labor law. He criticized northerners for failing to understand the facts of southern life in their false belief that a former slave was "the innocent victim of circumstances, a creature who needed only liberty to make him a man." In Wilson's view, black people were not ready for freedom or equality. Northerners who thought otherwise were wrong, he believed. From this false premise, Republicans in Congress had imposed a "revolutionary programme" on the white South. "Their leaders wished not only to give the negroes political privilege but also to put the white men of the South ... under the negroes' heels."[5]

Rejecting racial equality as unnatural, Wilson interpreted Radical Reconstruction as a revolutionary "social upheaval" that imposed black rule over white people. Behind the black politicians were corrupt northerners. Pennsylvania's Thaddeus Stevens, chief architect of this Republican congressional policy, had really enabled carpetbaggers to dominate both black and white southerners. They were "the new masters of the blacks.

of Race and Memory (Cambridge, MA, 2005); Charles W. Calhoun, Conceiving a New Republic: The Republican Party and the Southern Question, 1869–1900 (Lawrence, KS, 2006).

[4] Lang, Birth of a Nation, 94. For the original quotations, see Woodrow Wilson, A History of the American People, 5 vols. (New York, 1902), 5: 46, 49–50, 58, 60.

[5] Wilson, History, 5: 18, 22, 38.

They gained the confidence of the negroes, obtained for themselves the more lucrative offices, and lived upon the public treasury, public contracts, and their easy control of affairs." This threat to southern civilization, Wilson believed, justified illegal activities by white men in the Ku Klux Klan. "They took the law into their own hands," he explained, "and began to attempt by intimidation what they were not allowed to attempt by the ballot or by any ordered course of public action." The KKK directed its violence against anyone associated with interracial southern governments or even new schools for black students. "It became the chief object of the night-riding comrades to silence or drive from the country the principal mischief-makers of the reconstruction régime, whether white or black." Condoning this "reign of terror" to redeem the South for white supremacy, Wilson acknowledged that "brutal crimes were committed." White southerners united to "regain their mastery" by "intimidation and control of the negroes." They resisted efforts by President Ulysses S. Grant and Congress, with the Ku Klux Klan Act of 1871, to enforce civil rights of black citizens under the Fourteenth and Fifteenth Amendments. The heart of the problem, according to Wilson, was "the disfranchisement of the white men of the South. It was plain to see that the troubles in the southern States arose out of the exclusion of the better whites from the electoral suffrage no less than from the admission of the most ignorant blacks." White rule eventually solved this problem, removing "the more abnormal obstructions to the return of settled peace and a natural order of life at the South."[6]

In *Congressional Government* (1885), Wilson criticized the alleged abuses of Radical Reconstruction and offered his ideas for reform to ensure that such an episode would never again occur. He argued that the checks and balances of the Constitution were "no longer effective" in preventing the misuse of power that he perceived after "the war between the States." Union victory had demolished states' rights, destroying the original constitutional system of federalism. The equilibrium among the three branches of the national government also collapsed when Congress triumphed over President Johnson, leaving only the federal judiciary as a weak check on its abusive actions. "The balances of the Constitution are for the most part only ideal," he observed. "For all practical purposes the national government is supreme over the state governments, and Congress predominant over its so-called coördinate branches." What the founding fathers had created in 1787 was now "our *form of government*

[6] Wilson, *History*, 5: 44, 46, 59, 62, 64, 74, 82, 97.

rather in name than in reality."[7] Congressional committees now ruled the country. He identified this fundamental problem in *Congressional Government*, but had not yet found an effective remedy. Later he looked to a powerful presidency as the solution.

Wilson cited a few examples of what he regarded as the serious abuses that resulted from this alleged political crisis. He denounced the congressional assertion of national sovereignty over states' rights. Federal supervisors of state elections represented "the very ugliest side of federal supremacy." Their interference impaired "the self-respect of state officers of election by bringing home to them a vivid sense of subordination to the powers at Washington." Wilson found it unacceptably humiliating that white southerners were unable to control elections in their states because they were supervised by the national government. He criticized congressional efforts to protect black voting rights and also opposed the authorization of federal courts to restrict states in their actions to prevent African Americans from serving on juries. "The tide of federal aggression probably reached its highest shore," he asserted, "in the legislation which put it into the power of the federal courts to punish a state judge for refusing, in the exercise of his official discretion, to impanel Negroes in the juries of his court." White southerners, Wilson believed, should be able to discriminate against African Americans without interference by the federal judiciary. The white South's best hope, he thought, was for federal judges to limit the power of Congress and restore states' rights. The presidency was too weak to do so.[8] Restoring white power thus motivated Wilson's classic critique of the U.S. system of government and his pursuit of reforms to remedy the alleged problems that Radical Reconstruction had imposed on the South. This racial factor, however, has been almost totally ignored in otherwise excellent studies of his political and constitutional thought.[9]

WOODROW WILSON AND THOMAS DIXON, JR.

Wilson's first book launched his life-long academic and political career as a reformer who sought to protect the white South and expand its influence. Johns Hopkins University accepted *Congressional Government*

[7] Woodrow Wilson, *Congressional Government: A Study in American Politics* (Boston, 1885), 28, 53, 139–42.
[8] Wilson, *Congressional Government*, 39–43.
[9] Jeffrey K. Tulis, *The Rhetorical Presidency* (Princeton, NJ, 1987), 117–44; Niels Aage Thorsen, *The Political Thought of Woodrow Wilson, 1875–1910* (Princeton, NJ,

as his doctoral dissertation. Among those who praised the book was Dixon.[10] In the fall of 1883, he and Wilson had met in Baltimore, where they were new graduate students at Johns Hopkins. They studied with Professors Herbert Baxter Adams and Richard T. Ely, who had received their own PhD degrees from the University of Heidelberg. Sitting next to each other in Adams's seminar and spending considerable time together, these two southerners became what Dixon described as "intimate friends." He dropped out at the end of 1883 to pursue an acting career in the New York theater, while Wilson continued his education. Over the years, however, they maintained their friendship.[11]

What Wilson and Dixon learned at Johns Hopkins allowed them to place their existing southern views within a broader framework for understanding world history. Adams and Ely introduced them to German historicism. According to this Hegelian theory of history, modern nations grew like biological organisms from primordial racial roots. Anglo-Saxons accounted for the essential identity of the American people, including their democratic institutions. Wilson embraced this germ theory of history in writing about politics, while Dixon employed it in his novels. In *The State* (1889), Wilson traced the constitutional development of the United States back through England to "the first Teutons" who had come there with "a very fierce democratic temper." He emphasized that the English and subsequent American pursuit of liberty had grown from these primordial roots.[12] Identifying America's civic ideals with the Anglo-Saxon race, he drew the color line between white Europeans and black Africans to separate those who qualified for modern liberalism from others who did not. His liberalism was intertwined with a particular racial nationalism.

1988), 41–67; Daniel D. Stid, *The President as Statesman: Woodrow Wilson and the Constitution* (Lawrence, KS, 1998), 46–65; Ronald J. Pestritto, *Woodrow Wilson and the Roots of Modern Liberalism* (Lanham, MD, 2005), 33–65.

[10] Dixon to Wilson, Feb. 15, 1885, *The Papers of Woodrow Wilson* [hereafter *PWW*], ed. Arthur S. Link, 69 vols. (Princeton, NJ, 1966–93), 4: 258–59.

[11] Karen M. Crowe, "Southern Horizons: The Autobiography of Thomas Dixon, A Critical Edition" (PhD dissertation, New York University, 1982), 230–31; Raymond Allen Cook, *Fire from the Flint: The Amazing Careers of Thomas Dixon* (Winston-Salem, NC, 1968), 51–52; Dixon to Wilson, May 4, 1885, June 21, 1888, Nov. 8, 1888, May 12, 1890, *PWW*, 4: 558, 5: 738, 6: 19, 628; Stockton Axson, *"Brother Woodrow": A Memoir of Woodrow Wilson*, ed. Arthur S. Link (Princeton, NJ, 1993), 202.

[12] Woodrow Wilson, *The State: Elements of Historical and Practical Politics* (Boston, 1889), 366–67, 469; Edward L. Ayers, *The Promise of the New South: Life after Reconstruction* (New York, 1992), 372, 423; Ambrosius, *Wilsonianism*, 21–29; Pestritto, *Woodrow Wilson and the Roots of Modern Liberalism*, 33–65.

Only white people, Wilson believed, were ready for democracy. In 1885, he attributed American democracy to "a truly organic growth." Its success had originated "in our history, in our experiences as a Teutonic race set apart to make a special English character." He added: "The present trend of all political development the world over towards democracy is no mere episode in history. It is the natural resultant of now permanent forces which have long been gathering, which brought modern lights out of mediaeval shades, and which have made the life of the most advanced nations of our day." Democracy, he believed, required "several all-important conditions," including "homogeneity of race and community of thought and purpose among the people.... The nation which is to try democracy successfully must not only feel itself an organic body, but must be accustomed to *act* as an organic body." Wilson conceived of the modern democratic state as "the rule of the *whole.*" "Democracy is truly government by the whole–for the rule of the majority implies and is dependent upon the coöperation, be it active or passive, of the minority." Although he did not refer explicitly to African Americans, Wilson expected such minorities to acquiesce. Only modern nations that reached this stage in their development were ready for democratic government. This historical process would culminate in "the most humane results of the world's peace and progress."[13]

Dixon and Wilson pursued different careers but maintained their friendship. Giving up acting after a few months, Dixon returned to his hometown of Shelby, where he was elected in 1884 to the North Carolina legislature as a Democrat. His major success, as he proudly informed Wilson in 1885, was passage of a bill to provide pensions to former Confederate soldiers. Walter Hines Page, a reporter for the Raleigh *Daily Chronicle*, covered Dixon's maiden speech, which justified these pensions by combining the Lost Cause ideology with the New South emphasis on economic development. They formed a close friendship at this time. Years later, after Page had become a publisher in New York City, he approved Dixon's manuscript for *The Leopard's Spots.* Doubleday, Page & Company published it, and also *The Clansman* and some of Dixon's other novels. For Page, these business decisions were not just a matter of promoting racist ideas, although he did not hesitate to do so. Wilson later appointed Page as his ambassador to Great Britain. In 1885, Dixon finished his law studies in Greensboro, where he befriended Josephus Daniels. He briefly practiced in his hometown. Giving up both the law

[13] "The Modern Democratic State" [c. Dec. 1–20, 1885], *PWW*, 5: 58–92.

and politics, he became a Baptist preacher. He advanced from a small church in Goldsboro in 1886 to a larger one in Raleigh in 1887, then to Boston in 1888, and to New York City in 1889.[14]

Dixon's prowess as a Baptist preacher led Wake Forest College, his alma mater, to invite him back to deliver a commencement address. After his oration, a prominent member of the Baptist college's board of trustees told him that he planned to nominate him for an honorary degree. Dixon persuaded the trustee that the college should confer an honorary degree on Wilson instead. As Dixon remembered it, he praised his friend as a rising academic star. Referring to *Congressional Government*, he said: "His study of our form of government in his thesis will become a classic in the literature of Democracy." The faculty, some of whom had known Wilson at Johns Hopkins or read his book in the library, gave their approbation. After some hesitation from Wake Forest trustees, who were not certain they wanted to honor a Presbyterian who had attended rival Davidson College, they approved Dixon's proposal in June 1887. His role in persuading Wake Forest to confer on Wilson his first honorary degree enhanced the future president's national reputation as a leading scholar.[15]

NATIONAL UNITY AND MISSION

At Johns Hopkins, where he returned to deliver a series of lectures in 1889, Wilson met another graduate student, Frederick Jackson Turner, who helped him shift his focus from Europe to the American West. In the midst of writing *Division and Reunion* (1893), Wilson appealed to Turner for information about western contributions to "the growth of the national idea, and of nationality, in our history." The young historian belatedly sent him a copy of "Problems in American History" but Wilson had already finished writing his book. On his own he concluded that the American frontier had produced "a new epoch" with Andrew Jackson's presidency in 1829. This was Wilson's own frontier thesis. Turner praised his friend's book for emphasizing the West and "the doctrine of American

---

[14] Crowe, "Southern Horizons," 245–47, 259, 359–66; Cook, *Fire from the Flint*, 59–102, 108–34; Dixon to Wilson, Feb. 15, 1885, July 18, 1887, *PWW*, 4: 258–59, 5: 529–30; John Milton Cooper, Jr., *Walter Hines Page: The Southerner as American, 1855–1918* (Chapel Hill, NC, 1977), 69–70, 168–69, 206.

[15] Crowe, "Southern Horizons," 272–75; Dixon to Wilson, June 7, 1887, Joseph Ruggles Wilson to Wilson, June 11, 1887, *PWW*, 5: 515–16; George C. Osborn, *Woodrow Wilson: The Early Years* (Baton Rouge, LA, 1967), 169.

development, in contrast to Germanic *germs.*"[16] As Wilson shifted his focus from the Anglo-Saxon or Teutonic roots of the United States to the origins of American democracy on the western frontier, he mostly abandoned the rhetoric of racial nationalism in favor of civic nationalist ideals of liberty and democracy. Yet the subtext of racism remained in Wilson's modern liberalism. Like Dixon's, his vision of America's world mission called for white supremacy. In the 1890s, the Civil War's legacy still divided the United States. Nevertheless, Wilson anticipated sectional reconciliation in the making of the nation.[17] But he expected African Americans to accommodate themselves to a subordinate position in the emerging Jim Crow system of racial segregation.

White southerners were experiencing what Wolfgang Schivelbusch called "the culture of defeat." Suffering the trauma of their failure to create an independent nation, they sought a new identity that would reassure them in their despair and promise eventual recovery. He compared the American South after the Civil War, France after the Franco-Prussian War of 1870–71, and Germany after World War I. Despite military defeat, the losers saw themselves as defenders of civilization against their enemies and strove to move "from glory to justice."[18] Religion played a key role in the South's Lost Cause. It provided, as Charles Reagan Wilson emphasized, the "cultural dream" of a separate identity for white southerners despite the collapse of their political dream of a Confederate nation. "Religion was at the core of this dream, and the history of the attitude known as the Lost Cause was the story of the use of the past as the basis for a Southern religious-moral identity, an identity as a chosen people." Not restricted to a single Christian denomination, the Lost Cause offered a civil religion for the white South. It provided moral justification for a new crusade. Its imagery of "baptism of blood" evoked "the role of war in

[16] Wilson to Turner, Aug. 23, 1889, Turner to Wilson, Aug. 31, 1889, Jan. 23, 1890, July 16, 1893, Dec. 20, 1893, *PWW*, 6: 368–71, 381–84, 478–79, 8: 278–79, 417; Fulmer Mood, "Turner's Formative Period," in *The Early Writings of Frederick Jackson Turner*, ed. Louise P. Kellogg (Madison, WI, 1938), 36–38; Woodrow Wilson, *Division and Reunion: 1829–1899* (New York, 1893), 2–3, 10–11, 23, 118. See also Lloyd E. Ambrosius, *Wilsonian Statecraft: Theory and Practice of Liberal Internationalism during World War I* (Wilmington, DE, 1991), 3–10.

[17] Woodrow Wilson, "The Making of the Nation," *Atlantic Monthly* 80 (July 1897): 1–14, *PWW*, 10: 217–36, and *The Public Papers of Woodrow Wilson* [hereafter *PPWW*], eds. Ray Stannard Baker and William E. Dodd, 6 vols. (New York, 1925–27), 1: 310–35.

[18] Wolfgang Schivelbusch, *The Culture of Defeat: On National Trauma, Mourning, and Recovery* (New York, 2004), 18–19. Foster, *Ghosts of the Confederacy*, also emphasized the Lost Cause's forward-looking aspects that enabled the New South to overcome the trauma of defeat.

bringing a redemption from past sins, an atonement, and a sanctification for the future."[19] Clergy espoused the Lost Cause by lifting up military heroes, such as Generals Robert E. Lee and Thomas "Stonewall" Jackson, as prime examples of virtue, thus linking the South's military tradition with a manly kind of religion. They also identified white women, especially their sexual purity, with southern virtue. White men asserted their male dominance over their wives and daughters to defend them against the perceived threat of black men. Placing white women on a pedestal and targeting black men, the Lost Cause affirmed a moral code of honor that exalted white men as defenders of southern civilization. Out of this culture emerged both Dixon and President Wilson. During World War I, they transformed the South's Lost Cause into American patriotism, which the revived Ku Klux Klan took to the extreme.[20]

Sectional reconciliation in the late nineteenth century enabled the white South to deal with its culture of defeat by joining the North in a patriotic war against their common enemy. The Lost Cause provided Dixon's southern framework for interpreting the Spanish-American War of 1898 as a national triumph. Already a successful Baptist preacher, Dixon established a church without any denominational affiliation in New York City in 1895. Under his leadership, this People's Church provided the meeting place for the revolutionary Cuban junta to organize support for Cuba's independence from Spain. In *The Leopard's Spots,* Dixon reaffirmed the message he had preached. The war helped heal the North-South division as patriotic Americans united to win military victory and establish the United States as a great nation in the world. It was the test for southerners as Americans. "America," he rejoiced, "united at last and invincible, waked to the consciousness of her resistless power. And, most marvelous of all, this hundred days of war had re-united the Anglo-Saxon race. This sudden union of the English speaking people in friendly alliance disturbed the equilibrium of the world, and confirmed the Anglo-Saxon in his title to the primacy of racial sway."[21] The nation, united by the war, emerged as a great power among European colonial empires.

[19] Charles Reagan Wilson, *Baptized in Blood: The Religion of the Lost Cause, 1865–1920* (Athens, GA, 1980), 1, 5.
[20] Wilson, *Baptized in Blood,* 37–111. See also Nell Irvin Painter, *Southern History Across the Color Line* (Chapel Hill, NC, 2002), 112–33; David Goldfield, *Still Fighting the Civil War: The American South and Southern History* (Baton Rouge, LA, 2002), 1–120; W. Fitzhugh Brundage, "Thomas Dixon: American Proteus," and Cynthia Lynn Lyerly, "Gender and Race in Dixon's Religious Ideology," in Gillespie and Hall, *Thomas Dixon Jr.,* 23–45, 80–104.
[21] Crowe, "Southern Horizons," 326; Dixon, *Leopard's Spots,* 406–09; Cook, *Fire from the Flint,* 89–94; Raymond A. Cook, *Thomas Dixon* (New York, 1974), 45–46. See also

In *The Leopard's Spots*, Dixon elaborated his vision of global white supremacy in "A Speech That Made History." The novel's hero, Charles Gaston, proclaimed America's world mission. He delivered this speech to defend his racist platform and launch his successful candidacy for North Carolina governor. White Americans, having subordinated blacks and overcome their sectional division, had created a new nation that was ready for a global role. He wanted Anglo-Saxon men – "that world-conquering race of men" – to protect white civilization. General Daniel Worth, who would give his daughter in marriage to him, admired Gaston's "elemental manhood." Anglo-Saxon men, the hero affirmed, should dominate the world. "The Anglo-Saxon is entering the new century with the imperial crown of the ages on his brow and the sceptre of the infinite in his hands," he announced, welcoming "the resistless tide of the rising consciousness of Nationality and World-Mission.... Our old men dreamed of local supremacy. We dream of the conquest of the globe." Modernization and industrialization, which had helped unite the American nation, now enabled it to proceed with hegemonic globalization. Gaston identified this mission with God's will for Anglo-Saxons to dominate others: "We believe that God has raised up our race, as he ordained Israel of old, in this world-crisis to establish and maintain for weaker races, as a trust for civilisation, the principles of civil and religious Liberty and the forms of Constitutional Government." He foresaw the American flag waving over "semi-barbaric black men in the foulest slave pen of the Orient." Now was the time for the nation "to master the future or be mastered in the struggle."[22]

As Dixon's fictional hero, Gaston identified democracy with the Anglo-Saxon race and with Christianity. "I believe in God's call to our race to do His work in history," he affirmed. This required white supremacy because Africans were incapable of making any progress. He cited Haiti and San Domingo as total failures. African Americans in the North, who had enjoyed freedom for a century, had likewise not "added a feather's weight to the progress of humanity." Unlike Anglo-Saxons, whose determination to be "freemen" was "in their blood," they were not fit for

Foster, *Ghosts of the Confederacy*, 145–59; Tennant S. McWilliams, *The New South Faces the World: Foreign Affairs and the Southern Sense of Self, 1877–1950* (Baton Rouge, LA, 1988), 47–67; and Joseph A. Fry, *Dixie Looks Abroad: The South and U.S. Foreign Relations, 1789–1973* (Baton Rouge, LA, 2002), 119–31. For TR's similar "racialized nation," see Gary Gerstle, *American Crucible: Race and Nation in the Twentieth Century* (Princeton, NJ, 2001), 25–43.
[22] Dixon, *Leopard's Spots*, 433–36.

liberty. If they sought to govern this "superior race," they should "look for another world in which to rule." Thus Gaston wanted to preserve North Carolina's historic role as "the cradle of American Democracy and the typical commonwealth of freemen." His racist fantasy was global in scope. "The Anglo-Saxon race is united and has entered upon its world mission," he announced. To make the world safe for democracy, it was necessary to disfranchise African Americans. He equated his avowedly provincial Anglo-Saxon American identity with the nation's worldwide mission. What was good for the white South was good for the United States, and what was good for the United States was good for the world. "The true citizen of the world loves his country. His country is a part of God's world."[23]

Wilson too applauded the Spanish-American War and the subsequent creation of an overseas empire. The continental frontier's closing by 1890 required Americans to look abroad. This search for "new frontiers for ourselves beyond the seas" had led the United States into war with Spain for Cuba's freedom and into annexation of the Philippines. Americans had become, in Wilson's view, "apostles of liberty and of self-government." "The country was thrilled with a new sense of union and of enthusiasm for a common cause," he affirmed. "There was no longer any thought of differences between section and section when the flag was in the field." Reunion between white southerners and northerners enabled the nation to become a world power. "Of a sudden, as it seemed, and without premeditation, the United States had turned away from their long-time, deliberate absorption in their own domestic development ... and given themselves a colonial empire, and taken their place of power in the field of international politics." Sectional reconciliation, allowing the white South to dominate African Americans, laid the foundation for peace at home and abroad. "The southern States were readjusting their elective suffrage so as to exclude the illiterate negroes and so in part undo the mischief of reconstruction; and yet the rest of the country withheld its hand from interference," Wilson observed. "Sections began to draw together with a new understanding of one another. Parties were turning to the new days to come and to the common efforts of peace."[24] The United States was ready to rule over other peoples, bringing them democracy. But they would first have to acquiesce in its benevolent tutelage, just as African Americans were subjected to Jim Crow ascendancy. Wilson

[23] Dixon, *Leopard's Spots*, 437–42.
[24] Woodrow Wilson, "The Ideals of America," *Atlantic Monthly* 90 (December 1902): 721–34, *PWW*, 12: 208–27, and *PPWW*, 1: 416–42; Wilson, *History*, 5: 275–76, 294–95, 300.

thus reaffirmed racial hierarchy in his vision of America's global mission at the beginning of the new century.

JIM CROW AND PROGRESSIVISM

During the Progressive Era, both Dixon and Wilson altered their careers and reached the zenith of their public influence. In 1899, Dixon resigned his pastorate at the People's Church to devote his time fully to the lecture circuit. He had established his reputation as a great preacher and brilliant orator. He soon began to write historical novels. Moving from the South's Lost Cause to triumphal Americanism, he contended that his novels were historically accurate. He combined personal experience and memory with white supremacist history and mythology to create a past that never existed and to imagine a future that would fulfill his racist fantasy.[25] Returning to his earlier interest in theater, he converted his books into scripts for plays. He based "The Clansman" on his first two novels. Dixon later transformed this play into the scenario for the famous motion picture, eventually retitled *The Birth of a Nation*.[26]

Wilson saw presidential leadership as the solution to the alleged race problem he had identified in *Congressional Government*. In a new preface in 1900, he rejoiced that the Spanish-American War had resulted in "the greatly increased power and opportunity for constructive statesmanship given the President, by the plunge into international politics and into the administration of distant dependencies." He elaborated this insight in a series of lectures at Columbia University, published as *Constitutional Government in the United States* (1908).[27] Turning theory into practice, Wilson entered politics in 1910 as the Democratic candidate for New Jersey governor, resigning his presidency of Princeton University. Upon winning the election, he aimed toward the U.S. presidency. Dixon encouraged this prospect while promoting his latest play in the South. "Let me know if I can

[25] Dixon, *The Leopard's Spots*, preface. Dixon fictionalized and reinforced North Carolina's white supremacist history. See David S. Cecelski and Timothy B. Tyson, eds., *Democracy Betrayed: The Wilmington Race Riot of 1898 and Its Legacy* (Chapel Hill, NC, 1998) and Glenda Gilmore, *Gender and Jim Crow: Women and the Politics of North Carolina, 1896–1920* (Chapel Hill, NC, 1996), 66–71, 135–38.

[26] Crowe, "Southern Horizons," 382–95; Cook, *Fire from the Flint*, 135–60; The Clansman (First Sketch Unrevised), The Birth of a Nation (Play), and The Birth of a Nation (Fragments of Scenario), Box–Writings: A-K, Thomas Dixon Papers, Manuscript Department, Duke University Library, Durham, NC.

[27] Wilson, *Congressional Government*, 22; Woodrow Wilson, *Constitutional Government in the United States* (New York, 1908).

help you to the White House," he told Wilson, adding that he would "like to see you there."[28]

Wilson's victory in the 1912 presidential election fulfilled their hopes for more southern influence in the nation. Dixon recommended Daniels for a cabinet appointment. Wilson agreed, naming him as secretary of the Navy. He thanked Dixon for dedicating *The Southerner: A Romance of the Real Lincoln* (1913) to him.[29] In the first year of Wilson's presidency, Dixon urged him to draw the color line. He wanted him, moreover, to withdraw the nomination of a black man for a job in the Treasury department where he might supervise white women, warning that "the South can never forgive this." Such an appointment, he emphasized, was "a serious offense against the cleanness of our social life. I have confidently hoped that you would purge Washington of this iniquity."[30] Dixon did not need to worry. The new president was pursuing that goal. He intended to impose the Jim Crow system on the national government, although he would do so deftly to avoid public controversy as much as possible. "We are handling the force of colored people who are now in the departments in just the way in which they ought to be handled," Wilson assured Dixon. "We are trying – and by degrees succeeding – a plan of concentration which will put them all together and will not in any one bureau mix the two races." Because Treasury Secretary William G. McAdoo, a southerner who shared the Lost Cause ideology, had already set about segregating the bureau where the black appointee would work, the problem that Dixon had identified would no longer exist in this case. Wilson told his friend that it was unnecessary to remind him about the white South's expectations in race relations, which he intended to fulfill "with entire comprehension of the considerations which certainly do not need to be pointed out to me."[31]

A few days before the president assured Dixon that his administration was implementing the Jim Crow agenda, he reaffirmed the Lost Cause ideology. On July 4, 1913, the fiftieth anniversary of the Battle of Gettysburg, Wilson addressed the Union and Confederate soldiers who had fought each other but now came together in reunion. Some 53,407 veterans assembled for this "Peace Jubilee." The ceremony followed the ritual of

---

[28] Dixon to Wilson, Nov. 15, 1910, *PWW*, 22: 96.
[29] Wilson to Dixon, Dec. 3, 1912, *PWW*, 25: 578–79.
[30] Dixon to Wilson, July 27, 1913, *PWW*, 28: 88–89.
[31] Wilson to Dixon, July 29, 1913, *PWW*, 28: 94; Joel Williamson, *The Crucible of Race: Black-White Relations in the American South Since Emancipation* (New York, 1984), 365–71.

celebration that had developed in the South to commemorate the heroism
of veterans and remember the dead who had given the ultimate sacrifice in
the war. Honoring "these gallant men in blue and gray," Wilson shared his
interpretation of the meaning of the past fifty years. He emphasized sectional reconciliation. The nation that had emerged, he said, was "a great
people, great with every force that has ever beaten in the lifeblood of
mankind." Seeking to fulfill "its own great standards set up at its birth,"
it continued to strive for "righteousness and humanity." Unlike Lincoln,
who had reaffirmed the founding fathers' civic ideals of liberty and equality in his famous Gettysburg address, Wilson stressed national unity. He
did not proclaim "a new birth of freedom" for all Americans. Black veterans were excluded from the "Peace Jubilee." It celebrated white supremacy
and reunion. Wilson's concept of democracy was less inclusive and more
elitist than Lincoln's "government of the people, by the people, and for the
people." He wanted white Americans to join together to "make blessed the
nations of the world in peace and righteousness and love."[32]

African Americans understood the serious implications of Wilson's
drawing the color line in accordance with the Lost Cause ideology. As
the new administration segregated the federal government, they quickly
recognized the racism in Wilson's liberalism. The National Independent
Political League, with Boston *Guardian* editor William Monroe Trotter
as its secretary, circulated a petition against the president's new Jim Crow
policy. Gathering more than 20,000 signatures from thirty-six states, the
League sent a delegation to the White House on November 6, 1913. As
its spokesman, Trotter told Wilson, "There can be no equality, freedom
or respect from others, in segregation by the very nature of the case."
This "inequality of citizenship" violated the Constitution, he said, noting
the new discriminatory practices at the Post Office, Treasury, and Navy
departments. There was no good justification for making southern "race
prejudice and race discrimination" the official national policy. Trotter
appealed to the "apostle of the 'New Freedom'" to remove the barriers
to equal citizenship.[33]

Pretending that he was just learning about his administration's discriminatory practices, Wilson told Trotter's delegation that he had not

[32] Foster, *Ghosts of the Confederacy*, 36–179, 193–98; Bright, *Race and Reunion*, 6–15;
Garry Wills, *Lincoln at Gettysburg: The Words That Remade America* (New York,
1992), 263; Address, July 4, 1913, *PWW*, 28: 23–26, and *PPWW*, 3: 41–44.
[33] Trotter's Address, Nov. 6, 1913, *PWW*, 28: 491–95; Nicholas Patler, *Jim Crow and the
Wilson Administration: Protesting Federal Segregation in the Early Twentieth Century*
(Boulder, CO, 2004).

adopted an official policy of segregation. Contrary to what he had assured
Dixon, he claimed that "there is no policy on the part of the administration looking to segregation." He wanted the black delegation to believe
that any reports to the contrary were exaggerations. When challenged,
Wilson explained that neither he nor any cabinet officer had announced
such a policy. He dismissed one newspaper's account as "an inexcusable
misrepresentation" of a statement he had made. "It was," he asserted,
"not a statement of policy, but it was a statement of fact." Beyond this
duplicitous parsing of words, the president appealed for patience from
African Americans.[34]

African Americans wanted modern liberal democracy to include racial
justice. Trotter returned to the White House with another delegation to
appeal for an end to segregation. On November 12, 1914, reiterating that
the color line imposed "public humiliation and degradation" on black
citizens, Trotter reminded Wilson of his promise to investigate race relations in the federal government. Instead of improvement, the situation
had worsened as segregation spread beyond the Post Office, Treasury,
and Navy departments into others. Trotter also recalled that during the
presidential campaign in 1912, "you were heralded as perhaps the second Lincoln, and now the Afro-American leaders who supported you
are hounded as false leaders and traitors to their race. What a change
segregation has wrought!" Once more he appealed for equal treatment in
federal employment. Trotter bluntly asked: "Have you a 'new freedom'
for white Americans and a new slavery for your 'Afro-American fellow
citizens'? God forbid!" He wanted Wilson to issue an executive order to
end segregation based on race and color.[35]

Wilson resented Trotter's critique of his imposition of racial segregation on the national government. He regarded the black leader's reference to the 1912 election as political blackmail. He insisted that the race
question was "a human problem, not a political problem." It was a simple
fact, claimed the president, that the "two races" would inevitably experience friction in their relations. He now argued that segregation would
help both races deal with this reality, asserting that "the best way to help
the Negro in America is to help him with his independence." Mixing
the two races could not accomplish that goal. He said racial prejudice
would take the world generations to overcome. Only self-improvement
by African Americans, not protests like Trotter's, would promote racial

---

[34] Wilson's Reply and a Dialogue, Nov. 6, 1913, *PWW*, 28: 496–98.
[35] Trotter's Address, Nov. 12, 1914, *PWW*, 31: 298–301.

harmony, he warned. When Trotter told him that the humiliating condition of segregation would not advance black improvement and that "we are not here as wards," Wilson resorted to blaming the victim. But Trotter refused to allow him to shift the blame to African Americans for allegedly experiencing humiliating discrimination when nothing of the sort was intended by racial segregation. He told Wilson, "this is a very serious thing with us. We are sorely disappointed that you take the position that separation itself is not wrong, is not injurious, is not rightly offensive to you." At this point the president became angry, telling Trotter that his tone was offensive. Without backing down, Trotter tried to resume the dialogue but Wilson cut him off, telling him to show "a Christian spirit." Trotter epitomized the case he was arguing against the degradation of racial discrimination. His assertion of his own equality outraged Wilson, who told Trotter to leave the White House.[36] In retrospect, Wilson wished he had handled this confrontation with more restraint and duplicity. He said, as Daniels recalled, it would be preferable to "never raise an incident into an issue."[37] If he could, he would have changed the style, but not the substance, of his role in this particular episode. He did not waver in his commitment to white supremacy.

THE BIRTH OF A NATION

Wilson's friendship with Dixon and his contributions to *The Birth of a Nation* revealed their common dedication to its racist agenda. Dixon tried to make the film on his own but finally succeeded by joining in partnership with Harry E. Aitken in 1913. Griffith, who had once acted in one of Dixon's plays, was director of Aitken's small company, Epoch Producing Corporation. He persuaded Aitken to produce the motion picture. From Louisville, Kentucky, Griffith shared Dixon's ultra-racism and saw the potential for using *The Clansman* as the basis for an epic film. They worked for months on the screenplay for what would become the longest and most successful silent motion picture ever produced. Griffith took it to Hollywood for production in 1914. The film, entitled *The Clansman*, previewed in Riverside, California, on January 1 and 2, 1915, and opened in Los Angeles on February 8. After seeing it, Dixon suggested and Griffith agreed to change the title. Even before the official opening in New York City, they faced a serious obstacle. A protest arose,

[36] Wilson's Remarks and a Dialogue, Nov. 12, 1914, *PWW*, 31: 301–08.
[37] News Report, Nov. 12, 1914, Daniels to F. D. Roosevelt, June 10, 1933, *PWW*, 31: 308–09.

organized by the National Association for the Advancement of Colored People (NAACP), with the aim of preventing *The Birth of a Nation* from showing across the land. Led by Boston attorney and NAACP president Moorfield Storey, W. E. B. Du Bois, editor of the NAACP journal *The Crisis*, and Oswald Garrison Villard, editor of the New York *Evening Post*, this backlash threatened the film's potential success. As Dixon saw it, "the sinister forces that had provoked me to write the story were gathering to suppress it." Given the censorship laws that prohibited the showing of motion pictures that might result in public disturbances or riots, Dixon and Griffith recognized a real danger. "In the emergency," Dixon recalled, "our minds turned to Woodrow Wilson." Dixon expected his old friend in the White House to help. With the president's backing, he anticipated, "we would have a powerful weapon with which to fight the Sectional conspiracy."[38]

Without disclosing the purpose, Dixon requested an interview with Wilson, which he granted on February 3, 1915. At the White House, the old friends spent a few minutes reminiscing about college days. Then Dixon requested his favor, inviting Wilson to watch his new three-hour motion picture. He told him that he had written the story and a southerner had directed the film. Moreover, he added, "this picture made clear for the first time that a new universal language had been invented. That in fact it was a new process by which the will could be overwhelmed with conviction." Dixon must have said more to Wilson during their half hour-long discussion, but neither of them left a contemporary record. He surely did not need to explain the political importance of his request, given the public controversy over censorship of the motion picture. In any case, Wilson readily agreed to see it. Rather than going to a theater, he asked for a private showing at the White House. Instructing Dixon to make the arrangements with his daughter Margaret, Wilson offered to invite his cabinet and their families for this occasion. He also requested Dixon not to share news of this event with the press. He told him that he was pleased to return this "little" favor out of gratitude for Dixon's earlier role in Wake Forest's decision to confer an honorary degree on him.[39]

At the White House on February 18, 1915, Wilson and his guests viewed *The Birth of a Nation*. Dixon rejoiced at their positive response. "The effect of the picture in the White House was precisely what I knew

---

[38] Lang, *Birth of a Nation*, 25–33; Crowe, "Southern Horizons," 403–06; Cook, *Thomas Dixon*, 161–69.

[39] Crowe, "Southern Horizons," 406–08; Dixon to Tumulty, Jan. 27, 1915, *PWW*, 32: 142.

it would be," he recalled. Margaret Wilson served refreshments, while Dixon, Griffith, and Aitken received praise from this special audience. If Wilson made any comment on the film, no one recorded it at the time. He was later reported to have said: "It is like writing history with lightning. And my only regret is that it is all so terribly true." One young woman, who was present at the East Room showing, recalled in 1977 that he simply walked out of the room without saying anything. Whether Wilson expressed an opinion or not, he did what Dixon and his associates had most desired. On their behalf, Dixon thanked the president for "the gracious and beautiful way" he had received them. They regarded him, he added, as "the foremost exemplar of true American Democracy."[40]

After this triumph at the White House, Dixon suggested to Griffith that they show the film to the Supreme Court and Congress. He wanted the name of the chief justice, Edward D. White, to appear on the invitations as the honorary guest who would preside at this showing. Daniels intervened to arrange a meeting with White at his home on February 19. Dixon told the chief justice that Wilson and his cabinet had watched a motion picture the night before and that he wanted the other two branches of the federal government to see it too. White initially resisted until Dixon explained that the film dealt with post–Civil War Reconstruction and depicted the rise of the Ku Klux Klan. As a former clansman in Louisiana, the chief justice now agreed to allow his name to be used on the invitations to members of the Supreme Court and the Senate and House of Representatives. Dixon and Griffith acted very quickly to invite the special guests to watch *The Birth of a Nation* that very evening along with the National Press Club at the Raleigh Hotel. Once more it evoked a positive response from the audience. Dixon now planned to use these triumphs in Washington, DC, against "our enemies" in New York City, who were seeking to block the film's official opening there two weeks later.[41]

Success in Washington brought the desired results. *The Birth of a Nation* opened in New York on March 3, 1915, and in other cities across the land. Lawyers for the NAACP had earlier convinced a deputy commissioner in the New York Police Department to ban the film at the Liberty Theatre. At the time, motion pictures were not protected as a form of free speech under the Constitution, as interpreted by the Supreme Court. To

---

[40] Crowe, "Southern Horizons," 408; Cook, *Thomas Dixon*, 170; Dixon to Wilson, Feb. 20, 1915, *PWW*, 32: 267; "Movies at the White House," *The Washington Post*, February 19, 1915, 4.

[41] Crowe, "Southern Horizons," 408–12; "Movies at Press Club," *The Washington Post*, February 20, 1915, 5.

overcome New York's censorship, the Epoch Producing Corporation's lawyer informed the city's chief police magistrate that Wilson and his cabinet had seen the film, and so too had the Supreme Court and Congress. Once the chief magistrate verified this startling news by calling the White House, he decided to lift the ban and allow the showing. This triumph in New York cleared the way in most other cities, as they too abandoned their initial efforts at censorship. Resistance from African Americans and their white associates in the NAACP failed to stop the film.[42]

At no time did Wilson ever denounce *The Birth of a Nation*. His continuing friendship with Dixon and his exchange of letters with Griffith indicated that he found their film quite acceptable, despite his preference for avoiding controversy that might result from his public association with it. On March 2, Griffith wrote to express his "most sincere gratitude" for "the honor you conferred on us" at the White House. "If we carry out the proposed series of motion pictures dealing with matters historical and political, of which I spoke with you," Griffith added, "I should be most happy to have someone representing your views to pass upon our ideas before beginning the initial work." On March 5, Wilson agreed to help as much as his time permitted. "I am very much interested in what you intimate as to your plans with regard to future motion pictures and if it is possible for me to assist you with an opinion about them at any time, I shall certainly try to do so," he promised.[43] This was not the kind of letter Wilson would have written if he disliked *The Birth of a Nation* or felt betrayed by the publicity. Later attempts by historians to suggest that Wilson did not approve the film, or that he had been duped into watching it by not knowing its message in advance, ignored this evidence of his positive response and also missed the larger point. The film itself included quotations from Wilson's *A History of the American People*. He never repudiated the use of his words to lend credibility to its version of history. It did not matter whether he knew about its contents before the White House showing or what he might have said about it on that occasion. All viewers of this most popular American motion picture before *Gone with*

---

[42] Crowe, "Southern Horizons," 413–15. See also John David Smith, "'My Books Are Hard Reading for a Negro': Tom Dixon and His African American Critics, 1905–1939," and Louis Menard, "Do Movies Have Rights?," in Gillespie and Hall, *Thomas Dixon Jr.*, 46–79, 183–202. For the film's reception and reviews, see Thomas Cripps, *Slow Fade to Black: The Negro in American Film, 1900–1942* (New York, 1977), 41–69; Lang, *Birth of a Nation*, 159–213; and Arthur Lennig, "Myth and Fact: The Reception of *The Birth of a Nation*," *Film History* 16 (2004): 117–41.

[43] Griffith to Wilson, March 2, 1915, Wilson to Griffith, March 5, 1915, *PWW*, 32: 310–11, 325. Griffith's reference to his ideas for future motion pictures "of which I spoke

the Wind in 1939 would have seen the president's identification with its racist message, even without the White House premiere.

Both the chief justice and the president sought to avoid publicity about their complicity in helping promote the film, although neither of them privately criticized or publicly repudiated either it or its racist message. Upon learning that "rumors about my having sanctioned the show" were circulating in New York City, White asked his informant to warn Aitken to stop the further use of his name. Otherwise he might make a public statement that he did not approve the film. He notified Joseph P. Tumulty, the president's secretary, that the film's promoters were also using Wilson's name.[44] Sharing White's concern, Tumulty advised Wilson to clarify that he did not approve *The Birth of a Nation*. The president refused, fearing that any such denial would appear to endorse Trotter's efforts to prevent the film from being shown in Boston. Trotter and others had appealed to Mayor James Michael Curley to ban the film. The mayor, however, permitted its showing after a few scenes were cut. It opened at the Tremont Theatre on April 10. After serious disturbances a week later, Trotter appealed to Massachusetts governor David I. Walsh to prosecute the theater's manager under the state's 1910 censorship law. Aware of this situation, Wilson did not want to appear to support Trotter. Yet he did allow Tumulty to pass along a disingenuous statement, which Wilson wrote, to a former Democratic congressman from Massachusetts. In it the president acknowledged that he and his family had watched *The Birth of a Nation* but claimed that he was "entirely unaware of the character of the play before it was presented and has at no time expressed his approbation of it." Even now he did not criticize the film. He had viewed it, he explained, as "a courtesy extended to an old acquaintance."[45] It was unlikely that Wilson had been as ignorant of the film's character as he claimed in this statement, given the public controversy. A mere mention of its title, *The Clansman*, would have alerted him. At the time he agreed to see the film, its title was still the same as Dixon's book and play. Wilson even called it a "play" in his denial. He knew Dixon well as a southerner who shared the Lost Cause ideology. The president had assured him that he understood the white South's expectation that he segregate

with you" at the White House suggests that Wilson probably spoke with him after seeing *The Birth of a Nation*, thus calling into question Marjorie Brown King's recollection in 1977 "that he walked out of the room without saying a word when the movie was over"; *PWW*, 32: 267 n. 1.

44 White to Tumulty, Apr. 5, 1915, *PWW*, 32: 486–87.

45 Tumulty to Wilson, Apr. 24, 1915, Wilson to Tumulty, Apr. 24, 1915, Apr. 28, 1915, *PWW*, 33: 68, 86.

the national government, which he was already doing. Whatever he knew about *The Birth of a Nation* before seeing it, Wilson would have known the kind of film Dixon would have made, given the racist content of his books and plays. Dixon had told the president at their February 3 meeting that he had written the story for the motion picture and a southerner had directed its production. Moreover, when Wilson watched it at the White House, he would have read his quotations from *A History of the American People*. He never disavowed this implicit endorsement of *The Birth of a Nation*, although he sought some political cover from the public furor that it generated. Like White, he preferred to handle race relations quietly behind closed doors.[46]

RACE AND DEMOCRACY IN AMERICA'S INTERNATIONAL RELATIONS

Wilson could not have repudiated *The Birth of a Nation* without destroying his southern political base and denying his own cultural values. Its message affirmed his own understanding of democracy and of America's mission in international relations. Although the president used the text of liberal civic ideals to define his policies, the subtext of white racism also shaped them. His rhetoric and practices were often not the same. In 1915, he ordered the military occupation of Haiti, which continued for the next two decades. He promised to bring liberal democracy and economic development to this black republic, but its citizens did not receive the blessings of freedom and prosperity. Interactions of U.S. troops with the Haitians evidenced more racism and paternalism than liberalism. White Americans, especially from the South, brought the racial hierarchy of the Jim Crow system to Haiti, although with some modifications because they were vastly outnumbered by the black Haitians. The consequences of this military occupation were quite different from

---

[46] For Wilson's quotation that some historians have taken out of context to suggest his later disapproval of the film, see Hildebrand to Tumuly, Apr. 20, 1918, Wilson to Tumulty, c. Apr. 22, 1918, *PWW*, 47: 388. Wilson regarded "the forthcoming production" or showing of the film in a Washington, DC theater as "a very unfortunate production and I wish most sincerely that its production might be avoided, particularly in communities where there are so many colored people." His statement about "a very unfortunate production" referred to "the forthcoming production" or showing, not to the film's original production. For the misuse of Wilson's quotation, see Arthur S. Link, *Wilson: The New Freedom* (Princeton, NJ, 1956), 254. See also Wilson to Dixon, Aug. 2, 1919, *PWW*, 62: 115, for the president's affirmation that "I am of course genuinely interested in any play you may put on the boards," an indication of their continuing friendship.

Wilsonian promises. Rather than freeing the Haitian people for their own self-government, the president extended U.S. imperialism to the Caribbean island. Illiberal practices overwhelmed the civic ideals of modern liberalism.[47] Nevertheless, Wilson persisted in his pursuit of a so-called democratic foreign policy. Leading the United States into World War I in 1917, he promised to make the world safe for democracy to fulfill the nation's global mission.

Triumphal Americanism during World War I gave the white South another opportunity to escape its culture of defeat. Under Wilson's leadership as the first southern president since the Civil War, the United States overcame its sectional – but not racial – division in its crusade for democracy. Southern members of Congress, who strongly supported militant interventionism, joined Wilson's campaign to create a new international order.[48] Before he led the United States into a righteous war against Imperial Germany for this purpose, *The Birth of a Nation* proclaimed the millennial promise of world peace, identifying it with the Lost Cause. The official souvenir program for the film summarized its story of post-1865 triumph. It concluded that, "To the American people, the outcome of four years of fratricidal strife, the nightmare of Reconstruction, and the establishment of the South in its rightful place, is the birth of a new nation.... The new nation, the real United States, as the years glided by, turned away from the blood-lust of War and anticipated with hope the world-millennium in which a brotherhood of love should bind all the nations together."[49] The film affirmed this triumphal hope that war would culminate in eternal peace. Out of the terrible conflict of the Civil War and Reconstruction had emerged the "real United States" that now

[47] Frederick S. Calhoun, *Power and Principle: Armed Intervention in Wilsonian Foreign Policy* (Kent, OH, 1986), 69–113; Mary A. Renda, *Taking Haiti: Military Occupation and the Culture of U.S. Imperialism, 1915–1940* (Chapel Hill, NC, 2001). See also Hans Schmidt, *The United States Occupation of Haiti, 1915–1934* (New Brunswick, NJ, 1971) and Mark T. Gilderhus, *Pan American Visions: Woodrow Wilson in the Western Hemisphere, 1913–1921* (Tucson, AZ, 1986).

[48] Anthony Gaughan, "Woodrow Wilson and the Rise of Militant Interventionism in the South," *Journal of Southern History* 65 (November 1999): 771–801; McWilliams, *New South Faces the World*, 89–120; Fry, *Dixie Looks Abroad*, 139–74; David Stricklin, "'Ours Is a Country of Light': Dixon's Strange Consistency," in Gillespie and Hall, *Thomas Dixon Jr.*, 105–23. Jeanette Keith, *Rich Man's War, Poor Man's Fight: Race, Class, and Power in the Rural South during the First World War* (Chapel Hill, NC, 2004), recorded southern resistance to World War I, showing that the South was not monolithic in its militant interventionism.

[49] "D. W. Griffith's *The Birth of a Nation*" [cover] or *Souvenir: The Birth of a Nation, ... produced under the personal direction of D. W. Griffith* [title page] (New York, 1915).

looked forward to a new millennium of peace among nations. Wilson proclaimed this message during the Great War.

The Birth of a Nation depicted America's providential passage from war to peace in its final climactic scenes. It showed black soldiers pillaging and threatening white southerners during Reconstruction. Dr. and Mrs. Richard Cameron, and their daughter Margaret, aided by faithful black servants who had been their slaves, endeavored to escape along with Phil Stoneman. When black soldiers found them, they took refuge in the small cabin of two Union soldiers who helped defend them – a symbol of sectional reconciliation. As the much larger force of black soldiers almost broke into the cabin, Ben Cameron arrived with his fellow clansmen, riding to the rescue. Earlier he had saved Elsie Stoneman from the black lieutenant governor. The clansmen killed several black soldiers and frightened others into retreat. With this triumph, they ensured white victory at the next election, thus redeeming the South. The two couples, Phil and Margaret as well as Ben and Elsie, went on a double honeymoon. Sitting on a bluff overlooking the sea, Ben pondered whether they could dream of a future without war. The film depicted the God of War swinging a sword in the midst of dead bodies, but quickly shifted the scene to show the figure of Christ with arms outstretched to a crowd of happy people in a celestial city. This vision of the kingdom of God provided the answer to Ben's question. But, as the sequence of scenes had shown, the Klan's violence against black soldiers had been necessary to create the possibility for the coming of God's kingdom on earth. Triumphal warfare was the essential prelude to blissful, millennial peace.[50]

Dixon wanted the United States to enter the war against Imperial Germany earlier than Wilson did. The phenomenal box office success of *The Birth of a Nation* convinced him of Hollywood's power to shape public opinion. Deciding to use that influence to convince the American people to support the British in the Great War, he produced a film on the "burning issue" of military preparedness. As a warning to Americans that they were living in "a fool's paradise," he began writing *The Fall of a Nation* (1916) and the corresponding screenplay. He wanted to use the power of the motion picture to deal with "the problem of saving civilization" in this "hour of supreme world crisis."[51] Dixon saw triumphal

---

[50] Lang, *Birth of a Nation*, 149–56. For this motif in U.S. foreign relations throughout the twentieth century, often in language less explicitly religious, see Robert A. Divine, *Perpetual War for Perpetual Peace* (College Station, TX, 2000).

[51] Crowe, "Southern Horizons," 421–25.

warfare as the way to protect civilization and attain peace. Again he turned to Wilson, asking permission to film target practice on battleships in the U.S. navy. This time, however, the president declined. On September 7, 1915, he replied that "there is no need to stir the nation up in favor of national defense. It is already soberly and earnestly aware of its possible perils and of its duty, and I should deeply regret seeing any sort of excitement stirred in so grave a matter." Moreover, he would not ask Daniels to grant special permission to Dixon for the filming, which the navy's general policy prohibited.[52] Dixon completed the film, which premiered in June 1916. The book appeared later in the year. In its preface he linked the future of democracy with war to protect Anglo-American civilization.[53]

When Wilson finally led the United States into the European war against Imperial Germany, he too justified American belligerency as the way to protect democracy and attain permanent peace, thereby saving civilization. "The world must be made safe for democracy," he proclaimed in his war message to Congress on April 2, 1917. "Its peace must be planted upon the tested foundations of political liberty." He blamed Germany's government, not its people, for the war. He anticipated a new postwar international community with a league of democratic nations to sustain the peace. "A steadfast concert for peace can never be maintained except by a partnership of democratic nations," he said. Germany, if it could achieve self-government, might join this league. It would need to undergo the kind of liberal revolution that appeared underway in Russia. He thought the czar's recent abdication opened the way to democracy there. Removal of autocratic regimes, which had prevented the people of Europe from fulfilling their hopes for liberty and democracy in accordance with national self-determination, could inaugurate an era of peace. This redemptive vision of a new world order, based on America's liberal civic ideals, justified its intervention into the European war.[54] As Congress voted to declare war, Wilson's triumphal words would have reminded representatives and senators who had watched *The Birth of a Nation* of its message that the promise of democracy and peace required the use of violence to save white civilization from barbarism.

---

[52] Wilson to Dixon, Sept. 7, 1915, *PWW*, 34: 426–27.

[53] Thomas Dixon, *The Fall of a Nation: A Sequel to The Birth of a Nation* (New York, 1916), preface.

[54] Address to Congress, Apr. 2, 1917, *PWW*, 41: 519–27, and *PPWW*, 5: 6–16. See also Wilson to Dixon, Jan. 25, 1917, *PWW*, 41: 12.

Wilson identified America's wartime mission with God's will on earth, justifying U.S. involvement as the way to save the world. He expressed this redemptive theme during World War I. Social Gospel theologian George D. Herron emphasized it in *Woodrow Wilson and the World's Peace* (1917), noting that the president's ultimate goal was to build the kingdom of God on earth. "The uttermost democracy, the democracy that scales the whole human octave, is to him the certain issue of the idea for which Jesus lived and died." Wilson's crusade to make the world safe for democracy aimed toward the world's redemption. "He cunningly hopes, he divinely schemes, to bring it about that America, awake at last to her selfhood and calling, shall become as a colossal Christian apostle, shepherding the world into the kingdom of God." The president, Herron further noted, "stands for a universal politic so new, so revolutionary, so creative of a different world than ours, that few have begun to glimpse his vision or to apprehend his purpose. His eyes are fixed upon a goal that is far beyond the present faith of nations." In his address to the League to Enforce Peace on May 27, 1916, calling for a postwar league of nations, he had most clearly expressed this purpose, Herron explained. The theologian had not misunderstood. On October 1, 1917, Wilson wrote to the book's New York publisher, affirming that: "I have read it with the deepest appreciation of Mr. Herron's singular insight into all the elements of a complicated situation and into my own motives and purposes."[55] After the war at the Paris Peace Conference of 1919, Wilson gave top priority to founding the League of Nations. He included the Covenant – the League's legal framework with a Calvinist religious name – in the Versailles peace treaty with Germany. On July 10, 1919, when he submitted this treaty to the U.S. Senate, he said, "It has come about by no plan of our conceiving, but by the hand of God who led us into this way.... America shall in truth show the way."[56]

Wilson regarded the League of Nations as the central feature of his new world order of freedom and democracy, but racism still characterized his statecraft. His close friend Edward M. House, a Texan who shared the Lost Cause ideology, had collaborated with him during the

[55] George D. Herron, *Woodrow Wilson and the World's Peace* (New York, 1917), 68–69, 76–77; Wilson to Kennerley, Oct. 1, 1917, *PWW*, 44: 287, and Mitchell Pirie Briggs, *George D. Herron and the European Settlement* (Stanford, CA, 1932), 249.

[56] Address to the Senate, July 10, 1919, *PWW*, 61: 436, and *PPWW*, 5: 551–52; Ambrosius, *Woodrow Wilson*, 12–13; Richard M. Gamble, *The War for Righteousness: Progressive Christianity, the Great War, and the Rise of the Messianic Nation* (Wilmington, DE, 2003).

earlier drafting and final adoption of the Covenant at Paris.[57] The peace settlement Wilson sought to establish after World War I would depend on the League to protect the collective security of democratic states against external aggression, thereby permitting them to enjoy the benefits of national self-determination and peaceful commerce. In his advocacy of the League, he emphasized modern liberalism as the foundation for enduring peace. Yet he also revealed race prejudice. On April 11, 1919, in the commission that was drafting the Covenant, Japanese delegates introduced an amendment to affirm racial equality, arguing that "the principle of equality of nations and the just treatment of their nationals should be laid down as a fundamental basis of future relations in this world organization." British delegates opposed the amendment. In the commission, only Wilson and a Polish delegate joined the British to criticize it. Others advocated the racial equality amendment. When the president called a vote, eleven of the seventeen delegates at this meeting favored the amendment. Nevertheless, he arbitrarily ruled that it was defeated because the vote was not unanimous. In no other instance did he require unanimity in the voting. Japanese delegates raised the issue once more at a plenary session of the peace conference on April 28. Again they lost to the combined British and American rejection of racial equality. Wilson also affirmed the hierarchy of race to define the stages of development that would characterize the various types of League mandates (A, B, and C) for the former empires of the defeated Central Powers. He thought Europeans were ready for self-government, but people of color outside Europe were not. In the Near East, some nations that had arisen from the former Ottoman Empire, and were regarded as fairly advanced, would be placed under "A" mandates. "B" and "C" mandates would be created for so-called less-developed peoples of Germany's former African and Pacific island colonies. In Wilson's mind, Africans were the least developed. He assigned the task of implementing these League mandates to House, who served as the chief U.S. delegate at a conference in London during the summer of 1919. Thus Wilson's foreign policy, like his advancement of racial segregation at home, revealed his dedication to white supremacy.[58]

[57] Godfrey Hodgson, *Woodrow Wilson's Right Hand: The Life of Colonel Edward M. House* (New Haven, CT, 2006).

[58] Ambrosius, *Woodrow Wilson*, 119–21; Paul Gordon Lauren, *Power and Prejudice: The Politics and Diplomacy of Racial Discrimination* (Boulder, CO, 1988), 76–101; Derek Heater, *National Self-Determination: Woodrow Wilson and His Legacy* (New York, 1994), 177–205; Margaret MacMillan, *Paris 1919: Six Months That Changed the World* (New York, 2001), 98–106, 306–21; Ambrosius, *Wilsonianism*, 21–29; Marc Gallicchio,

Wilson never revised his racist perspective. In 1918, the publisher of *A History of the American People* issued a new edition of this work, adding original documents to supplement the text.[59] The president left his interpretation exactly as it had been published in 1902. In the midst of the Great War to make the world safe for democracy, he reaffirmed his commitment to white supremacy and his rejection of racial equality. The South's Lost Cause continued to shape his worldview, as it did *The Birth of a Nation*. While Dixon's novels affirmed the essential racial nationalism of white supremacy, Wilson combined this perspective with the civic nationalism of modern liberalism. They both thought that assimilation across the color line would destroy the national identity and that the Anglo-Saxon race provided the source of modern progress. While Dixon blatantly proclaimed white racism, Wilson was more subtle. He used the language of civic ideals, yet retained the subtext of racism within the text of his liberalism. The color line restricted his civic nationalist ideals in practice. He thought different European nationalities could and should assimilate, but not with people of color. Making the world safe for democracy did not mean racial equality. His ideas for progressive reform at home and abroad started with the Lost Cause's premise that white men should rule the world.

HISTORIOGRAPHY

Subsequent generations have largely ignored the nexus between liberalism and racism in Wilson's progressivism. American historians in the last half-century, having embraced anti–Jim Crow liberal values of the civil rights movement, have usually not identified him as a proponent of global white supremacy. In their interpretations, the progressive president typically appeared as an advocate of civic rather than racial nationalism. As a liberal, he championed freedom and democracy at home and abroad. His vision of a new world order thus promised international peace and human rights. This generally positive view of Wilson's statecraft highlighted his liberalism, not his dedication to white supremacy. Even outstanding historical scholarship on race relations has not linked Wilson with Dixon's ultra-racist definition of America's national identity.[60]

The African American Encounter with Japan and China: Black Internationalism in Asia, 1895–1945 (Chapel Hill, NC, 2000), 15–27; Erez Manela, "Imagining Woodrow Wilson in Asia: Dreams of East-West Harmony and the Revolt against Empire in 1919," American Historical Review 111 (December 2006): 1327–51.
[59] Woodrow Wilson, *A History of the American People*, 10 vols. (New York, 1918).
[60] Gerstle, *American Crucible*, 83–115, omitted Dixon and *The Birth of a Nation* from his history of race and nation in twentieth-century America. Identifying Wilson only with

This rendition confused style with substance. It failed to recognize that Wilson's preference for handling the race question quietly behind closed doors did not mean that he disregarded the color line. It was central to his statecraft. "Negroes soon learned," Rayford W. Logan observed at the time and wrote later, "that the war by which the world was to be 'made safe for democracy' would not revolutionize their subordinate status in American society."[61]

Wilson's biographers and historians of the Progressive Era have downplayed or ignored his friendship with Dixon and his contributions to *The Birth of a Nation*. Recounting its White House premiere, Arthur S. Link exonerated the president as "an unwitting accomplice in the success of one of the most violent pieces of anti-Negro propaganda in modern American history." Presumably unaware of what he was doing to help promote the film, or unable to correct his mistake afterward, Link argued that "Wilson fell into Dixon's trap, as, indeed, did also members of the Supreme Court and both houses of Congress."[62] Kendrick A. Clements too denied that his viewing of the film was "proof of rampant racism," claiming that "Wilson allowed it to be shown at the White House because Dixon told him that film was the new medium of universal communication."[63] Other biographers altogether omitted *The Birth of a Nation* from their accounts of Wilson's life.[64] However, as Anthony Slide noted,

the civic nationalist tradition, he described him as the champion of liberal ideals to make the world safe for democracy during World War I, but not of exclusive racial nationalism like TR's "racialized nation." Williamson, *The Crucible of Race*, 140–79, 364–95, saw *The Leopard's Spots* as "a codification of the Radical dogma" (140) of white racism. But he did not associate Wilson with Dixon and denied the president's affinity for the virulently racist views of *The Birth of a Nation*. He categorized southerners in Wilson's cabinet (Albert Sydney Burleson, David F. Houston, and Josephus Daniels) and his ambassador to Italy (Thomas Nelson Page) as Radicals, yet did not see Wilson as one of the "racial extremists," claiming instead that "the administration as a whole ultimately did not regard race as a vital matter" (368).

[61] Rayford W. Logan, *The Betrayal of the Negro: From Rutherford B. Hayes to Woodrow Wilson* (New York, 1965), 369. Even Logan did not identify Wilson with *The Birth of a Nation*. Nor did John Hope Franklin and Alfred A. Moss, Jr., *From Slavery to Freedom: A History of African Americans* (New York, 1994), 323–60, or Nell Irvin Painter, *Creating Black Americans: African-American History and Its Meaning, 1619 to the Present* (New York, 2006), 185.

[62] Link, *Wilson: The New Freedom*, 250–51.

[63] Kendrick A. Clements, *Woodrow Wilson: World Statesman* (Boston, 1987), 100; he also incorrectly identified Dixon as "one of Wilson's students at Johns Hopkins in the 1890s."

[64] Arthur Walworth, *Woodrow Wilson* (Second Edition Revised; Baltimore, MD, 1969); John Milton Cooper, Jr., *The Warrior and the Priest: Woodrow Wilson and Theodore Roosevelt* (Cambridge, MA, 1983); August Heckscher, *Woodrow Wilson: A Biography* (New York, 1991); Jan Willem Schulte Nordholt, *Woodrow Wilson: A Life for World Peace* (Berkeley, CA, 1991); John A. Thompson, *Woodrow Wilson* (London, 2002).

Dixon and Wilson were "far closer in racial philosophy than most liberal biographers of the president might have one believe."[65] Kenneth T. Jackson, Nell Irvin Painter, and John Milton Cooper, Jr. noted the film's contribution to the KKK revival after 1915, but they left Wilson out of this story.[66] Other Progressive Era historians barely mentioned or totally ignored the film.[67]

Wilson's statecraft in international relations combined the text of modern liberalism with the subtext of racism. He called for making the world safe for democracy, but he also restricted this promise in practice by drawing the color line. Both liberal civic ideals and race prejudice characterized his legacy of Wilsonianism. As the United States defined its role in world affairs during the so-called American Century, it struggled with the choice between its inclusive civic ideals and its exclusive historic identity as a white Anglo-Saxon Christian nation. This struggle over cultural values profoundly affected America's democracy at home and its involvement abroad. U.S. leaders after World War II pursued America's global vision for human rights with considerable success. Their liberal civic ideals shaped the new international order.[68] Yet these same leaders ensured that the United Nations would not jeopardize the American South's Jim Crow system, thereby thwarting the African-American struggle for human rights.[69] Wilson had protected the same southern interest

[65] Slide, *American Racist*, 83. See also Rogers M. Smith, *Civic Ideals: Conflicting Visions of Citizenship in U.S. History* (New Haven, CT, 1997), 410–69, and Michael Rogin, "'The Sword Becomes a Flashing Vision': D. W. Griffith's *The Birth of a Nation*," in Lang, *Birth of a Nation*, 250–93.

[66] Kenneth T. Jackson, *The Ku Klux Klan in the City, 1915–1930* (New York, 1967), 3–4; Nell Irvin Painter, *Standing at Armageddon: The United States, 1877–1919* (New York, 1987), 219–20, 304; John Milton Cooper, Jr., *Pivotal Decades: The United States, 1900–1920* (New York, 1990), 209.

[67] David M. Kennedy, *Over Here: The First World War and American Society* (New York, 1980), 281; Robert H. Zieger, *America's Great War: World War I and the American Experience* (Lanham, MD, 2000), 126–35; Michael McGerr, *A Fierce Discontent: The Rise and Fall of the Progressive Movement in America* (New York, 2003), 256; David Traxel, *Crusader Nation: The United States in Peace and the Great War, 1898–1920* (New York, 2006), 187; Maureen A. Flanagan, *America Reformed: Progressives and Progressivisms, 1890s-1920s* (New York, 2007). Exceptional among Progressive-era historians, Alan Dawley, *Changing the World: American Progressives in War and Revolution* (Princeton, NJ, 2003), 66, 250, linked Wilson's racism to *The Birth of a Nation* and noted the implications for his public policies at home and abroad.

[68] Elizabeth Borgwardt, *A New Deal for the World: America's Vision for Human Rights* (Cambridge, MA, 2005). See also Micheline R. Ishay, *The History of Human Rights: From Ancient Times to the Globalization Era* (Berkeley, CA, 2004).

[69] Carol Anderson, *Eyes Off the Prize: The United Nations and the African American Struggle for Human Rights, 1944–1955* (Cambridge, 2003). See also Thomas

in white supremacy during the drafting of the League Covenant in 1919. The rhetoric of U.S. foreign policy proclaimed the universal values of liberal democracy as the foundation for world peace, but the practice was often quite different. The odd mixture of inclusive civic ideals with exclusive racist and nationalist prejudices, which Wilson's friendship with Dixon and his contributions to *The Birth of a Nation* had epitomized, continued to influence American democracy and international relations. Deciding which cultural values to give higher priority after 9/11 during President George W. Bush's global war on terrorism was still a critical question for Americans in the twenty-first century.[70] Once more, in this new historical context, they needed to decide which aspects of the Wilsonian legacy – its best universal ideals of freedom and democracy or its worst prejudices of racism and religious intolerance – to embrace at home and abroad.

Borstelmann, *Apartheid's Reluctant Uncle: The United States and Southern Africa in the Early Cold War* (New York, 1993) and *The Cold War and the Color Line: American Race Relations in the Global Arena* (Cambridge, MA, 2001).

[70] Melani McAlister, *Epic Encounters: Culture, Media, and U.S. Interests in the Middle East since 1945* (Updated Edition; Berkeley, CA, 2005), 266–307; Michael Lind, *Made in Texas: George W. Bush and the Southern Takeover of American Politics* (New York, 2003); Lloyd E. Ambrosius, "Woodrow Wilson and George W. Bush: Historical Comparisons of Ends and Means in Their Foreign Policies," *Diplomatic History* 30 (June 2006): 509–43.

4

The Others in Wilsonianism

President Woodrow Wilson affirmed modern liberalism as the foundation for America's foreign policy when he led the United States into World War I. Liberal ideals, which he proclaimed as potentially applicable throughout the world, should define America's wartime purposes and guide its postwar peacemaking. In his war message he called for making the world safe for democracy. In subsequent speeches he outlined his vision of a new world order that, he hoped, would replace the old, discredited European order, which had collapsed in 1914. The president's liberal vision, later known as Wilsonianism, was apparently universal. His rhetoric suggested that it could apply to all nations. Yet in practice he did not believe in the universality of his modern liberal principles and did not plan to implement them for the benefit of all peoples. Although apparently universal, Wilson's vision left some peoples on the outside at least in the foreseeable future. He saw real or potential enemies, whether at home or abroad, as disqualified in some way from full participation in his new world order. Unless or until they conformed to his vision, if they could, these others would be kept out. Thus a fundamental paradox of apparent universality and actual exclusivity characterized Wilsonianism.

WILSON'S NEW WORLD ORDER VERSUS
THE OLD WORLD

Wilson's liberal ideology shaped his progressive presidency in the United States and abroad. He had defined a program of New Freedom during the 1912 presidential election and implemented it as his domestic agenda during the first years of his administration. Similar goals characterized his foreign policy as he called for peace, human rights, and equality among nations in a new world order. He defined four key tenets of Wilsonianism in his famous Fourteen Points address and in subsequent wartime speeches in 1918. First, he called for the self-determination of nations. This principle combined the traditional concept of state sovereignty, which had prevailed in European international relations since 1648, with the American (and also Western European) idea of democracy. Accordingly, all peoples were entitled to self-rule or popular sovereignty. Second, Wilson advocated an "open door" for international trade and investment across borders. Breaking down national or colonial barriers to commerce and finance would open the world to American-style capitalism. Third, the president proposed a new system of international collective security. His emerging idea of the League of Nations would become the central feature in his peacemaking after the war. Fourth, Wilson's vision of a new world order affirmed and depended on the idea of progressive history. He wanted to reform international relations so as to replace the old order with a new one, while guarding against radical or revolutionary changes – or at least against such extreme changes as defined by the norms of the United States. He sought orderly progress toward his liberal goals at home and abroad.[1]

Wilson outlined his global agenda of reform in his Fourteen Points address to a joint session of Congress on January 8, 1918. Emphasizing its ostensibly universal applicability, he proclaimed:

What we demand in this war, therefore, is nothing peculiar to ourselves. It is that the world be made fit and safe to live in; and particularly that it be made safe for every peace-loving nation which, like our own, wishes to live its own life,

---

[1] For various perspectives on Wilsonianism, see N. Gordon Levin, Jr., *Woodrow Wilson and World Politics: America's Response to War and Revolution* (New York, 1968); Thomas J. Knock, *To End All Wars: Woodrow Wilson and the Quest for a New World Order* (New York, 1992); Tony Smith, *America's Mission: The United States and the Worldwide Struggle for Democracy in the Twentieth Century* (Princeton, NJ, 1994); Frank Ninkovich, *The Wilsonian Century: U.S. Foreign Policy since 1900* (Chicago, 1999); G. John Ikenberry, *After Victory: Institutions, Strategic Restraint, and the Rebuilding of Order after Major Wars* (Princeton, NJ, 2001), 117–62; Lloyd E. Ambrosius, *Wilsonianism: Woodrow Wilson and His Legacy in American Foreign Relations* (New York, 2002); Alan Dawley, *Changing the World: American Progressives in War and Revolution* (Princeton, NJ, 2003); Joan Hoff, *A Faustian Foreign Policy from Woodrow Wilson to George W. Bush: Dreams of Perfectibility* (Cambridge, 2008); Lloyd E. Ambrosius, "Democracy, Peace, and World Order," in *Reconsidering Woodrow Wilson: Progressivism, Internationalism, War, and Peace*, ed. John Milton Cooper, Jr. (Washington, DC, 2008), 225–49; Ross A. Kennedy, *The Will to Believe: Woodrow Wilson, World War I, and America's Strategy for Peace and Security* (Kent, OH, 2009).

determine its own institutions, be assured of justice and fair dealing by the other peoples of the world as against force and selfish aggression. All the peoples of the world are in effect partners in this interest, and for our own part we see very clearly that unless justice be done to others it will not be done to us.

Peaceful nations were entitled to freedom at home and security against aggressive neighbors. "An evident principle runs through the whole program I have outlined," he affirmed. "It is the principle of justice to all peoples and nationalities, and their right to live on equal terms of liberty and safety with one another, whether they be strong or weak."[2] The war, he asserted, should end with the creation of this kind of new world order.

Wilson's principles of global reform maintained America's traditional antipathy toward the old world, thereby combining exclusivity with universality. Since the Americans had gained their independence from the British Empire in the eighteenth century, they had drawn a contrast between the new and old worlds as a defining feature in their nationalism, marking an ideological as well as geographical division between the new nation and old Europe. This contrast had justified America's isolationism during the nineteenth century and continued to influence its global role during the Great War. Wilson's policy of neutrality from 1914 to 1917 expressed his traditional belief that the United States should not entangle itself in Europe's wars and diplomacy. When Imperial Germany's submarine warfare finally convinced him in 1917 to intervene in the world war, the president still saw the United States as different from the others of the old world. America represented the values of freedom and democracy for all nations, not the special or selfish interests of the European belligerents on either side, whether the Allies or the Central Powers. Although the United States would align with the United Kingdom and France against Germany, it would do so only as an "associated power" and not as an ally. It would seek to transform international relations, thus presumably avoiding entanglement in the old world that earlier American presidents since George Washington had warned against.[3]

In his address to Congress on April 2, 1917, while calling for a declaration of war against Germany, Wilson defined America's purpose. To protect and promote his liberal ideals, he thought the United States

[2] Address to Congress, Jan. 8, 1918, Woodrow Wilson, *The Public Papers of Woodrow Wilson: War and Peace* [hereafter *PPWW: War & Peace*], eds. Ray Stannard Baker and William E. Dodd (New York, 1927), 1: 158–59, 162; Woodrow Wilson, *The Papers of Woodrow Wilson* [hereafter *PWW*], ed. Arthur S. Link (Princeton, NJ, 1984), 45: 534–39.

[3] Robert W. Tucker, *Woodrow Wilson and the Great War: Reconsidering America's Neutrality, 1914–1917* (Charlottesville, VA, 2007).

should now intervene in the war. It should fight for a new world order against the enemies of this global mission. Germany's unrestricted submarine attacks against neutral as well as belligerent ships challenged Wilson's "open door" vision of the international economy. "The present German submarine warfare against commerce is a war against mankind. It is a war against all nations," he claimed. To protect freedom for all nations, he called for the United States to join a new democratic partnership – not one of Europe's old alliances – to restore and preserve world peace. "A steadfast concert for peace can never be maintained except by a partnership of democratic nations," he explained. "No autocratic government could be trusted to keep faith within it or observe its covenants." Russia's recent revolution, which had replaced the Romanov czarist regime with a new provisional government, encouraged Wilson to believe that history was moving in the right direction. "Russia was known by those who knew it best to have been always in fact democratic at heart," he asserted. "The autocracy that crowned the summit of her political structure, long as it had stood and terrible as was the reality of its power, was not in fact Russian in origins, character, or purpose; and now ... the great, generous Russian people have been added in all their naive majesty and might to the forces that are fighting for freedom in the world, for justice, and for peace." The Russians could now join the Americans, alongside the British and the French, to defend democracy and create a peaceful world. "We are glad ... to fight thus for the ultimate peace of the world and for the liberation of its peoples, the German peoples included: for the rights of nations great and small and the privilege of men everywhere to choose their way of life and of obedience. The world must be made safe for democracy. Its peace must be planted upon the tested foundation of political liberty."[4] A new ideological and military partnership of democratic nations would create this new world order.

Wilson heralded America's purpose in the Great War as a providential mission. What Americans had achieved at home would now define their global role. As he explained on May 30, 1917, "we are saying to all mankind, 'We did not set this Government up in order that we might have a selfish and separate liberty, for we are now ready to come to your assistance and fight out upon the field of the world the cause of human liberty.' ... Such a time has come, and in the providence of God

---

[4] Address to Congress, April 2, 1917, *PPWW: War & Peace*, 1: 8, 12–14; *PWW* (1983), 41: 519–27.

America will once more have an opportunity to show to the world that she was born to serve mankind."[5] It was the nation's calling to redeem others.

America's God-given mission, in Wilson's view, promised to transcend the historic failures of the old world's statecraft. On February 11, 1918, he explained that "the United States has no desire to interfere in European affairs or to act as arbiter in European territorial disputes." It should remain aloof from Europe's traditional system of international relations, which had produced the war. "This war had its roots in the disregard of the rights of small nations and of nationalities which lacked the union and the force to make good their claim to determine their own allegiances and their own forms of political life," he asserted. "Covenants must now be entered into which will render such things impossible for the future; and those covenants must be backed by the united force of all the nations that love justice and are willing to maintain it at any cost." The new world order, Wilson emphasized, would guarantee "essential justice" and peace, replace "the great game, now forever discredited, of the balance of power," ensure "every territorial settlement ... for the benefit of the population concerned," and provide each "well-defined national aspiration ... the utmost satisfaction." In short, it would fulfill the "true spirit of America ... for justice and for self-government."[6]

Throughout the war Wilson reiterated the contrast between the new and old worlds. Europe still represented the other in his traditionally American nationalist thinking. On September 27, 1918, he summarized the kind of peace he favored. He advocated "impartial justice" with "no special or separate interest." Within the new League of Nations that he envisaged, there should be "no leagues or alliances or special covenants and understandings" and "no special, selfish economic combinations." Instead of secret accords, "all international agreements and treaties" should be known to the entire world. This new diplomacy would fulfill rather than abandon the American diplomatic tradition. "We still read Washington's immortal warning against 'entangling alliances' with full comprehension and an answering purpose," Wilson emphasized. "But only special and limited alliances entangle; and we recognize and accept the duty of a new day in which we are permitted to hope for a general

[5] Memorial Day Address, May 30, 1917, *PPWW: War & Peace*, 1: 53; *PWW* (1983), 42: 422–23; Richard M. Gamble, *The War for Righteousness: Progressive Christianity, the Great War, and the Rise of the Messianic Nation* (Wilmington, DE, 2003).
[6] Address to Congress, Feb. 11, 1918, *PPWW: War & Peace*, 1: 180–84; *PWW* (1984), 46: 318–24.

alliance which will avoid entanglements and clear the air of the world for common understandings and the maintenance of common rights."[7]

The new world order, with its League of Nations, would transcend the old European statecraft of military alliances and balances of power that had culminated in the Great War. Wilsonianism thus promised a new internationalism without requiring the United States to sacrifice its historic aloofness or isolation from the old world. The president stressed this point at a plenary session of the Paris Peace Conference. "In coming into this war," he reminded the delegates on January 25, 1919, "the United States never for a moment thought that she was intervening in the politics of Europe or the politics of Asia or the politics of any part of the world. Her thought was that all the world had now become conscious that there was a single cause which turned upon the issues of this war. That was the cause of justice and of liberty for men of every kind and place."[8]

IMPERIAL GERMANY AND BOLSHEVIK RUSSIA

After the United States entered the world war, Wilson denounced Imperial Germany as the principal enemy. It became the foremost other in Wilsonianism. Although the president generally distrusted the old world, Germany's autocratic and militaristic government ranked as his chief nemesis. It directly threatened his new world order. Wilson blamed Kaiser Wilhelm II's regime but not the German people. "The military masters of Germany denied us the right to be neutral," he asserted in his Flag Day address on June 14, 1917. "They filled our unsuspecting communities with vicious spies and conspirators and sought to corrupt the opinion of our people in their own behalf." The German government dominated not only its own people but also the other Central Powers. "The war was begun by the military masters of Germany, who proved to be also the masters of Austria-Hungary." German leaders sought to extend their power well beyond their homeland. "Their plan was to throw a broad belt of German military power and political control across the very center of Europe and beyond the Mediterranean into the heart of Asia; and Austria-Hungary was to be as much their tool and pawn as Serbia or Bulgaria or Turkey or the ponderous states of the East." Imperial Germany's global ambitions not only involved military force but

---

[7] Address, New York City, Sept. 27, 1918, *PPWW: War & Peace*, 1: 257–58; *PWW* (1985), 51: 127–33.
[8] Address to Plenary Session of Paris Peace Conference, Jan. 25, 1919, *PPWW: War & Peace*, 1: 397; *PWW* (1986), 54: 264–71.

also subversive activity in the United States and throughout Europe. "The sinister intrigue is being no less actively conducted in this country than in Russia and in every country in Europe to which the agents and dupes of the Imperial German Government can get access." To counter Germany's autocratic and militaristic regime, Wilson called upon all democratic nations to fight against this global challenge. He affirmed that "this is a People's War, a war for freedom and justice and self-government amongst all the nations of the world, a war to make the world safe for the peoples who live upon it and have made it their own, the German people themselves included." The president expressed his firm revolve to win this war. "For us there is but one choice. We have made it," he avowed. "Woe be to the man or group of men that seeks to stand in our way in this day of high resolution when every principle we hold dearest is to be vindicated and made secure for the salvation of the nations."[9] After winning the war against Imperial Germany and the other Central Powers, the democratic partners under American leadership should establish a new world order to preserve the peace.

Russia's Bolshevik Revolution in November 1917 challenged Wilson's plan for a global democratic partnership. In a message to Russia on May 26, while still expecting the provisional government to establish a liberal democracy, he had affirmed: "We are fighting for the liberty, the self-government, and the undictated development of all peoples, and every feature of the settlement that concludes this war must be conceived and executed for that purpose."[10] But the Bolsheviks replaced the provisional government with their new socialist or communist regime under Vladimir I. Lenin's leadership. Contrary to the president's expectation of orderly progress toward liberal democracy in Russia, its radical new government now became another enemy. He discounted the authenticity of this dangerous development, viewing the Bolsheviks as German agents or dupes and thus regarding them as illegitimate representatives of the country. Refusing to recognize the Bolshevik government, he continued to hope that moderate liberals would defeat the radicals and keep Russia as a democratic partner.[11]

---

[9] Flag Day Address, June 14, 1917, *Public Papers: War and Peace*, 1: 61–63, 66–67; *PWW*, 42: 498–504.

[10] Message to Russia, May 26, 1917, *PPWW: War & Peace*, 1: 50.

[11] David S. Fogelsong, *America's Secret War Against Bolshevism: U.S. Intervention in the Russian Civil War, 1917–1920* (Chapel Hill, NC, 1995); Norman E. Saul, *War and Revolution: The United States and Russia, 1914–1921* (Lawrence, KS, 2001); Donald E. Davis and Eugene P. Trani, *The First Cold War: The Legacy of Woodrow Wilson in U.S.-Soviet Relations* (Columbia, MO, 2002).

Shortly after the Bolsheviks seized power in Petrograd, Wilson identified
them with Imperial Germany and denounced them as opponents of his
new world order. Speaking to the American Federation of Labor convention on November 12, 1917, he expressed his amazement that the
Bolsheviks or "any group of persons should be so ill-informed as to suppose, as some groups in Russia apparently suppose, that any reforms
planned in the interest of the people can live in the presence of a Germany
powerful enough to undermine or overthrow them by intrigue or force."
He thought that "any body of free men that compounds with the present German Government is compounding for its own destruction. But
that is not the whole of the story. Any man in America or anywhere else
that supposes that the free industry and enterprise of the world can continue if the Pan-German plan is achieved and German power fastened
upon the world is as fatuous as the dreamers in Russia." Wilson criticized
Bolshevik Russia as an enemy for aligning with Imperial Germany. But
he also warned American workers not to identify with the radical revolution in Russia. "Let us show ourselves Americans by showing that we do
not want to go off in separate camps or groups by ourselves, but that we
want to cooperate with all other classes and all other groups in the common enterprise which is to release the spirits of the world from bondage.
I would be willing to set that up as the final test of an American. That is
the meaning of democracy." The president expected American workers
to remain patriotic, rejecting the radical class politics of the Bolsheviks
and adhering to the moderate liberal democracy of the United States.
"We claim to be the greatest democratic people in the world, and democracy means first of all that we can govern ourselves. If our men have not
self-control, then they are not capable of that great thing which we call
democratic government."[12]

Wilson viewed the Bolsheviks as others and hoped that the Russian
people would reject their radical revolution. To counter their appeal for
peace with the Central Powers, he announced his alternative vision of
a new world order in the Fourteen Points. He sought to prevent Russia
from concluding a separate peace on the eastern front, which might allow
Germany to defeat the Allies on the western front before the United States
could send a sufficient military force under General John J. Pershing's
command to help them win the war. However, the president could not
stop Lenin's government from signing the Treaty of Brest-Litovsk on

[12] Address to American Federation of Labor, Nov. 12, 1918, *PPWW: War & Peace*, 1: 120,
122–23; *PWW* (1984), 45: 11–17.

March 3, 1918. Even now he still tried to encourage the Russians to resist both the Bolsheviks and the Germans. In a message to the Russian people on March 11, he reiterated that "the whole heart of the people of the United States is with the people of Russia in the attempt to free themselves forever from autocratic government and become the masters of their own life."[13] Throughout the war Wilson maintained his anti-German and anti-Bolshevik stance as a posture against external enemies of liberal democracy.

HYPHENATED AMERICANS AND PATRIOTISM

Counterparts to these external enemies posed internal threats in the United States, as the president perceived them. He distinguished between patriotic Americans and others who were potentially subversive or disloyal. Hyphenated Americans, he feared, might identify more with their ancestral lands than with their adopted country. German-Americans and Irish-Americans topped his list of suspects. He distrusted them far more than Anglo-Americans, who appeared simply as Americans to Wilson. Even before the United States had entered the war, he had questioned the patriotism of some foreign-born citizens as well as resident aliens. In an address on citizenship on July 13, 1916, he emphasized that loyalty means self-sacrifice. "Certain men – I have never believed a great number – born in other lands, have in recent months thought more of those lands than they have of the honor and interest of the government under which they are now living." They needed to sacrifice their old national identities to become loyal Americans, which required them to accept America's "vision of real liberty and real justice and purity of conduct."[14]

Before the Great War, the United States had experienced a massive influx of European immigrants at the same time that it was expanding its empire abroad. These immigrants brought the old world into the new, while Americans were also encountering others through imperial expansion, as with the annexation of the Philippines after the Spanish-American War of 1898.[15] Long before he became president,

[13] Message to Russia, March 11, 1918, *PPWW: War & Peace*, 1: 191; *PWW* (1984), 46: 598.
[14] Address on Citizenship, July 13, 1916, Woodrow Wilson, *The Public Papers of Woodrow Wilson: The New Democracy* [hereafter *PPWW: New Democracy*], eds. Ray Stannard Baker and William E. Dodd (New York, 1926), 2: 251–52; *PWW* (1982), 37: 414–18.
[15] Matthew Frye Jacobson, *Barbarian Virtues: The United States Encounters Foreign Peoples at Home and Abroad, 1876–1917* (New York, 2000); Paul A. Kramer, *The*

Wilson contemplated the historical implications of these interacting developments. Writing about "The Significance of American History" in 1902, he claimed that "a virgin continent discovered in the West" had opened a place where "men out of an old world" could undertake their "work as pioneers." They brought their "old civilization" and transplanted it in the "wilderness" of the new world. "Men out of every European race, men out of Asia, men out of Africa, have crowded in, to the bewilderment alike of statesmen and historians," he observed. European immigrants in the new world had created the "new race" of Americans through "the mixture of races." Wilson viewed the creation of this new nation as a process of liberal assimilation. European nationalities – or races, as he described them – became American as they acquired the cultural values and embraced the institutions that the United States had derived from its English origins. American national identity could be traced back to the Anglo-Saxons, although it was the product of history more than of biology. Wilson affirmed the idea of civic rather than racial or ethnic nationalism, even though he still believed that the core of Americanism came from the nation's British heritage. Acculturation, later called the "melting pot," had transformed European immigrants, such as the Dutch and the French, into Americans. Their new national identity, he affirmed, was as genuine as if "we kept the pure Saxon strain." He explained: "All peoples have come to dwell among us, but they have merged their individuality in a national character already formed; have been dominated, changed, absorbed." In Wilson's view, history provided a better explanation than biology or race for the enduring British legacy in the United States. Although the nation's origins could be traced back to the Anglo-Saxons, historical developments were more important than primordial roots in shaping the American identity. "Nations grow by spirit, not by blood," he avowed, "and nowhere can the significant principle of their growth be seen more clearly, upon a more fair and open page, than in the history of the United States." American history, he elaborated, was "an offshoot of European history and has all its antecedents on the other side of the sea, and yet it is so much more than a mere offshoot." He anticipated that in the twentieth century the United States would play an even larger global role. "The life of the new world grows as complex as the life of the old. A nation hitherto wholly devoted to domestic developments now finds its first tasks of the great world at large, seeking its

Blood of Government: Race, Empire, the United States, and the Philippines (Chapel Hill, NC, 2006).

special part and place of power. A new age has come which no man may forecast. But the past is the key to it; and the past of America lies at the center of modern history."[16]

Although early in his academic career Wilson had espoused the germ theory of history, he later embraced the civic nationalism of modern liberalism. During the 1880s, he had traced the origins of the United States back through English history to the Anglo-Saxons. But after meeting Frederick Jackson Turner at Johns Hopkins in 1889, he began to shift his focus from primordial roots to the frontier experience in the American West as the critical factor in shaping the national identity.[17] This transition in Wilson's historical thinking undergirded his confidence in liberal assimilation of even the so-called new immigrants from Southern and Eastern Europe. The historical process of orderly progress, which the frontier had epitomized, could transform the newcomers into Americans. He did not join strong advocates, such as President Theodore Roosevelt, of a "racialized nation."[18] Less optimistic than Wilson about liberal assimilation of immigrants, such proponents of a racialized nation adopted a harder line on Americanization. Wilson also resisted new restrictions on immigration. Yet he obviously preferred the old immigrants from Western Europe. In *A History of the American People* (1902), he noted a change in the pattern of immigration after 1890 from "the sturdy stocks of the north of Europe" to "the lowest class of the south of Italy and men of the meaner sort out of Hungary and Poland." He added that "the Chinese were more to be desired, as workmen if not as citizens, than most of the coarse crew that came crowding in every year at the eastern ports."[19]

During the Great War, Wilson reaffirmed his belief in liberal assimilation. He reminded the Daughters of the American Revolution on October 11, 1915, that "America has not grown by the mere multiplication of the original stock." Instead, the nation had preserved the ideals of its founders by teaching their principles to subsequent generations of immigrants. "It is easy to preserve tradition with continuity of blood," he acknowledged,

[16] Woodrow Wilson, "The Significance of American History," in *Woodrow Wilson: Essential Writings and Speeches of the Scholar-President*, ed. Mario R. DeNunzio (New York, 2008), 212–17; *PWW* (1972), 12: 179–84.
[17] Lloyd E. Ambrosius, *Wilsonian Statecraft: Theory and Practice of Liberal Internationalism during World War I* (Wilmington, DE, 1991), 3–13; Ronald J. Pestritto, *Woodrow Wilson and the Roots of Modern Liberalism* (Lanham, MD, 2005).
[18] Gary Gerstle, *American Crucible: Race and Nation in the Twentieth Century* (Princeton, NJ, 2001), 14–80; Gary Gerstle, "Race and Nation in the Thought and Politics of Woodrow Wilson," in *Reconsidering Woodrow Wilson*, 93–123.
[19] Woodrow Wilson, *A History of the American People* (New York, 1902), 5: 212–13.

"... but it is not so easy when that race is constantly being renewed and augmented from other sources, from stocks that did not carry or originate the same principles." Nevertheless, under proper American tutelage, they too embraced the national legacy of liberty. "So from generation to generation strangers have had to be indoctrinated with the principles of the American family, and the wonder and beauty of it all has been that the infection has been so generously easy." Thus, later immigrants from various lands became foreign-born citizens who were just as patriotic as those born in the United States. With few exceptions, they too were ready to fulfill their duties as Americans.[20]

Wilson interpreted the closing of America's western frontier in 1890 as the turning point in its history. Whereas the United States had previously concentrated on internal developments, it subsequently began to assume global responsibilities. He reminded his Omaha audience on October 5, 1916, that the war with Spain, which came only eight years after the frontier's closing, left the United States as the guardian of Cuba and the possessor of Puerto Rico. "And," he added, "that frontier which no man could draw upon this continent in 1890 had been flung across the sea 7,000 miles to the untrodden forests of some part of the Philippine Islands." The president believed that America's history at home prepared it for a new role in world affairs. Seeking to link his audience's local experience with America's global mission, he explained: "Nebraska was once, as I have phased it, the melting pot in which the various elements of America were fused together for the purpose of American life. Now it is our great duty to fuse the elements of America together for the purpose of the life of the world." He anticipated that the United States would help create a postwar league of nations to preserve the peace. "What disturbs the life of the whole world is the concern of the whole world," he avowed, "and it is our duty to lend the full force of this nation, moral and physical, to a league of nations which shall see to it that nobody disturbs the peace of the world without submitting his case first to the opinion of mankind."[21] From this same perspective, Wilson outlined his ideas for a "peace without victory" to end the European war. "These are American principles, American policies," he affirmed in his address to the Senate on January 22, 1917.[22]

[20] Address to Daughters of American Revolution, Oct. 11, 1915, *PPWW: New Democracy*, 1: 376; *PWW* (1980), 35: 47–51.
[21] Address, Omaha, Nebraska, Oct. 5, 1916, *PPWW: New Democracy*, 2: 345, 348; *PWW* (1982), 38: 343–49.
[22] Address to Senate, Jan. 22, 1917, *PPWW: New Democracy*, 2: 410, 414; *PWW* (1982), 40: 533–39.

After the United States entered the Great War, Wilson stressed national unity. To defeat foreign enemies, the American people needed to fulfill their duties as U.S. citizens. They should support the war effort by volunteering for military service or contributing in other ways. But if they neglected these obligations, he resolved to use the federal government's powers of coercion. The wartime experience thus contributed to the making of the modern American citizen. Under Wilson's leadership, the United States intensified the liberal assimilation or Americanization of European immigrants and their descendants. Expecting all patriots to support the American principles that he articulated, he stifled dissent and rejected cultural pluralism.[23] In his view, the "melting pot" on the western frontier had created the prototypical Americans out of European immigrants of various nationalities. In a telegram to the Northwest Loyalty Meeting at Saint Paul, Minnesota, on November 16, 1917, he called upon all Americans to unite to win the war. "You have come together as the representatives of that Western Empire in which the sons of all sections of America and the stocks of all the nations of Europe have made the prairie and the forest the home of a new race and the temple of a new faith," the president wrote. "The time has come when that home must be protected and that faith affirmed in deeds. Sacrifice and service must come from every class, every profession, every party, every race, every creed, every section. This is not a banker's war or a farmer's war or a manufacturer's war or a laboring-man's war—it is a war for every straight-out American whether our flag be his by birth or by adoption."[24] By identifying "a new race" of Americans as including "the stocks of all the nations of Europe," Wilson reaffirmed his belief in the nation's ability to transform immigrants from the old world into citizens of the new world. Like other Americans who had expanded their understanding of "whiteness" to include Irish Catholics and the new immigrants from Southern and Eastern Europe, many of whom were Jews or Catholic or Orthodox Christians, he no longer restricted the national identity to Anglo-Saxon Protestants or Anglo-Americans. But, notably, he omitted any reference to Asian or African Americans. His liberal inclusiveness excluded people

---

[23] Desmond King, *Making Americans: Immigration, Race, and the Origins of the Diverse Democracy* (Cambridge, MA, 2000), 1–165; Christopher Capozolla, *Uncle Sam Wants You: World War I and the Making of the Modern American Citizen* (New York, 2008); Geoffrey R. Stone, *Perilous Times: Free Speech in Wartime* (New York, 2004), 135–233; Geoffrey R. Stone, "Mr. Wilson's First Amendment," in *Reconsidering Woodrow Wilson*, 189–224.

[24] Telegram, Nov. 16, 1917, *PPWW: War & Peace*, 1: 127.

of color. Nonwhite Americans did not fit his ideal of U.S. citizenship. They were others.[25]

Wilson drew a sharp color line despite his apparently universal liberal rhetoric. During his presidency, the racial segregation of the Jim Crow South became the common practice in the federal government. In 1915, he watched the racist film *The Birth of a Nation* at the White House as a favor to his Johns Hopkins classmate and friend, Thomas Dixon, Jr., who had joined David W. Griffith to make this movie about the Civil War and Reconstruction. They included Wilson's quotations from *A History of the American People* in this silent film to give credibility to their historical interpretation of the "war between the states" and the postwar reconstruction of the South. They used his words to exonerate the Ku Klux Klan, which had inflicted violence and terror to overturn the interracial governments and restore white supremacy. Whatever he might have said in private after viewing the film, the public knew that the president had seen it and had not criticized its virulently racist message. Thus, although he never publicly praised the film, he implicitly endorsed its glorification of the KKK and white supremacy. All viewers, after reading the quotations from Wilson's book between the first and second parts of the film, would have identified him with its message. Nevertheless, he refused to express any public criticism of this most popular silent movie. Deeply embedded in the text of his liberalism was the subtext of white racism. Despite his universal rhetoric, the president's idea of freedom and democracy marginalized black people.[26]

Wilson sought to unite white Americans from the North and the South but denied African Americans equal rights as citizens. Speaking to Confederate veterans on June 5, 1917, he emphasized their place in the reunited nation. He affirmed "the great ends which God in His mysterious Providence wrought through our instrumentality, because at the heart of the men of the North and of the South there was the same love

---

[25] Matthew Frye Jacobson, *Whiteness of a Different Color: European Immigrants and the Alchemy of Race* (Cambridge, MA, 1998).

[26] Lloyd E. Ambrosius, "Woodrow Wilson and *The Birth of a Nation*: American Democracy and International Relations," *Diplomacy and Statecraft* 18 (December 2007): 689–718. See also Glenda Sluga, *The Nation, Psychology, and International Politics, 1870–1919* (New York, 2006).

of self-government and of liberty, and now we are to be the instrument in the hands of God to see that liberty is made secure for mankind." White Americans from the North and the South, who shared a common "passion for human freedom" even when they had fought against each other, should now unite to help liberate the old world.[27]

Wilson's concept of national self-determination projected his American belief in the "melting pot" onto the peacemaking. His Fourteen Points outlined the new map of Europe and the Middle East. He thought all Europeans, if they practiced self-control like Americans, were capable of governing themselves. They could establish liberal democracy throughout the old world. When he announced the Armistice at a joint session of Congress on November 11, 1918, the president shared his vision of orderly progress toward the new world order. He urged the emerging nations to "preserve their self-control and the orderly processes of their governments." He warned that "peoples who have just come out from under the yoke of arbitrary government and who are now coming at last into their freedom will never find the treasures of liberty they are in search of if they look for them by the light of the torch. They will find that every pathway that is stained with the blood of their own brothers leads to the wilderness, not to the seat of their hope."[28] Wilson wanted viable nation-states to establish democratic governments and join the League of Nations but he greatly underestimated the problems of competing nationalities in Russia, Central Europe, and the Middle East after the collapse of the Romanov, Habsburg, Hohenzollern, and Ottoman empires. The various peoples in the lands of these former empires embraced racial or ethnic nationalism rather than Wilson's civic nationalism.[29] New nation-states, such as Poland, Czechoslovakia, and Yugoslavia, experienced ethnic conflicts within their borders as well as with their neighbors. A civil war in Russia, which the Bolsheviks eventually won, prevented it from becoming the democratic partner Wilson expected in Eastern Europe. It was not easy for him to apply American liberal principles in the old world.

Leaders of the new Weimar Republic, which replaced Kaiser Wilhelm II's government after the 1918 German Revolution, also held a different concept of national self-determination. They wanted the president to help

---

[27] Address to Confederate Veterans, June 5, 1917, *PPWW: War & Peace*, 1: 55; *PWW*, 42: 451–53.

[28] Address to Congress, Nov. 11, 1918, *PPWW: War & Peace*, 1: 301–02; *PWW* (1986), 53: 35–43.

[29] Aviel Roshwald, *Ethnic Nationalism and the Fall of Empires: Central Europe, Russia, and the Middle East, 1914–1923* (London, 2001).

them keep or acquire all lands in Central Europe that were inhabited by Germans. That was their understanding of his Fourteen Points. They were deeply disappointed, of course, when he expected them to accept territorial losses to Poland, France, Belgium, and Denmark, and when he opposed their annexation of Austria or German-speaking parts of Czechoslovakia. Wilson's belief, based on the liberal American idea of the "melting pot," that Germans outside the new borders of the Weimar Republic could assimilate into other nations made no sense from their perspective of racial or ethnic nationalism. They did not think that fellow Germans should be absorbed into Poland, France, Belgium, or Denmark, or kept apart in Austria and Czechoslovakia. When the German delegation received the peace treaty from Wilson and Allied leaders at Versailles on May 7, 1919, and immediately demanded revisions, believing that he had betrayed his promise of the Fourteen Points, he stiffened his resolve to require them to sign the treaty anyway. Until they accepted and fulfilled the peace conditions, he agreed with the Allies that Germany should be excluded from membership in the new League of Nations. Even with a republican government, it did not qualify for this partnership of democratic nations. Still an enemy, Weimar Germany remained one of the others in Wilsonianism.[30]

People of color around the world also found the peace settlement deeply disappointing. The president's call for a new order based on self-determination and equality of nations resonated in, among other places, Egypt, India, China, and Korea. Anticolonial nationalists appropriated his words to advocate their independence from the great powers that dominated the Paris Peace Conference. Expecting him to bolster their claims, these leaders used Wilson's rhetoric to justify their causes. They felt betrayed, however, because he never gave them the kind of support they expected. Given his Eurocentric orientation, he had not even imagined that so many peoples outside of Europe would think he was promising them self-determination anytime soon. In his view, colonial peoples were not yet sufficiently civilized to qualify as nations ready for self-government. They still needed tutoring by the advanced nations. Although the president's liberal ideals were apparently universal, he did not apply them in the colonial empires of the victorious Allies. He agreed that Egypt and India should remain in the British Empire and that Japan

[30] Ambrosius, *Wilsonianism*, 125–34; Lloyd E. Ambrosius, "Nationale Selbstbestimmung im Ersten und Zweiten Weltkrieg: Eine Vergleichsstudie von Wilson bis Roosevelt," in *Deutschland und die USA in der Internationalen Geschichte des 20. Jahrhunderts*, eds. Manfred Berg and Philipp Gassert (Stuttgart, 2004), 237–62.

would keep Korea and take over Germany's assets in China, notably in Shandong. Some anticolonial nationalists, in their disillusionment with Wilsonianism, subsequently turned to Bolshevism. Lenin promised self-determination to all nations, including colonial peoples. Given Wilson's attitude toward these others, he was not ready for "the Wilsonian moment."[31]

Wilson's vision of a new world order drew a global color line. Yet, while protecting the colonial empires of the victorious Allies, he expected them to accept minimal supervision by the League of Nations under a system of mandates for their new acquisitions of the defeated empires' former possessions outside of Europe. New nations emerging from conquered empires in Europe were presumably ready for self-government. But Germany's former colonies and some peoples in the former Ottoman Empire were deemed not yet ready. For them Wilson advocated mandates that would authorize the mandatory powers, under the League's oversight, to provide tutelage for the local peoples. The various mandates affirmed a racial hierarchy. Some new nations in the former Ottoman lands, which were regarded as fairly advanced and thus closer to eligibility for self-government, would be placed in so-called "A" mandates. Other "less-developed" peoples of Germany's Pacific-island and African colonies would be assigned "B" and "C" mandates. Although Wilson's rhetoric seemed to promise an end to colonialism, the League mandates perpetuated its legacy in a new form. These peoples were still others in his new world order.[32]

At the peace conference, Wilson rejected the idea of racial equality. During the drafting of the Covenant for the League of Nations, Japanese delegates introduced an amendment to affirm that "the principle of equality of nations and the just treatment of their nationals should be laid down as a fundamental basis of future relations in the world organization." British delegates vociferously opposed the amendment. In the commission that drafted the Covenant, only Wilson and a Polish delegate joined the British to criticize it. Other delegates favored the amendment. At the meeting on April 11, 1919, eleven of the seventeen delegates voted for it. But as chair of the commission, the president ruled that the amendment was defeated because the vote was not unanimous. At no other time did he require such unanimity. Japanese delegates then raised the issue at

[31] Erez Manela, *The Wilsonian Moment: Self-Determination and the International Origins of Anticolonial Nationalism* (New York, 2007).
[32] Margaret MacMillan, *Paris 1919: Six Months That Changed the World* (New York, 2001), 98–106.

a plenary session on April 28, but they lost again to the British and the Americans, who did not want their empires open to Japanese or other Asian immigrants. By his crucial role in defeating the Japanese racial equality amendment, Wilson, along with the British, drew a global color line. His liberal ideals, although ostensibly universal, were exclusive in practice. The full benefits of Wilsonianism were available only for white nations of the West.[33]

African Americans wanted Wilson's ostensibly universal promise of freedom and democracy for themselves. With few exceptions, they loyally supported the war effort. But he saw their assertive claims for human or civil rights as a danger. His administration used its wartime coercive powers to investigate and control them. During the peace conference, he confided to his physician Dr. Cary Grayson his fear that "the American negro returning from abroad would be our greatest medium in conveying bolshevism to America."[34] The president identified African Americans with foreign foes of Wilsonianism, although – or because – they, like anticolonial nationalists abroad, affirmed its evident promise of racial equality. They too learned that Wilson still excluded them. His modern liberalism at home revealed the same fundamental paradox of apparent universality and actual exclusivity that characterized Wilsonianism abroad. For him, there were many others who did not – or at least not yet – qualify for his new world order.

FAILURE OF WILSON'S NEW WORLD ORDER

Despite its limitations, Wilson touted his new world order. On July 10, 1919, when he submitted the Versailles Treaty to the Senate, he acknowledged that "it was not easy to graft the new order of ideas on the old, and some of the fruits of the grafting may, I fear, for a time be bitter." To overcome the evil influences, purposes, and ambitions that had produced the "sinister designs of Germany," he heralded "the League of Nations as an

---

[33] Paul Gordon Lauren, *Power and Prejudice: The Politics and Diplomacy of Racial Discrimination* (Boulder, CO, 1988), 82–107; Marilyn Lake and Henry Reynolds, *Drawing the Global Colour Line: White Men's Countries and the International Challenge of Racial Equality* (Cambridge, 2008), 284–309.

[34] Diary of Dr. Grayson, March 10, 1919, *PWW* (1986), 55: 471; Mark Ellis, *Race, War, and Surveillance: African Americans and the United States Government during World War I* (Bloomington, IN, 2001); Theodore Kornweibel, Jr., *"Investigating Everything": Federal Efforts to Compel Black Loyalty during World War I* (Bloomington, IN, 2002); Jonathan Rosenberg, *How Far the Promised Land?: World Affairs and the American Civil Rights Movement from the First World War to Vietnam* (Princeton, NJ, 2006), 15–72.

indispensable instrumentality for the maintenance of the new order" in "the world of civilized men." To replace the old order, "the united power of free nations must put a stop to aggression, and the world must be given peace." The League was "the only hope of mankind." "The stage is set, the destiny disclosed," Wilson proclaimed. "It has come about by no plan of our own conceiving, but by the hand of God who led us into this way.... It was of this that we dreamed at our birth. America shall in truth show the way. The light streams on the path ahead, and nowhere else."[35]

Yet others still resisted Wilson's new world order and he blamed them for it. In private conversations with Secretary of State Robert Lansing, he denounced Great Britain, France, Italy, Romania, and Greece, confessing that "I am almost inclined to refuse to permit this country to be a member of the League of Nations when it is composed of such intriguers and robbers. I am disposed to throw up the whole business and get out." He condemned the old world for "the inordinate cupidity and disregard of right by all nations."[36] Nevertheless, he sought American support for the League of Nations. During his western tour in September 1919, he questioned the loyalty of its critics. "Opposition is the specialty of those who are Bolshevistically inclined," he asserted.[37] Helping whip up the Red Scare, he claimed that "there are apostles of Lenin in our own midst."[38] Denouncing hyphenated Americans, especially German-Americans, he alleged that "the most un-American thing in the world is a hyphen."[39] Pro-German and pro-Bolshevik propagandists sought to keep the United States out of the League and defeat this "progressive reform." If they were to win the treaty fight, it would serve the interests of America's foreign enemies, Weimar Germany and Bolshevik Russia.[40] It would prevent the United States from fulfilling its providential mission to guarantee the new world order.[41] Despite his patriotic appeal against all these others, Wilson failed. Republicans, who controlled the Senate under Henry

---

[35] Address to Senate, July 10, *PPWW: War & Peace*, 1: 541, 545, 548, 551–52; *PWW* (1989), 61: 426–36.

[36] Memorandum by Robert Lansing, Aug. 20, 1919, *PWW* (1990), 62: 428–29.

[37] Address, Kansas City, Missouri, Sept. 6, 1919, *PPWW: War & Peace*, 2: 10; *PWW* (1990), 63: 66–75.

[38] Address, Billings, Montana, Sept. 11, 1919, *PPWW: War & Peace*, 2: 108; *PWW*, 63: 170–80.

[39] Address, St. Paul, Minnesota, Sept. 9, 1919, *PPWW: War & Peace*, 2: 78; *PWW*, 63: 125–31.

[40] Address, Coeur D'Alene, Idaho, Sept. 12, 1919, *PPWW: War & Peace*, 2: 143; *PWW*, 63: 212–21.

[41] Address, San Francisco, California, Sept. 18, 1919, *PPWW: War & Peace*, 2: 249–62; *PWW*, 63: 341–50.

Cabot Lodge's leadership, rejected the treaty and kept the United States out of the League.[42]

Both at home and abroad, Wilsonianism generated a backlash. Although ostensibly universal, it excluded or disappointed others and they reacted negatively. African Americans and anticolonial nationalists felt that the president had betrayed his promise of freedom and democracy for all peoples by drawing a global color line. The Japanese too suffered from his rejection of racial equality. The Germans also blamed him for not supporting their nationalist claims as they had expected. Other Europeans strove to create new nation-states that would achieve their hopes for racial or ethnic self-determination, simply ignoring his preference for civic nationalism based on liberal ideals. Bolsheviks in Russia identified him as an enemy, and he held a reciprocal view of them. Even the Allies resisted his vision of a new world order and pursued their own interests. Wilson painfully perceived, although he did not acknowledge it publicly, that the old world was rejecting Wilsonianism. Ironically, like the others whom he saw as real or potential enemies and sought to exclude from his new world order, he too was eventually marginalized in the peacemaking after the Great War.

---

[42] Lloyd E. Ambrosius, *Woodrow Wilson and the American Diplomatic Tradition: The Treaty Fight in Perspective* (Cambridge, 1987); John Milton Cooper, Jr., *Breaking the Heart of the World: Woodrow Wilson and the Fight for the League of Nations* (Cambridge, 2001).

5

The Great War, Americanism Revisited, and the Anti-Wilson Crusade

From the beginning of the Great War in 1914 to his death in 1919, Theodore Roosevelt identified the national interests of the United States with the European Allies. He blamed the Central Powers for starting the war, and especially Imperial Germany for its brutal aggression against neutral Belgium. The former president soon directed sharp criticism against President Woodrow Wilson, who called upon the American people to remain neutral in thought as well as deed. Never neutral in his attitude toward the two sides, TR expressed his views in private letters and public speeches, and in published articles and books. He sharply criticized the Wilson administration for its aloofness from the global conflict and for its lack of military preparedness in anticipation of America's entry into the war. Even after the United States declared war against Germany on April 6, 1917, Roosevelt persisted in his anti-Wilson crusade. He advocated Allied military victory over the Central Powers. He blamed Wilson for failing to mobilize U.S. military force more quickly and for favoring a negotiated peace with the Central Powers that would not require their unconditional surrender. Identifying Americanism and patriotism with the all-out pursuit of total victory, TR attacked the Wilson administration for its continuing weakness and ineptitude in the Great War.

TR VERSUS WILSON

Roosevelt expressed his early wartime critique of Wilson and his secretary of state William Jennings Bryan in a letter to his English friend, Arthur Hamilton Lee. He thought that, in contrast to British foreign secretary

Edward Grey and the English people, America's leaders had failed to recognize the seriousness of the European conflict. They shared the pacifist illusion that universal arbitration treaties could have prevented the war. "One curious feature of the professional pacifists, the peace-at-any-price men," TR wrote, "is that in the crisis they always tend to support the apostles of brutal violence. Most of them now have a sneaking admiration for Germany."[1] In contrast, Roosevelt clearly identified with the Allies, and especially with Belgium whose neutrality the Germans had violated. Given that Germany had willfully broken its commitments to respect Belgian neutrality and its obligations under the Hague conventions of 1899 and 1907, he did not think arbitration could have prevented the war or could end it now, although he approved its use for some limited disputes.[2] Only military force could turn back German aggression.

Denouncing Germany for invading Belgium, and justifying the British decision to enter the war for that reason, Roosevelt apprehended the future implications for the United States of a German victory. If the Germans defeated the British Empire after destroying its navy, they would, he anticipated, seek within one or two years to dominate Latin America. He did not want that outcome. Nor did he want the Allies to dismember Germany if they won. In essence, he favored a stable post-war balance among the great powers, including the United States, which would depend on military force, not on treaties alone. "I regard the Wilson-Bryan attitude of trusting to fantastic peace treaties, to impossible promises, to all kinds of scraps of paper without any backing in efficient force, as abhorrent," TR wrote to Harvard professor Hugo Münsterberg. "It is infinitely better for a nation and for the world to have the Frederick the Great and Bismarck tradition as regards foreign policy than to have the Bryan or Bryan-Wilson attitude as a permanent national attitude, for the Bryan-Wilson attitude is one that would Chinafy the country and reduce us to the impotence of Spain when it was under the leadership of Godoy – 'The Prince of Peace,' as he was officially entitled."[3] Unless Wilson and Bryan intended to act under the Hague conventions to assist Belgium, and they did not, Roosevelt saw no reason for them to negotiate new arbitration treaties. He deplored their "spiritless 'neutrality'."[4]

---

[1] TR to Lee, Sept. 4, 1914, *The Letters of Theodore Roosevelt*, ed. Elting E. Morison (Cambridge, MA, 1954), 8: 818.
[2] TR to Apponyi, Sept. 17, 1914, TR to Spring Rice, Oct. 3, 1914, *Letters*, 8: 819–22.
[3] TR to Münsterberg, Oct. 3, 1914, *Letters*, 8: 824–25.
[4] TR to White, Nov. 1, 1914, TR to Kipling, Nov. 4, 1914, TR to Derby, Nov. 4, 1914, *Letters*, 8: 831.

In TR's view, Wilson was essentially weak and self-serving, strong on rhetoric but short on action. "He is certainly a timid man in all that affects sustaining the honor and the national interests of the United States and justice by force of arms," Roosevelt asserted to the British ambassador Cecil Arthur Spring Rice. "He is also a shifty and rather unscrupulous man. Finally, he is entirely cold-blooded and selfish." TR criticized the president for appealing to pacifist and German-American voters, and also "extreme" Irish-Americans, by inaction regarding Belgium, knowing that England and France would nevertheless eventually welcome him as a mediator between them and Germany, thus enabling him to become "the righteous peacemaker."[5]

Roosevelt also candidly shared his views with Friedrich von Stumm, a career diplomat in the German foreign ministry. He acknowledged, "If I were a German, I should now be fighting for Germany; but most emphatically as soon as the opportunity came I would advocate Germany undoing and atoning for the dreadful wrong it has committed on Belgium." In view of that aggression, he distrusted German promises not to threaten America's interests in the Western Hemisphere. He asked: "What is the use of Germany assuring the United States, as it has done, that it never intends to seek territorial aggrandizement in America, when we have before our eyes the fate of Belgium and must know that if Germany destroyed the British Empire, it would act toward the Panama Canal and toward the Western Hemisphere generally precisely as it deemed German interest required?" Roosevelt reaffirmed his preference for a postwar balance of power. "I have also stated as emphatically as possible, having in view certain statements made in Russia, France and England, that I should regard any attempt to break up the German Empire or to reduce Germany to the condition in which it was prior to half a century ago as being a calamity to mankind, as great a calamity as the annihilation of France or the destruction of the British Empire. If I had my way, I would actively interfere to prevent any one of these calamities." TR did not clarify whether his kind of interference would have involved quick military as well as diplomatic intervention. He depicted himself not only as "a practical man" but also an "an idealist," who hoped to turn ideals into practice. He added that "one of these ideals is to strive to bring about the era when international wrongdoing shall be actively discouraged by civilized nations."[6]

[5] TR to Spring Rice, Nov. 11, 1914, *Letters*, 8: 841.
[6] TR to Stumm, Dec. 2, 1914, *Letters*, 8: 856–57.

Roosevelt made the same points about the danger of aggression to Bernhard Dernburg, a Darmstadt bank director who had opened the German Information Service in New York in 1914 to explain Berlin's perspective on the war. "If Germany became master of the seas," TR asked, "what earthly reason is there to suppose that she will refrain from seizing the Panama Canal or establishing a colonial empire in America, if she deems it her interest so to do, without paying any more regard to international morality than she had paid in the case of Belgium?"[7] Germany's potential threat to the Monroe Doctrine, in view of its aggression against Belgium, indicated to him that the United States should not rely only on international morality.

Believing that deterrence by "civilized nations" against future aggression depended on preparedness, Roosevelt regarded the U.S. navy as a crucial defense against Germany's potential threat to America's interests in the event of a British defeat. He criticized Wilson's navy secretary Josephus Daniels, along with Bryan and the president himself, for neglecting to foresee this danger. "Wilson, Bryan and Daniels represent the nadir of American misconduct as regards foreign affairs and national self-defense," TR charged. A victorious Germany might also join Japan in a new alliance against the United States. "If Germany smashes England I should regard it as certain that this country either had to fight or to admit that it was an occidental China. In any event I feel that an alliance between Germany and Japan, from which we would suffer, is entirely a possibility, if Germany comes out even a little ahead in the present war."[8]

Roosevelt shared his critique of the Wilson administration with British foreign secretary Grey in 1915, while affirming London's response to Germany's aggression. "To me the crux of the situation has been Belgium," he wrote. "If England or France had acted toward Belgium as Germany has acted I should have opposed them, exactly as I now oppose Germany. I have emphatically approved your action as a model for what should be done by those who believe that treaties should be observed in good faith and that there is such a thing as international morality." He denounced Wilson as "a pacifist, with apparently no adequate understanding of any military problems." Although the president seemed most desirous of keeping the United States out of the Great War, TR anticipated that he would be driven into it anyway. "I need not point out to you that it is often pacifists who, halting and stumbling and not knowing

---

[7] TR to Dernburg, Dec. 4, 1914, *Letters*, 8: 860.
[8] TR to Foulke, Dec. 12, 1914, *Letters*, 8: 865–66.

whither they are going, finally drift helplessly into a war, which they have rendered inevitable, without the slightest idea that they were doing so."[9]

TR AND A RIGHTEOUS PEACE

At the beginning of the new year, Roosevelt published his first wartime book, *America and the World War* (1915), a collection of articles that had previously appeared in newspapers and magazines.[10] He expanded on the points he had already made in his critique of the Wilson administration. "The kind of 'neutrality' which seeks to preserve 'peace' by timidly refusing to live up to our plighted word and to denounce and take action against such wrong as that committed in the case of Belgium," he proclaimed, "is unworthy of an honorable and powerful people.... The only peace of permanent value is the peace of righteousness." He wanted the United States to join the Allies "to put the combined power of civilization back of the collective purpose of civilization to secure justice." This would require preparedness against war now and potentially "a world league for peace" in the future.[11]

TR emphasized America's duty not only of self-defense but also of helping secure a righteous peace throughout the world. The Belgian tragedy had taught the lesson that nations could not depend on treaties of neutrality or arbitration to protect them against aggression. "But in view of what has occurred in this war," he wrote, "surely the time ought to be ripe for the nations to consider a great world agreement among all the civilized military powers *to back righteousness by force.*"[12] He did not blame Germany's aggression solely on Kaiser Wilhelm II, because the German ruler acted with the overwhelming support of the German people. The war also enjoyed widespread popularity among the people in other European countries. "It is idle to say that this is not a people's war."[13] Given this reality, Roosevelt recognized that peacemaking would be difficult. Governments that had justified war to protect the vital interests of their people were committed to fight for victory. No more than President Abraham Lincoln during the American Civil War could

---

[9] TR to Grey, Jan. 22, 1915, *Letters*, 8: 876–77, 879.
[10] Theodore Roosevelt, *America and the World War* (New York, 1915), republished in *The Works of Theodore Roosevelt*, ed. Hermann Hagedorn (New York, 1926), 18: xvii–xxiv, 1–185.
[11] *Works*, 18: xxi–xxiii.
[12] *Works*, 18: 29–30.
[13] *Works*, 18: 46.

they be expected to negotiate a compromise peace and abandon their stakes. In TR's view, Wilson and Bryan, and the pacifists who applauded them, had failed to understand this fundamental attribute of the war. The civilized nations needed to form an international posse comitatus to restore order and render justice for the victims. "Above all," he asserted, "we should not do as the present administration does; for it refuses to take any concrete action in favor of any nation which is wronged; and yet it also refuses to act so that we may ourselves be sufficient for our own protection."[14] He denied that preparedness for defense would promote militarism in the United States. "I advocate that our preparedness take such shape as to fit us to resist aggression, not to encourage us in aggression."[15] TR viewed a larger American navy as "our peacemaker." "Until an efficient world league for peace is in more than mere process of formation," he explained, "the United States must depend upon itself for protection where its vital interests are concerned."[16] He advocated "preparedness against war," suggesting that weakness invited contempt and aggression from other great powers. He charged that "the most striking instance of the utter failure of unpreparedness to stop war has been shown by President Wilson himself," who was "the great official champion of unpreparedness in military and naval matters."[17] He and Bryan exemplified "the cult of cowardice," whereas TR thought they should act with manliness to defend America's interests and uphold its commitments under the Hague conventions in pursuit of a righteous peace.[18]

Roosevelt recognized the limits of American power to shape the postwar peace. Even while contemplating a world league for peace to facilitate the restoration of international order and prevention of future aggression, he advocated military and naval preparedness primarily for American national defense. Preparedness by the United States would not threaten others, he argued. "Autocracy may use preparedness for the creation of an aggressive and provocative militarism that invites and produces war; but in a democracy preparedness means security against aggression and the best guaranty of peace."[19] He did not expect the United States to impose its conditions of peace on the European belligerents. "Peace in Europe will be made by the warring nations," he wrote. "They and they

[14] *Works*, 18: 79.
[15] *Works*, 18: 104.
[16] *Works*, 18: 107.
[17] *Works*, 18: 123–24.
[18] *Works*, 18: 153.
[19] *Works*, 18: 181.

alone will in fact determine the terms of settlement. The United States may be used as a convenient means of getting together; but that is all." He warned Americans not to think of themselves as morally superior to the Europeans:

If the nations of Europe desire peace and our assistance in securing it, it will be because they have fought as long as they will or can. It will not be because they regard us as having set a spiritual example to them by sitting idle, uttering cheap platitudes, and picking up their trade, while they have poured out their blood like water in support of the ideals in which, with all their hearts and souls, they believe. For us to assume superior virtue in the face of the war-worn nations of the Old World will not make us more acceptable as mediators among them. Such self-consciousness on our part will not impress the nations who have sacrificed and are sacrificing all that is dearest to them in the world.[20]

Quite the opposite of calling for an American crusade in the Great War, Roosevelt advocated closer alignment with the European Allies and rapid preparedness to defend the United States. He spoke about a righteous peace but criticized Wilson's self-righteousness. TR's was an anti-Wilson crusade.

Determined to shift the debate in the United States, Roosevelt appreciated the praise of English journalist John St. Loe Strachey for *America and the Great War*. Although explaining that "I am trying to look at things as dispassionately as possible," TR affirmed to Strachey that "England had made all peace lovers her debtors by her action toward Belgium." He confided that, if he had been president in 1914, he would have protested "very emphatically" against Germany's invasion of Belgium and "I should have backed the protest by force." He denounced Wilson as "an absolutely cold and self-seeking man" for failing to act. "More and more I come to the view that in a really tremendous world struggle, with a great moral issue involved, neutrality does not serve righteousness," Roosevelt concluded.[21]

In contrast to Strachey, George Sylvester Viereck denounced TR's book. In a heated exchange of letters, Roosevelt condemned this German-American editor and other hyphenated Americans for their divided loyalty. In his view, patriotism required complete Americanism. "No man can retain his self-respect if he ostensibly remains as an American citizen while he is really doing everything he can to subordinate the interests and duty of the United States to the interests of a foreign land," he bluntly

---

[20] *Works*, 18: 185.
[21] TR to Strachey, Feb. 22, 1915, *Letters*, 8: 897, 899, 903.

told Viereck. "You have made it evident that your whole heart is with the country of your preference, Germany, and not with the country of your adoption, the United States. Under such circumstances you are not a good citizen here."[22] Viereck violated TR's sense of American patriotism.

Seeking to align the United States with the Allies, Roosevelt hoped that British statesmen would avoid giving approval of the president while he kept aloof from the European war and catered to pacifists and hyphenated Americans for their votes in 1916. TR urged his friend and former British ambassador James Bryce not to praise or collaborate with Wilson because that would give him credibility, thereby weakening TR's own critique and jeopardize American support for the Allies. The British, he advised, should call upon the United States to adopt a policy that distinguished between right and wrong. "This appeal could not be made save by fervently setting forth that the Allies are right; that Germany has been terribly wrong; and that America should not be neutral between right and wrong."[23] Rather than seeming to approve Wilson's neutrality between the Allies and the Central Powers by making favorable references to him, the British should expect him to honor U.S. commitments under the Hague conventions. Until he could be persuaded to act in this way rather than remain aloof from the European war to woo pacifists and hyphenated Americans, TR urged Bryce to say nothing positive about him. Moreover, it was premature for anyone in England to collaborate with the president even to develop plans for a future world league for peace. In contrast to his current policy of neutrality, a viable league would have to distinguish between aggressor and victim, which Wilson was still unwilling to do. Implicitly, TR questioned the president's manliness and Americanism too.

Roosevelt's anti-Wilson crusade intensified after a German submarine sank the *Lusitania* on May 7, 1915, off the southern coast of Ireland, killing 1,198 people, of whom 128 were Americans. Before this British liner embarked from New York, the German embassy had warned passengers not to travel on it through the war zone. On the eve of the sinking, TR expressed his outrage about the Germans' lack of respect for American rights and his belief that the United States ought to retaliate if they destroyed the ship. He confessed that he might "favor instant war with Germany."[24] After the tragedy, Roosevelt blamed Wilson as well as the Germans. "As a nation," he told his son Archibald, "we have thought

[22] TR to Viereck, March 15, 1915, *Letters*, 8: 911.
[23] TR to Bryce, March 31, 1915, *Letters*, 8: 916.
[24] TR to O'Laughlin, May 6, 1915, *Letters*, 8: 922.

very little about foreign affairs; we don't realize that the murder of the thousand men, women and children on the *Lusitania* is due, solely, to Wilson's abject cowardice and weakness in failing to take energetic action when the *Gulflight* was sunk but a few days previously." He charged that Wilson and Bryan were "morally responsible" for the loss of lives because "they won't go to war unless they are kicked into it, and they will consider nothing whatever but their own personal advantage in the matter." The only positive feature in the *Lusitania* crisis was the prospect that the Germans might drive them into the war. TR exulted that "there is a chance that Germany may behave in such fashion that they will have to go to war."[25]

Wilson's protests to Germany over the sinking of the *Lusitania* seemed to Roosevelt to substitute rhetoric for action. "I feel he is not carrying out any policy at all save one of words merely, which he tries to make strong enough to satisfy our people that something is being done and at the same time to enable him to dodge out of doing anything to Germany," TR confided to David Lloyd George, the new British minister of munitions and future prime minister. Wilson might drift into war but could not be expected to hold the Germans to strict accountability.[26] Roosevelt believed that if the president had done what he should have done since the beginning of the world war, he could have forced Germany to abstain from submarine warfare or else led the United States into the war on the side of the Allies. TR told Lee, "if we had done what we ought to have done after the sinking of the *Lusitania*, I and my four boys would now be in an army getting ready to serve with you in Flanders or else to serve against Constantinople." Although Bryan had resigned in dissent over Wilson's protests against Germany's sinking the *Lusitania* without comparable protests against British violations of U.S. neutral rights, TR thought that the president still relied on words alone. Even now he failed to prepare the nation for war. "President Wilson's delightful statement about the nation being 'too proud to fight' seemed to me," TR told his friend, "to reach the nadir of cowardly infamy."[27]

Instead of announcing that Americans were "too proud to fight," Roosevelt wanted the president to prepare the nation for war. "I very earnestly hope," he informed British author-businessman Frederick Scott Oliver, "Wilson makes up his mind at last that we must fight Germany."

[25] TR to Roosevelt, May 19, 1915, *Letters*, 8: 923.
[26] TR to Lloyd George, June 1, 1915, *Letters*, 8: 927.
[27] TR to Lee, June 17, 1915, *Letters*, 8: 937–38.

Focusing on the current war rather than the future peace, he asserted that "it is literally criminal to sacrifice to vague talk about this ultimate aim the duty of immediate action in the present." This duty would require military and naval preparedness by the United States. He explained that "the first lesson for the nation as for the individual to learn is that the surest way to invite aggression is to incur contempt; and the second lesson is that *no* nation acts properly all the time. Therefore a nation must be strong; otherwise it can neither preserve the friendship of friendly nations, or the respect of possibly hostile nations." TR accused Wilson of inviting such contempt and hostility, especially from Germany and potentially also Japan. He apprehended that "if this war ends with Germany even partially victorious, and if we Americans continue our policy of incessant peace talk, and general fatuity and utter reluctance to take any genuine steps in the way of preparation, why, this nation will have trouble with Germany even before it has trouble with Japan."[28]

TR identified America's vital interests with those of the European Allies. He claimed some success for his anti-Wilson crusade. "Perhaps the most immediately important result of my crusade," he told Lee, "has been that it has undoubtedly prevented Wilson from abject surrender to the Germans."[29] But he had gone far in that direction, nevertheless. In another letter to Lee, TR expressed his utter disdain for the president: "Wilson is a physically timid man. He is anxious to avoid war at all hazards. He is an entirely cold-blooded self-seeking man; and he is anxious at all hazards to keep the German-American vote and the pacifist vote. He had intended to have a neutrality which should really work in the German interest. He intended to favor Germany just as much as he safely could."[30] Without explicitly saying so, TR was questioning not just Wilson's foreign policy but also his manliness and Americanism.

Over the months after the *Lusitania* sinking, Roosevelt criticized Wilson's poor statecraft. He believed that forceful presidential leadership, like he could have offered, would have rallied the American people to oppose German aggression. He refused to exonerate Wilson for his timid or cautious response by attributing it to the nation's reluctance to support a stronger policy. The president, he thought, could have shaped public opinion. "I am perfectly sure that, if I had been President and had acted as I should have acted about Belgium and the *Lusitania* and these

[28] TR to Oliver, July 22, 1915, *Letters*, 8: 949, 952, 956–57.
[29] TR to Lee, Aug. 6, 1915, *Letters*, 8: 960.
[30] TR to Lee, Sept. 2, 1915, *Letters*, 8: 967.

bomb outrages in our munitions plants, the people would by a substantial majority, have been behind me," he told Bryce.[31] Because Wilson, instead of rising to the challenge, had apparently cowered before pacifist and hyphenated American voters, Roosevelt felt compelled to muster the nation against him. "In my judgment we are in a great world crisis," he confided to former U.S. ambassador Isaac Wayne MacVeagh. He saw himself as a one-man crusader. "No other public man has ventured to tell the truth of Germany, of the pacifists, of the German-Americans, of Wilson. I have told it and shall tell it as strongly as I know how and without regard to its effect on me."[32]

TR AND AMERICANISM

Early in the new year, Roosevelt published another collection of articles and speeches, *Fear God and Take Your Own Part* (1916).[33] He reiterated the same themes he had previously expressed. He advocated his brand of Americanism as the way to serve both God and mankind. "Unless we are thoroughly Americans and unless our patriotism is part of the very fibre of our being," TR proclaimed, "we can neither serve God nor take our own part.... The United States can accomplish little for mankind, save in so far as within its borders it develops an intense spirit of Americanism. A flabby cosmopolitanism, especially if it expresses itself through a flabby pacifism, is not only silly, but degrading. It represents national emasculation." Devotion to true Americanism, in his view, would benefit the world. "I stand for a nationalism of duty, to one-self and to others; and, therefore, for a nationalism which is a means to internationalism." He lambasted Wilson for lacking this kind of Americanism. "If President Wilson had shown the disinterested patriotism, courage, and foresight demanded by this stupendous crisis," TR wrote, "I would have supported him with hearty enthusiasm. But his action, or rather inaction, has been such that it has become a matter of high patriotic duty to oppose him. No man can support Mr. Wilson without opposing the larger Americanism, the true Americanism."[34] He dismissed the president's belated call for military and naval preparedness as wholly inadequate. He derided as well the idea of a future League to Enforce Peace, which former president

[31] TR to Bryce, Nov. 30, 1915, *Letters*, 8: 994.
[32] TR to MacVeagh, Jan.29, 1916, *Letters*, 8: 1010.
[33] Theodore Roosevelt, *Fear God and Take Your Own Part* (New York, 1916), republished in *The Works of Theodore Roosevelt*, 18: 197–457.
[34] *Works*, 18: 200–01, 203, 214.

William Howard Taft had begun to champion, unless its advocates also called for expanding the regular army and navy. "No person outside of an imbecile asylum should be expected to take such talk seriously at the present time," TR charged. "Leagues to Enforce Peace and the like may come in the future; I hope they ultimately will; but not until nations like our own are *not* too proud to fight, and *are* too proud not to live up to their agreements."[35] Action, not another empty promise, was needed. He denounced Wilson for having responded to the *Lusitania* sinking by writing "note after note, each filled with lofty expressions and each sterile in its utter futility, because it did not mean action, and Germany knew it did not mean action."[36]

Americanism, as Roosevelt defined it, was an inclusive ideology, although it excluded hyphenated Americans and overlooked some others. "The Americans in whom I believe," he wrote, "include Jews and Catholics and Protestants. They include men of old native American descent and other men of recent German, English, French, Irish, Italian, Scandinavian, Magyar, and Slavonic descent; but all are Americans entitled to be treated as such, and claiming to be nothing else." He expected undivided loyalty to the United States, and none at all to ancestral homelands. "I do not believe in hyphenated Americans," he explained. "I do not believe in German-Americans or Irish-Americans; and I believe just as little in English-Americans."[37] Notably, however, he did not refer to Americans of African or Asian descent. "We of the United States need above all things to remember that, while we are by blood and culture kin to each of the nations of Europe, we are also separate from each of them. We are a new and distinct nationality. We are developing our own distinctive culture and civilization," he emphasized. "We must be strong in purpose for our own defense and bent on securing justice within our borders. If as a nation we are split into warring camps, if we teach our citizens not to look upon one another as brothers but as enemies divided by the hatred of creed for creed or of those of one race against those of another race, surely we shall fail and our great democratic experiment on this continent will go down in crushing overthrow."[38] True Americanism required national unity and patriotism.

Roosevelt viewed the president's continuing inaction over the *Lusitania* as evidence of unmanly behavior. "Mr. Wilson's conduct in international

---

[35] *Works*, 18: 241.
[36] *Works*, 18: 272.
[37] *Works*, 18: 281.
[38] *Works*, 18: 388, 404.

matters," he told New York Life and J. P. Morgan executive George W. Perkins, "has been precisely that of a man whose wife's face is slapped by another man, who thinks it over and writes a note telling the other man he must not do it; and when the other man repeats the insult and slaps the wife's face again, writes him another note of protest, and then another and another and another; and lets it go for a year."[39] Even other Republicans seemed far too passive. Charles Evans Hughes, who would become the Republican Party's candidate for president in 1916, had not yet proposed a vigorous alternative. TR doubted that Hughes would take sufficiently strenuous action on "the great questions that face us, that is of Americanism, of Preparedness, of International Duty."[40] Nevertheless, he preferred Hughes over Wilson and consequently declined the Progressive party's nomination to run for president, so as not to divide the vote again, as in 1912, and give Wilson a second term.[41]

American voters, in Roosevelt's harsh judgment, also showed cowardice by reelecting Wilson in 1916, when they responded to the Democrats' slogan that "he kept us out of war." Unfortunately, Hughes failed to offer a clear alternative that would rally the nation to action. TR noted that, although the president had not led the United States into the Great War in Europe, he had entered other wars against countries weaker than Germany. With reference to California voters, who ensured Wilson's victory over Hughes, TR observed to journalist William Allen White: "They didn't mind his having put us into war with Hayti and San Domingo (& twice in Mexico); these were little wars in which only people for whom they didn't care were killed; what they meant was that they objected solely to wars in which their own comfort and skins were endangered."[42] A timid electorate, in the absence of strong leadership by Hughes, had reelected Wilson.

Roosevelt continued his anti-Wilson crusade despite his disappointment. Criticizing the president's peace note of December 18, 1916, which asked the belligerents for their war aims in the hope of helping them reach a compromise, TR called it a "poisoned chalice."[43] He did not want the United States even to attempt to persuade the Allies to stop fighting before they had defeated the Central Powers. He likewise voiced his

---

[39] TR to Perkins, Apr. 6, 1916, *Letters*, 8: 1031.
[40] TR to Noble, May 2, 1916, *Letters*, 8: 1035.
[41] TR to Progressive National Convention [June 11] & June 22, 1916, *Letters*, 8: 1062–63, 1067–74.
[42] TR to White, Jan. 1, 1917, *Letters*, 8: 1135.
[43] TR to Strachey, Jan. 1, 1917, *Letters*, 8: 1139.

dissent against Wilson's call for "peace without victory" on January 22, 1917. TR would not refrain from criticism when there was so much at stake in the war. Although he had briefly abstained from pubic attacks on Wilson's foreign policy for sixty days after the beginning of the Great War in 1914, he had soon begun to speak out. No longer willing to keep silent, TR explained, "I have never committed the error since, in connection with the *Lusitania*, or the too-proud-to-fight or peace-without-victory propaganda, or anything else!"[44]

Roosevelt almost despaired in his repeated attempts to force Wilson to act on behalf of the Allies and against Imperial Germany. Even after Kaiser Wilhelm II authorized unrestricted submarine warfare against neutral as well as belligerent shipping, beginning in February 1917, and despite Wilson's decision to break diplomatic relations with Germany, TR doubted that the president would take a sufficiently hard line. He agreed with Senator Henry Cabot Lodge that "Wilson won't break definitely with any man of whom he is afraid. Personally, I have begun to doubt whether he will go to war under any circumstances. He is evidently trying his old tactics; he is endeavoring to sneak out of going to war under any condition."[45] Preparations for war still did not characterize the Wilson administration even in response to the real prospect that German submarines would begin to sink American ships.

TR AND WILSON'S WAR FOR DEMOCRACY

Despite Roosevelt's doubts about Wilson, German submarine warfare drove him into the war, which he now justified as a defense of democracy. After the sinking of American ships in mid-March, the president called Congress into session and recommended a declaration of war. He proclaimed in his war message on April 2, 1917, "The world must be made safe for democracy."[46] Four days later, Congress voted for war against Germany. TR agreed that the outcome of the Great War would determine the fate of democracy, but this had been the case since its beginning. "It is at least possible that the conflict will result in a growth of democracy in Europe, in at least a partial substitution of the rule of the people for the

---

[44] TR to Morrell, Jan. 31, 1917, *Letters*, 8: 1148–49.
[45] TR to Lodge, Feb. 20, 1917, *Letters*, 8: 1156.
[46] Address to Congress, Apr. 2, 1917, Woodrow Wilson, *The Public Papers of Woodrow Wilson: War and Peace*, eds. Ray Stannard Baker and William E. Dodd (New York, 1927), 1: 14; Woodrow Wilson, *The Papers of Woodrow Wilson*, ed. Arthur S. Link (Princeton, NJ, 1983), 41: 519–27.

rule of those who esteem it their God-given right to govern the people,"
he had written in *Outlook* in September 1914. "This, in its turn, would
render it probably a little more unlikely that there would be a repetition
of such disastrous warfare."[47] "I absolutely agree that the present world
war is in its essence one between militarism and democracy," TR wrote to
Raymond Robins, a Progressive party reformer.[48] He believed that autocratic "Germany stands as the antithesis of democracy."[49] The war thus
pitted democracy against autocracy and militarism. "Let us without one
hour's unnecessary delay," he urged shortly after Congress had declared
war against Germany, "put the American flag on the battle front in this
great world war for democracy and civilization and for the reign of justice and fair dealing among the nations of mankind."[50]

But TR did not view Wilson as an authentic defender of democracy,
despite the rhetoric in his war message. He scolded White for crediting
the president as the champion of democracy. Its true defenders were the
western Allies who had fought heroically against the Central Powers since
1914. "Wilson did not come into this war for Democracy," Roosevelt
reminded White.

For two and one half years he announced again and again and again that he was
neutral and that we should all be neutral in the war; and he didn't know what
the different peoples were fighting about; that he didn't side with one party more
than with the other; and we had no concern with the purpose of the war, and
finally, that we ought to strive for a peace that did not bring victory.... He came
into this war purely because he couldn't stop the Germans from murdering our
citizens, and in the effort to stop murdering our citizens he was perfectly willing to betray the Allies and to see Democracy trampled underfoot by Prussian
Militarism.[51]

Roosevelt still worried that the Wilson administration might not fight
in Europe. He criticized its inadequate military preparedness and its
apparent willingness even now to postpone U.S. participation on the
battlefield. "Our nation has not prepared in any adequate way during
the last two and a half years to meet the crisis which now faces us," he
bluntly told Wilson's secretary of war Newton D. Baker. "You, therefore, propose that we shall pay billions of dollars to the Allies to do
our fighting for us, while we stay here in comfort and slowly proceed

[47] *Works*, 18 27-28.
[48] TR to Robins, June 3, 1915, *Letters*, 8: 928.
[49] *Works*, 18: 330.
[50] TR to Chamberlain, Apr. 12, 1917, *Letters*, 8: 1171.
[51] TR to White, May 28 & Aug. 3, 1917, *Letters*, 8: 1198, 1216–17.

to train an army to fight in the end, unless the war is over, one way or the other, before our army is ready." Such a delay was totally unacceptable to TR, who expected Baker to get the American Expeditionary Force to France and into the war quickly. "It is an ignoble thing for us not to put our men into the fighting line at the earliest possible moment. Such failure will excite derision and may have a very evil effect upon our national future."[52] To help remedy the damage from this negligence, he requested Baker to authorize him to raise an army corps of two divisions, which would quickly go to France and join the battle.[53] Baker denied this request, however.

In his anti-Wilson crusade, Roosevelt identified with the Allies. He wrote to the future French premier Georges Clemenceau that "the fundamental trouble with Mr. Wilson is that he is merely a rhetorician, vindictive and yet not physically brave; he cannot really face facts; he cannot help believing that inasmuch as sonorous platitudes in certain crises win votes they can in other crises win battles. Unfortunately pacifist voters, and brutal men with rifles in their hands, cannot be reached by the same arguments!"[54] TR also expressed his hope for "the great Russian democracy" to Prince George Eugenievich Lvov, Russia's new prime minister after its March 1917 revolution. He wanted Russians to maintain "orderly liberty" in their pursuit of self-government, and to continue fighting on the eastern front. "The only way by which to make sure the future of liberty is to secure the complete overthrow of the Germany of the Hohenzollerns."[55]

As he explained months later to a Republican congressman, all Americans should support "the efficient prosecution of the war" for the benefit of both the Allies and the United States. "We send our troops to fight beside our allies abroad," TR wrote, "because if we do not do so then sometime or other we shall have to fight without any allies at home.... We must fearlessly insist upon the utmost efficiency in the handling of the war."[56]

Wilson still, in Roosevelt's judgment, remained aloof and did not seek to win the war. When the Bolsheviks replaced the potentially democratic government in Russia with their November 1917 revolution, his concerns grew. With the Russians no longer fighting on the eastern front,

[52] TR to Baker, Apr. 23, 1917, *Letters*, 8: 1179–81.
[53] TR to Baker, May 8, 1917, *Letters*, 8: 1187–91.
[54] TR to Clemenceau, June 6, 1917, *Letters*, 8: 1201.
[55] TR to Lvov, July 20, 1917, *Letters*, 8: 1212.
[56] TR to Lundeen, Nov. 7, 1917, *Letters*, 8: 1251.

Germany might win before the United States could rescue the Allies. This raised the specter of a global realignment that would threaten America's interests. Roosevelt foresaw that "the danger of the future is an alignment or understanding between Germany and Japan if Germany wins."[57] Under these potential circumstances, which Wilson seemed totally incapable of comprehending, TR savagely criticized him to Lee. "Wilson is at heart a pacifist; he is not pro-German, but neither is he pro-Ally or pro-American – he is purely pro-Wilson," TR wrote in 1918. "Moreover, he is a rhetorician pure and simple, and an utterly inefficient administrator. He is a very adroit demagogue, skilled beyond any man we have ever seen in appealing to the yellow streak in people. But he has not the slightest understanding of the need of efficiency in a desperate crisis like this."[58] Although Wilson had led the United States into the war in 1917, a year later Roosevelt still doubted his commitment or ability to help the Allies defeat Germany. "It is maddening to see Russia break and Germany stride nearer triumph because my country failed to prepare," he confided to King George V.[59] He blamed Wilson for the collapse of the eastern front. "If we had prepared in advance, having begun as soon as the *Lusitania* was sunk," TR asserted to Bryce, "we could have put two million men in the field last spring; Russia would not have broken, and the war would have been over long ago."[60]

TR AND UNCONDITIONAL SURRENDER

By July 1918, after the western Allies has finally stopped Germany's spring offensive, Roosevelt began to anticipate triumph. "In this great war we stand unequivocally by all our allies, by every nation which has continued to fight, and which will continue to fight to the end, for the great common cause," he affirmed.[61] He wanted "a decisive victory over Germany, Austro-Hungary, Bulgaria and Turkey." For the peace settlement, he thought that "Europe must be reconstructed on the basis of the principle of nationalities; which means that, in addition to full reparation by Germany for the hideous injuries she has inflicted on mankind, both Austro-Hungary and Turkey should be dismembered. Neither is a nation. Each is a tyranny of one or two races over more numerous individuals of

[57] TR to Perkins, Dec. 21, 1917, *Letters*, 8: 1265.
[58] TR to Lee, Feb. 21, 1918, *Letters*, 8: 1289.
[59] TR to George V, March 12, 1918, *Letters*, 8:1300.
[60] TR to Bryce, May 2, 1918, *Letters*, 8: 1314.
[61] TR to Pepper, July 2, 1918, *Letters*, 8: 1345–46.

other races."[62] Roosevelt also approved the idea of a postwar League to Enforce Peace, which Taft had championed, but with a difference. "I will back it as an *addition to,* but not as a *substitute for,* our preparing our own strength for our own defense," he told Taft.[63] With that qualification, he affirmed, the victorious powers might continue their alliance as a postwar league to enforce the peace against the defeated enemies.

When Imperial Germany, after losing the war, appealed to Wilson in October 1918 for an armistice on the basis of his Fourteen Points, Roosevelt apprehended that the president might sacrifice military victory through peace negotiations. He asserted that "the greatest of all our interests at this time is to win the war and force Germany to an unconditional surrender."[64] He saw his stance as "the standpoint of straight Americanism and of winning the war." It was quite different, he claimed, from the Fourteen Points that Wilson had outlined to Congress on January 8, 1918. "The so-called fourteen points laid down by the President, and eagerly accepted by Germany would, if adopted by the American people, mean a surrender to Germany of some of the most vital things for which she has fought, and a failure on our part to accomplish the things we announced to be our objects in the war."[65] TR shared with Senator Lodge his deep concern that Wilson was standing aloof from the Allies "by continually referring to this country merely as the associate, instead of the ally of the nations with whose troops our own troops are actually brigaded in battle.... We ought to make it clear to the world that we are neither an untrustworthy friend nor an irresolute foe."[66] After Germany finally accepted the armistice's military and naval conditions, which the Allies had set, Roosevelt credited himself with stopping Wilson from double-crossing them and becoming an umpire between the Allies and the Central Powers. "The Fourteen Points were thoroughly mischievous and would have meant a negotiated peace with Germany," TR alleged, but his advocacy of unconditional surrender during the weeks leading up to the armistice had prevented Wilson from taking that path.[67]

Roosevelt rejoiced that Germany signed the armistice on November 11, 1918, but still doubted Wilson's approach to peacemaking. At the core of their differences was TR's firm commitment to the Allies. "I hope

---

[62] TR to Michailovitch, July 11, 1918, *Letters,* 8: 1350.
[63] TR to Taft, Aug. 15, 1918, *Letters,* 8: 1362.
[64] TR to Spencer, Oct. 15, 1918, *Letters,* 8: 1375.
[65] TR to Bartlett, Oct. 18, 1918, *Letters,* 8: 1377–78.
[66] TR to Lodge, Oct. 24, 1918, *Letters,* 8: 1380–81.
[67] TR to Lee, Nov. 19, 1918, *Letters,* 8: 1397.

that the League of Nations will begin by being a League of Allies who have just overthrown the hideous despotism of the central powers," he told an Australian journalist, "and I hope that no nation that has been acting as a criminal will be admitted to the League until after a sufficient number of years to satisfy us."[68] The president, in contrast, seemed to favor a universal league that might exalt himself at the expense of the Allies. TR apprehended that "Mr. Wilson intended to bring the war to a close by a negotiated peace with Germany, crowned by a League of Nations, with Germany in and Wilson as first president of the League."[69]

Until his death on January 6, 1919, Roosevelt persisted in his anti-Wilson crusade. Skeptical about how the president would interpret his Fourteen Points, he foresaw problems with the "absolute self-determination for all peoples." TR doubted that either American or British leaders would allow self-government for "African savages." "Yet," he told Bryce, "there are any number of people, including Wilson very often, and Lloyd George not infrequently, who like to use language which means this or nothing. In the same way at this moment the United States has deprived and is depriving Haiti and Santo Domingo of self-determination. It has destroyed democracy in these two little festering black republics."[70] Critical of the hypocritical contrast between the president's rhetoric and practice, TR assured English writer Rudyard Kipling, "I am carrying on as active a crusade as possible, and with considerable success, to make our people understand that they have got to see that Wilson stands by the allies – stands by England and France, in the peace terms, and devotes much more attention to thus standing by them than to carrying out plans to please himself and the Germans by advocating the 'freedom of the seas' so-called and the League of Nations."[71] Before the Paris Peace Conference opened in 1919, however, TR's death ended his crusade. He had done all he could to promote his brand of Americanism during the Great War.

---

[68] TR to Davies, Nov. 14, 1918, *Letters*, 8: 1393.
[69] TR to Putnam, Nov. 15, 1918, *Letters*, 8: 1394.
[70] TR to Bryce, Nov. 19, 1918, *Letters*, 8: 1401.
[71] TR to Kipling, Nov. 23, 1918, *Letters*, 8: 1404.

6

Woodrow Wilson, Alliances, and the
League of Nations

People in the United States and other countries, if they know anything about Woodrow Wilson, identify this American president with the League of Nations. They regard his role in its creation as his major contribution to world history. Beyond this general consensus, however, there is considerable disagreement.

Wilson's vision of the League and its place in a new international order after World War I evoked both praise and criticism at that time. It still does in the twenty-first century. He has remained a contested figure among historians, political scientists, and others. Looking back on his leadership during the Paris Peace Conference of 1919, scholars have variously lauded or condemned his statecraft, including his role in drafting the League Covenant. His responsibility for the U.S. Senate's rejection of the Versailles Treaty, which contained the Covenant as an integral part of the peace settlement with Germany, has likewise remained a subject of scholarly debate. Even among those who have affirmed Wilson's legacy, there are substantial differences over what it means. It has continued to stir controversy.[1]

These are not just academic disputes. They deal with vital issues because the president's legacy, known as Wilsonianism, still significantly defines the choices and shapes the behavior of the United States in world affairs. Ongoing debates among Americans over nation-building in the midst of war and revolution, peacemaking after either civil or international war, and peacekeeping within or among states have all given

---

[1] Lloyd E. Ambrosius, "Woodrow Wilson and World War I," *A Companion to American Foreign Relations*, ed. Robert D. Schulzinger (Malden, MA, 2003), 149–67.

the treaty fight in 1919–20 a continuing relevance. U.S. presidents – or those who might like to offer alternative policies or perspectives – must still deal with the crucial questions that Wilson confronted, concerning whether, when, and how the United States should join other nation-states in alliances or leagues. Americans are still struggling with these questions and still searching for ways to fulfill the Wilsonian promise of a better and more peaceful world.

WILSON'S LEAGUE OF NATIONS

What was Wilson's own understanding of the postwar League of Nations? Why did he make its creation his top priority at the Paris Peace Conference? How did he conceive of the League and its potential role in a new era of international relations? Which responsibilities did Wilson want the United States to assume in this international organization? What limits did he place on the new League's functions and thus on American obligations under the Covenant? Answers to these questions can help clarify the ongoing debates among scholars and in public discourse over Wilson's historical record and over his legacy for future generations after World War I.

Before the United States entered the war as a belligerent in 1917, the American president made a sharp distinction between old, entangling alliances, which he strongly condemned, and a new association or league of nations, which he began to advocate. He made this distinction on May 27, 1916, when he first announced his commitment to the idea of a postwar league of nations.[2] He reiterated it in his famous "peace without victory" address on January 22, 1917. The best method of peacekeeping, he now proclaimed, would be a League for Peace that the United States would help create after the two sets of belligerents, the Allies and the Central Powers, resolved their conflicts over competing war aims and negotiated a "peace without victory." Denouncing traditional European diplomacy that had relied on a balance of power and alliances, he called instead for a new partnership or community of nations. "There must be," he told the U.S. Senate, "not a balance of power, but a community of power; not organized rivalries, but an organized common peace."

---

[2] Address to League to Enforce Peace, May 27, 1916, Woodrow Wilson, *The Public Papers of Woodrow Wilson: The New Democracy* [hereafter *PPWW: New Democracy*], eds. Ray Stannard Baker and William E. Dodd (New York, 1926), 2: 184–88; Woodrow Wilson, *The Papers of Woodrow Wilson* [hereafter *PWW*], ed. Arthur S. Link (Princeton, NJ, 1982), 37: 113–16.

Identifying his vision of a new international order with the Monroe Doctrine, he proclaimed that this American doctrine should be extended beyond the Western Hemisphere to the entire world. "I am proposing," Wilson affirmed, "that all nations henceforth avoid entangling alliances which would draw them into competitions of power; catch them in a net of intrigue and selfish rivalry, and disturb their own affairs with influences intruded from without. When all unite to act in the same sense and with the same purpose all act in the common interest and are free to live their own lives under a common protection."[3] In Wilson's view, a new, universal league of nations under American leadership – or actually U.S. hegemony – should thus replace old-style alliances, and it should render obsolete the traditional military balances among Europe's great powers.[4]

Wilson used this vision of a new world order to justify American entry into the war against Imperial Germany. In his war message to Congress on April 2, 1917, he called for a new partnership of democratic nations to win the war and establish the postwar peace. He wanted the United States to participate in the peacemaking. "A steadfast concert for peace can never be maintained except by a partnership of democratic nations," he asserted. "No autocratic government could be trusted to keep faith within it or observe its covenants. It must be a league of honor, a partnership of opinion.... Only free peoples can hold their purposes and their honor steady to a common end and prefer the interests of mankind to any narrow interest of their own." In view of the recent Russian Revolution, which promised to give rise to a new liberal democratic state in place of the czarist regime, the president welcomed the new Russia as "a fit partner for a League of Honor." He wanted Imperial Germany to undergo a similar regime change from autocratic to democratic government. "The world must be made safe for democracy," he proclaimed. "Its peace must be planted upon the tested foundations of political liberty." Wilson denied that the United States had any "selfish ends to serve." This nation desired "no conquest, no dominion" and it sought "no indemnities for ourselves, no material compensation for the sacrifices we shall freely make." The United States, he said, should instead enter the war as "one of the champions of the rights of mankind. We shall be satisfied when those rights have been made as secure as the faith and the freedom of nations can

---

[3] Address to Senate, Jan. 22, 1917, *PPWW: New Democracy*, 2: 407–14; *PWW* (1982), 40: 533–39.
[4] For the ongoing debate over the balance of power and hegemony, see G. John Ikenberry, *America Unrivaled: The Future of the Balance of Power* (Ithaca, NY, 2002).

make them." In this new world order of democratic nations that Wilson envisioned, he pledged that the United States would join its partners to guarantee the peace.[5]

This new partnership of democratic nations – this new league of nations – would be profoundly different from the old world's traditional alliances, Wilson promised. He did not want the United States to join any old-style alliance to restore or preserve the traditional European balance of power. Accordingly, he determined that the United States would not become one of the Allied Powers. Instead, it merely associated itself with the Allies in the coalition, officially known as the Allied and Associated Powers. The United States was the only "associated" power in the coalition. This odd legal distinction reflected Wilson's typically American belief in the exceptional character or uniqueness of the United States. This belief in American exceptionalism undergirded Wilson's enduring distinction between the old and new worlds and his determination to replace Europe's old diplomacy with America's new diplomacy.[6] Prior to 1917, Wilson had attempted to protect U.S. neutrality, thereby keeping the United States out of the European conflicts that had culminated in the Great War. Now, leading the American nation into this war, the president wanted to transform the old European system of international relations into a new world order, in which the United States would provide hegemonic leadership in a new league of nations. This would, in the religious terms of progressive Christianity, turn the Great War into "the war for righteousness" as the United States fulfilled its role as the "messianic nation" to create the kingdom of God on earth.[7]

---

[5] Address to Congress, Apr. 2, 1917, Woodrow Wilson, *The Public Papers of Woodrow Wilson: War and Peace* [hereafter *PPWW: War & Peace*], eds. Ray Stannard Baker and William E. Dodd (New York, 1927), 1: 6–16; *PWW* (1983), 41: 519–27.

[6] C. Vann Woodward, *The Old World's New World* (New York, 1991); Peter Novick, *That Noble Dream: The "Objectivity Question" and the American Historical Profession* (Cambridge, 1988), 61–132; Ernst A. Breisach, *American Progressive History: An Experiment in Modernization* (Chicago, 1993); Seymour Martin Lipset, *American Exceptionalism: A Double-Edged Sword* (New York, 1996), 17–76. For recent attempts by the Organization of American Historians' Project on Internationalizing the Study of American History to escape the framework of American exceptionalism, see Thomas Bender, ed., *Rethinking American History in a Global Age* (Berkeley, CA, 2002). See also Hugh De Santis, *Beyond Progress: An Interpretive Odyssey to the Future* (Chicago, 1996).

[7] Richard M. Gamble, *The War for Righteousness: Progressive Christianity, the Great War, and the Rise of the Messianic Nation* (Wilmington, DE, 2003); Lloyd E. Ambrosius, *Woodrow Wilson and the American Diplomatic Tradition: The Treaty Fight in Perspective* (Cambridge, 1987), 12–13. See also Martin E. Marty, *Modern American Religion*, Vol. I: *The Irony of It All, 1893–1919* (Chicago, 1986), 398–416, Anders Stephanson, *Manifest Destiny: American Expansion and the Empire of Right* (New York, 1995), 113–29, and

WILSON'S LEAGUE VERSUS TRADITIONAL
ALLIANCES

Wilson thus reconciled two tendencies in the American diplomatic tradition that are often regarded as opposites, namely isolationism and internationalism. He wanted either to isolate the United States from Europe or to transform and redeem the old world. By preserving U.S. neutrality – which he attempted until 1917 – or by reforming European diplomacy and statecraft – which he attempted after 1917 – the president sought, in both cases, to avoid the entangling alliances that he regarded as one of the worst features of Europe's traditional international relations. Wilson provided the outlines of his vision of a new world order in his famous Fourteen Points of January 8, 1918. Point 14 called for a new league of nations: "A general association of nations must be formed under specific covenants for the purpose of affording mutual guarantees of political independence and territorial integrity to great and small states alike," he announced.[8] This new league, in his view quite different from traditional alliances, would unite the world rather than divide it into a new balance of power, and would guarantee peace rather than prepare for war. It would, moreover, enable the United States to participate in world affairs on its own terms as a new global power, paradoxically preserving the essential core of traditional American isolation from the old world's diplomacy and wars. Or, in current terminology, it would combine both unilateralism and multilateralism in America's new global role.

Wilson emphasized this point in a major wartime address on September 27, 1918, in which he reconciled his proposal for a new league of nations with traditional American avoidance of entanglements in Europe. He denied that U.S. involvement in this new league would violate this diplomatic tradition. President George Washington, in his farewell address in 1796, had advised his fellow Americans to protect their new nation's independence by avoiding unnecessary alliances with the old world. Wilson explained: "We still read Washington's immortal warning against 'entangling alliances' with full comprehension and an answering purpose. But only special and limited alliances entangle; and we recognize and accept the duty of a new day in which we are permitted to hope for a general alliance which will avoid entanglements and clear the air of the world

Walter A. McDougall, *Promised Land, Crusader State: The American Encounter with the World Since 1776* (Boston, 1997), 122–46.

[8] Address to Congress, Jan. 8, 1918, *PPWW: War & Peace*, 1: 155–62; *PWW* (1984), 45: 534–39.

for common understandings and the maintenance of common rights."[9]
Thus Wilson reconciled the traditional American rejection of entangling
alliances, which formed the essential core of isolationism, with his proposed global role for the United States in a new league of nations – a
new vision of internationalism. By renouncing traditional alliances in
favor of a new league of nations, Wilson affirmed both of the apparently
opposite isolationist and internationalist tendencies in twentieth-century
U.S. foreign relations. In other words, Wilson promised a new diplomacy
of multilateral cooperation to implement American – and presumably
universal – principles, but without sacrificing traditional American unilateral decision-making. Wilson's vision of a postwar league of nations
thus combined both internationalist and isolationist impulses, thereby
affirming but also reshaping the American diplomatic tradition.

   Wilson conceived of the League of Nations as a new international organization that could mobilize world public opinion – or the moral force of
humanity – to preserve peace. After arriving in Europe for the Paris Peace
Conference, he traveled to the major Allied capitals, sharing his views
with the people and seeking their support for a new world order. In Paris
on December 21, 1918, he told his French audience how he expected the
proposed league to function. "My conception of the League of Nations is
just this," Wilson explained, "that it shall operate as the organized moral
force of men throughout the world, and that whenever or wherever wrong
and aggression are planned or contemplated, this searching light of conscience will be turned upon them and men everywhere will ask, 'What
are the purposes that you hold in your heart against the fortunes of the
world?' Just a little exposure will settle most questions."[10] The absence
of a league of nations in 1914, Wilson claimed, had prevented the world
from rallying the moral force of its public opinion to compel the Central
Powers to choose peace over war. To remedy this problem with the old
diplomacy, he advocated the creation of a new league of nations to facilitate a global moral commitment to peace through rational discourse to
mobilize public opinion. Wilson's vision of the proposed league expressed
his liberal faith in the power of moral persuasion.

   At the peace conference the president gave top priority to the creation of the League of Nations. This new international organization,
he anticipated, would enable the United States to participate in world

[9] Address, New York City, Sept. 27, 1918, *PPWW: War & Peace*, 1: 253–61; *PWW* (1985),
   51: 127–33.
[10] Address at University of Paris, Dec. 21, 1918, *PPWW: War & Peace*, 1: 329–31; *PWW*
   (1986), 53: 461–63.

affairs without becoming entangled in the old world's politics. It could promote international justice without war. At a plenary session of the peace conference on January 25, 1919, he reiterated his affirmations of both isolationist and internationalist – or unilateralist and multilateralist – tendencies as he explained his paradoxical vision of a new league. Americans, Wilson said, had never regarded their entry into the war as "intervening in the politics of Europe or the politics of Asia or the politics of any part of the world." They had instead joined "the cause of justice and of liberty for men of every kind and place." Consistent with that explanation of American intervention in 1917, Wilson drew the conclusion that the United States should avoid entangling alliances even as it helped create a new league of nations. "Therefore," he continued, "the United States should feel that its part in this war had been played in vain if there ensued upon it merely a body of European settlements. It would feel that it could not take part in guaranteeing those European settlements unless that guarantee involved the continuous superintendence of the peace of the world by the associated nations of the world." [11]

Wilson devoted most of his time during the first weeks of the peace conference to drafting the Covenant for this new international organization. Upon completing that task, he presented the new Covenant to a plenary session of the peace conference on February 14, 1919. He emphasized its moral commitment. He told the delegates that "throughout this instrument we are depending primarily and chiefly upon one great force, and that is the moral force of the public opinion of the world." By exposing the sinister intrigues of those who might start wars to "the cleansing and clarifying and compelling influences of publicity," the League would preserve peace. Only in the last resort might it use armed force to stop aggression. [12]

Wilson viewed the League from the perspective of his Christian faith. He saw it as a redeeming influence. His emphasis on "moral force" expressed this orientation. Moreover, Wilson had chosen the word "covenant" as the name for the new League's founding document – rather than "charter" as later used for the United Nations, or some other word. For devout Presbyterians like himself, the word "covenant" communicated an important religious meaning. The president also determined that the new League's headquarters would be located in Geneva, Switzerland,

---

[11] Address to Plenary Session of Paris Peace Conference, Jan. 25, 1919, *PPWW: War & Peace*, 1: 395–400; *PWW* (1986), 54: 264–71.

[12] Address to Plenary Session of Paris Peace Conference, Feb. 14, 1919, *PPWW: War & Peace*, 1: 413–29; *PWW* (1986), 55: 164–78.

which had been John Calvin's home. Wilson's Calvinism was a modern, liberal version.[13] He identified with the Social Gospel movement, which advocated progressive reform at home and abroad. One of its leading theologians, George D. Herron, had recognized this missionary impulse in Wilson's new diplomacy in 1917, stressing that the president hoped "to bring it about that America, awake at last to her selfhood and calling, shall become as a colossal Christian apostle, shepherding the world into the kingdom of God." After reading this, Wilson praised "Herron's singular insight ... into my own motives and purposes."[14] Most historians have neglected or devalued this religious dimension in Wilson's vision of the new League. One outstanding exception was the Dutch historian Jan Willem Schulte Nordholt, who understood its centrality in Wilson's "life for world peace."[15]

Wilson believed that the new League of Nations, under American leadership, could redeem the old world, and yet allow the United States to avoid entangling alliances, against which President Washington had warned. On a brief trip home during the peace conference, Wilson told his New York City audience on March 4, 1919, that the Covenant provided for "an arrangement which will disentangle all the alliances in the world."[16] In place of those traditional alliances, nation-states would join the new system of what would later be called collective security. In Wilson's view, this universal guarantee of each nation's territorial integrity and political independence against external aggression would render old alliances obsolete.

While emphasizing its moral character, Wilson also recognized the League's importance for international law. The Covenant was, after all, a legal document. He had trained and briefly practiced as a lawyer. Yet unlike his secretary of state, Robert Lansing, he was less concerned with legal precedents than with infusing a new morality into international law. On May 9, 1919, two days after the Allied and Associated Powers had presented the peace treaty, including the final draft of the Covenant, to the German delegation at Versailles, the president addressed the International Law Society

---

[13] John M. Mulder, *Woodrow Wilson: The Years of Preparation* (Princeton, NJ, 1978); David T. Rowlands, "Democracy, American Nationalism and Woodrow Wilson's Search for Identity" (PhD dissertation, University of Sydney, 1999).

[14] Lloyd E. Ambrosius, *Wilsonian Statecraft: Theory and Practice of Liberal Internationalism during World War I* (Wilmington, DE, 1991), 11–13.

[15] Jan Willem Schulte Nordholt, *Woodrow Wilson: A Life for World Peace* (Berkeley, CA, 1991).

[16] Address, New York City, March 4, 1919, *PPWW: War & Peace*, 1: 444–55; *PWW*, 55: 413–21.

in Paris. "If we can now give to international law the kind of vitality which it can have only if it is a real expression of our moral judgment," the president explained, "we shall have completed in some sense the work which this war was intended to emphasize."[17] Some scholars have exaggerated Wilson's legal contribution to international relations. Law professor Frances Anthony Boyle credited him with successfully fusing "legalistic" and "moralistic" approaches to U.S. foreign policy. Although recognizing the tensions between legalism and Wilsonianism, Boyle regarded Wilson's role in creating the League of Nations as a major step forward toward establishing the legal foundations of world order.[18] For Wilson, however, the new League was not primarily an instrument of international law.

In contrast to him, leading Republicans adopted the legalistic approach to U.S. foreign policy. Notably, Elihu Root, who had served as secretary of war for both Presidents William McKinley and Theodore Roosevelt, and also as TR's secretary of state, plus all of Root's Republican successors in that office over the years to 1933, from Philander Knox to Charles Evans Hughes, Frank Kellogg, and Henry Stimson, were lawyers. Far more than Wilson, they all favored the legalistic approach to U.S. foreign policy. Root, for example, helped establish the World Court at The Hague after the war, while Wilson remained largely indifferent toward this new legal institution.[19]

In Wilson's view, the League of Nations promised a new postwar morality. It was, he told the Belgian Chamber of Deputies in Brussels on June 19, 1919, "a league of right."[20] Yet it was also an instrument of international law. After the peace treaty was signed at Versailles on June 28, 1919, the president sent a message to the American people, affirming that: "It associates the free Governments of the world in a permanent league in which they are pledged to use their united power to maintain peace by maintaining right and justice. It makes international law a reality supported by imperative sanctions."[21]

---

[17] Address, Paris, May 9, 1919, *PPWW: War & Peace*, 1: 478–81; *PWW* (1988), 58: 598–600.

[18] Francis Anthony Boyle, *Foundations of World Order: The Legalist Approach to International Relations, 1898–1922* (Durham, NC, 1999).

[19] Jonathan Zasloff, "Law and the Shaping of American Foreign Policy: From the Gilded Age to the New Era," *New York University Law Review* 20 (2001): 1–128; Jonathan Zasloff, "Law and the Shaping of American Foreign Policy: The Twenty Years' Crisis," *New York University Law Review* 20 (2002): 1–100.

[20] Address to Belgian Parliament, June 19, 1919, *PPWW: War & Peace*, 1: 509–15; *PWW* (1989), 61: 16–20.

[21] Cablegram, June 28, 1919, *PPWW: War & Peace*, 1: 523–24.

After returning home, Wilson reiterated these themes. On July 10, 1919, he submitted the Versailles Treaty to the Senate for its approval. It had not been easy, he said, to create the new world order because "old entanglements of every kind stood in the way." He believed, however, that he had largely succeeded, especially with the League of Nations, which was "an indispensable instrumentality for the maintenance of the new order" in "the world of civilized men." This new international organization would make "the accepted principles of international law" into "the actual rule of conduct among the governments of the world," he anticipated. It would replace the old balance of power, not with a new one, but with "the united power of free nations" to keep the peace and stop aggression. The peacemaking at Paris, Wilson concluded, had established the United States as the world's preeminent leader. He welcomed this hegemonic role, although he never explicitly acknowledged it as such. He used moral rhetoric rather than the candid language of power. The League, he believed, would enable this nation to provide global leadership largely through its influence over public opinion and thus fulfill its God-given destiny. "The stage is set, the destiny disclosed," the president proclaimed. "It has come about by no plan of our conceiving, but by the hand of God who led us into this way. We cannot turn back. We can only go forward, with lifted eyes and freshened spirit, to follow the vision. It was of this that we dreamed at our birth. America shall in truth show the way."[22]

CRITIQUES AND ALTERNATIVES

Republican senators were not so convinced, however. Under Henry Cabot Lodge's leadership, they challenged Wilson's vision of America's world role and rejected the Versailles Treaty. Without at least attaching reservations, they would not vote for the treaty, which contained the League Covenant. They wanted to know what obligations it would impose on the United States in the new League to protect other nations. Wilson's argument that America could play a global role in peacekeeping without becoming entangled in the politics and wars of the old world did not convince Republicans. Nor did his claim that Europeans would refrain from interfering with the Western Hemisphere. Lodge and other Republicans saw a threat to the Monroe Doctrine, not its worldwide extension. Article

[22] Address to Senate, July 10, 1919, *PPWW: War & Peace*, 1: 537–52; *PWW* (1989), 61: 426–36.

10 of the Covenant caused the greatest problem for them, because they feared its universal commitment to prevent aggression would entangle the United States in one foreign war after another. They did not trust his unique combination of unilateralism and multilateralism.[23]

Trying to address this concern, Wilson resorted to a dubious distinction between moral and legal obligations. On August 19, 1919, he told the Senate Foreign Relations Committee:

The United States will, indeed, undertake under Article X to 'respect and preserve as against external aggression the territorial integrity and existing political independence of all members of the League,' and that engagement constitutes a very grave and solemn moral obligation. But it is a moral, not a legal, obligation, and leaves our Congress absolutely free to put its own interpretation upon it in all cases that call for action. It is binding in conscience only, not in law.[24]

In a rather contradictory fashion, however, he said that moral commitments were more binding than legal ones, and hence the new League would guarantee peace, but that the United States would retain total freedom to decide its own involvement in future peacekeeping. Thus Wilson tried to explain how the United States could engage in multilateral diplomacy in the League as the world's preeminent leader, but without sacrificing its right to unilateral decision-making. In other words, he attempted to convince the Republican senators that the League of Nations – the key feature of his new internationalism – was consistent with the essential core of American isolationism. Wilson did not succeed in convincing them, either at this meeting of the Foreign Relations Committee or at any other time throughout the treaty fight in 1919–20.[25]

Wilson's unilateralism expressed his determination to keep out of an entangling alliance. To ensure that the League of Nations would never impose any obligation on the United States that he or future presidents did not approve, he absolutely insisted on giving all permanent members of the League Council a veto over its decisions. Even if the United States had joined the League, it would have retained a double veto over any use of economic sanctions or military force under Article 10. It could have vetoed any decision in the Council to recommend such action, and, like all League members, it would have reserved its sovereign right as a nation-state to decide whether to accept the Council's recommendation.

[23] Ambrosius, *Woodrow Wilson and the American Diplomatic Tradition*, 136–71.
[24] Statement to Senate Committee on Foreign Relations, Aug. 19, 1919, *PPWW*, 1: 574–80; *PWW* (1990), 62: 339–44.
[25] Ambrosius, *Woodrow Wilson and the American Diplomatic Tradition*, 172–250.

Although Article 10 might entail a universal moral commitment, it did not impose any binding legal obligation on the League members to take any action in a particular situation to preserve the territorial integrity or political independence of other members against external aggression. Thus the United States would have been totally free to decide whether to involve itself in any particular world crisis. The Covenant would not obligate the United States to any definite military commitment. In this way, as Wilson conceived it, the League was profoundly different from an alliance. It conformed to the historic reluctance of Americans to entangle themselves in the old world's wars and politics, while also promising a new opportunity for the United States to exercise global leadership through moral persuasion.[26]

Keenly aware of this unilateralist feature of the new League, French leaders at the peace conference sought a more traditional alliance with the United Kingdom and the United States to guarantee France's security against future German aggression. As part of a complex compromise over the occupation and possible annexation of the Rhineland, French premier Georges Clemenceau extracted commitments from Wilson as well as British prime minister David Lloyd George to a tripartite alliance. Under separate Franco-American and Anglo-French security treaties, the American and British governments gave joint promises to guarantee French security against a potentially revengeful Germany. Wilson, however, never favored the French security treaty, which would have created an alliance that entangled the United States in Europe. He reconciled himself to this obligation only by viewing it as a particular instance of what the League might do in any case. When he returned to the United States, the president made no effort to win the Senate's approval for the French security treaty. He focused instead on the League.[27]

Ironically, it was the Republican leadership that most favored the French security treaty. Henry Cabot Lodge, Elihu Root, and Philander Knox, among others, advocated the maintenance of the wartime coalition against Germany during the postwar years. They favored a definite military alliance limited to Western Europe rather than the indefinite but potentially universal commitments of the League under Article 10. They wanted to defend France against future German aggression, but refused to delegate to Wilson or any president the right to decide, without a

[26] Lloyd E. Ambrosius, "Wilson's League of Nations," *Maryland Historical Magazine* 65 (Winter 1970): 369–93.
[27] Lloyd E. Ambrosius, "Wilson, the Republicans, and French Security after World War I," *Journal of American History* 59 (Sept. 1972): 341–52.

Congressional resolution or declaration of war, whether to use American military force to preserve the territorial integrity and political independence of all nation-states in the League. Republican leaders were willing for the United States to enter a limited alliance with the United Kingdom and France, but opposed the vague, universal commitment that Wilson advocated under Article 10. In other words, preferring a different kind of multilateralism, Lodge and his Republican colleagues reversed Wilson's priorities: they favored the French security treaty, which he really did not like because it was an entangling alliance with the United Kingdom and France, while they also rejected his vision of universal collective security. It was Wilson, not the Republicans, who killed the French security treaty in the Senate by subordinating it to his League.[28]

Rather than compromise with the Republicans over Article 10 in the Covenant or seek the Senate's approval for the French security treaty, Wilson went on a speaking tour of western states in a futile attempt to persuade American public opinion to support the League of Nations. He refused to consider any reservations to the Covenant as he had drafted it. He emphasized the contrast between the new League and old alliances. In San Diego, California, on September 19, 1919, he told his audience: "I know the difficulties which arise when we speak of anything which seems to involve an alliance. But I do not believe that when Washington warned us against entangling alliances he meant for one moment that we should not join with the other civilized nations of the world if a method could be found to diminish war and encourage peace."[29] Wilson returned to this theme the next day in Los Angeles. He acknowledged that Washington had advised his fellow Americans against entangling alliances, but rejected the use of that warning by Republican senators as "an argument against the League of Nations. What Washington had in mind," Wilson explained, giving his view of what Washington had warned against in his farewell address, "was exactly what these gentlemen want to lead us back to. The day we have left behind us was a day of alliances. It was a day of balances of power.... This project of the League of Nations is a great process of disentanglement."[30] Wilson advocated the new League as the

---

[28] Ambrosius, "Wilson, the Republicans, and French Security," 341–52; Ambrosius, *Woodrow Wilson and the American Diplomatic Tradition*, 108–13, 123, 137, 139–40, 152–53, 164–65, 211–14. See also William C. Widenor, *Henry Cabot Lodge and the Search for an American Foreign Policy* (Berkeley, CA, 1980), 266–348.

[29] Address, San Diego, California, Sept. 19, 1919, *PPWW: War & Peace*, 2: 277–92; *PWW* (1990), 63: 371–82.

[30] Address, Los Angeles, California, Sept. 20, 1919, *PPWW: War & Peace*, 2: 299–310; *PWW*, 63: 400–07.

best alternative to old alliances. Through it the United States would help establish a new world order, which would replace the old diplomacy that had led to the Great War.

HISTORIOGRAPHY ON WILSONIANISM

Most American scholarship on Woodrow Wilson and the League of Nations, and on his role at the Paris Peace Conference, has used his own categories to assess his ideology and statecraft. In other words, conventional historiography has interpreted Wilsonianism from within the perspective of Wilsonianism. Historians and political scientists have usually embraced American exceptionalism. In this framework, which expressed the historic polarity in American nationalism between the new and old worlds, they have typically contrasted America's new diplomacy with Europe's old diplomacy, Wilson's League of Nations with Europe's alliances, and his progressive liberal internationalism with reactionary Republican isolationism. For half a century after World War I, most U.S. scholars accepted Wilson's own categories to depict him as the great internationalist and to denounce Lodge as the obstructive isolationist.

But this conventional historical framework distorted important features of Wilson's ideology and statecraft. Emphasizing his internationalism, it obscured his reluctance to entangle the United States in the old world. His insistence on unilateral decision-making in the League and his antipathy toward the French security treaty, as well as the willingness of Lodge and other Republicans to make a multilateral American commitment to help defend France against future German aggression, did not fit that traditional Wilsonian interpretation of the treaty fight in 1919–20. In two articles published in the early 1970s, and later reprinted in *Wilsonianism* (2002), I challenged this conventional viewpoint.[31] Then I reinterpreted Wilson's role in creating the League of Nations and in the treaty fight in *Woodrow Wilson and the American Diplomatic Tradition* (1987), by placing him within the context of international history rather than viewing him within the traditional framework of the internal American debate.

Some other scholars have also escaped Wilsonian categories, derived from American exceptionalism, in their assessments of the president's ideology and statecraft. Sharing my critical perspective, they have

---

[31] Lloyd E. Ambrosius, *Wilsonianism: Woodrow Wilson and His Legacy in American Foreign Relations* (New York, 2002), 51–64, 91–99.

incorporated my reinterpretation of his place in the American diplomatic tradition into their studies while developing their own larger themes about war and peace. For his chapter on Wilsonianism in *Promised Land, Crusader State* (1997), historian Walter A. McDougall relied on my book. He too recognized the inherent weaknesses in Wilson's liberal internationalism, and its false promise of peace through redemption of the old world – a greatly exaggerated promise it could not possibly fulfill after World War I. "As a blueprint for world order," McDougall concluded, "Wilsonianism has always been a chimera, but as an ideological weapon against 'every arbitrary power anywhere,' it has proved mighty indeed. And that, in the end, is how Wilson did truly imitate Jesus. He brought not peace but a sword."[32]

Political scientist G. John Ikenberry also embraced my interpretation of Wilson's failure. In *After Victory* (2001), his comparative study of peacemaking in 1815, 1919, 1945, and 1989, he used my work on Wilson in his chapter on the settlement of 1919 to develop his broader themes about liberal international institutions and their foundation in a postwar balance among the victorious and defeated great powers. Ikenberry emphasized the contrast between Wilson's vision and diplomacy after World War I and that of earlier European statesmen at the Congress of Vienna after the Napoleonic Wars and of later American and European leaders who constructed the "long peace" after World War II. Like Wilson, they sought to build new international institutions to help preserve peace among the great powers, including the defeated enemies. But unlike him, they willfully formed alliances with firm commitments to deter potential aggressors and assure possible victims. With alliances and regular forums for ongoing diplomatic consultation, and with realistic appreciation of the existing balance of power and of the importance of sustaining it, they managed to create stable and peaceful international orders that survived for decades. As a result, the prolonged nineteenth century (1815–1914) and the Cold War era (1945–1989) escaped major wars. Long periods of peace characterized Europe's international history after the Napoleonic Wars and after World War II. In comparison to those earlier and later achievements in statecraft, peacemaking failed after World War I. Wilson's vision of a new world order did not become the postwar reality as he had hoped.[33]

[32] McDougall, *Promised Land, Crusader State*, 122–46.
[33] G. John Ikenberry, *After Victory: Institutions, Strategic Restraint, and the Rebuilding of Order after Major Wars* (Princeton, NJ, 2001). References in chapters on the settlements of 1815, 1919, and 1945 show Ikenberry's extensive reliance on three historical

Ikenberry understood that the president himself was a major obstacle to the achievement of his liberal peace program "to create a stable and legitimate postwar order organized around democratic countries that operate within liberal institutions and uphold collective security." Wilson had sought in vain to rebuild international order after World War I. "The war brought the United States to a new position of power," Ikenberry noted, "but the way the war ended and Wilson's lost opportunities left the United States unable to dictate the terms of the peace. Wilson's own conceptions of commitment and global historical change undercut an institutional agreement that was within his reach."[34] In short, Wilson was largely responsible for this failure.

Contrary to my reinterpretation and critique of Wilson's peacemaking, and those of McDougall and Ikenberry, other scholars have continued to praise the president and to affirm Wilsonian ideology. They have looked back to him as the chief architect of a new international order, which did not succeed in the short term after World War I but eventually triumphed throughout the world by the end of the twentieth century. Thomas J. Knock[35] and John Milton Cooper, Jr.[36] believed that Wilson's quest for a new world order through the creation of the League of Nations failed largely because of lack of political support at home; his stroke also contributed to this failure. They saw his new diplomacy, however, as a positive contribution to world history, although it was not able "to end all wars" at this time. In their interpretations, Wilson's foes from both the left and right wings of American politics were responsible for "breaking the heart of the world" by defeating the Versailles Treaty and thereby preventing the United States from joining the League of Nations. Yet neither Knock nor Cooper studied foreign countries to determine whether other governments or peoples outside the United States actually welcomed Wilsonianism. Without analyzing international relations after World War I, they essentially assumed that Wilson's vision of the League as an instrument of peace was relevant to postwar Europe and could have

studies: Paul W. Schroeder, *The Transformation of European Politics, 1763–1848* (Oxford, 1994); Ambrosius, *Woodrow Wilson and the American Diplomatic Tradition*; Marc Trachtenberg, *A Constructed Peace: The Making of the European Settlement, 1945–1963* (Princeton, NJ, 1999). See also John Lewis Gaddis, *The Long Peace: Inquiries into the History of the Cold War* (New York, 1987).
[34] Ikenberry, *After Victory*, 117–62.
[35] Thomas J. Knock, *To End All Wars: Woodrow Wilson and the Quest for a New World Order* (New York, 1992).
[36] John Milton Cooper, Jr., *Breaking the Heart of the World: Woodrow Wilson and the Fight for the League of Nations* (Cambridge, 2001).

succeeded there if only the U.S. Senate had given it a chance. Focusing on the League, they disregarded the significance of Republican support for an Anglo-American alliance with France to guarantee its security. They interpreted the fight between the president and the Senate over the Versailles Treaty from Wilson's own viewpoint, not from the comparative perspective of international history. American exceptionalism thus defined the parameters of their historical inquiries.[37]

Despite Wilson's obvious failure to transform or redeem the old world with the League of Nations, he appeared to many Americans in retrospect to have offered the right approach to world affairs. In the post–Cold War era, many historians and political scientists concluded that he had laid the foundations for fundamental changes in the world. Historian Akira Iriye credited him with reshaping international relations in the twentieth century. "Because the globalizing of America has been a major event of the century," Iriye argued, "Wilsonianism should be seen not as a transient phenomenon, a reflection of some abstract idealism, but as a potent definer of contemporary history."[38] Wilson's vision contributed to the creation of a "global community."[39] Political scientist Tony Smith praised the president for defining "America's mission" in the worldwide struggle for democracy in the twentieth century.[40] Historian Frank Ninkovich developed this same idea. In his view, this was not just the American Century; it was "the Wilsonian century."[41] Political scientist Amos Perlmutter likewise interpreted international history from World War I through the Cold War as a global struggle between Wilsonianism and its totalitarian

[37] Despite efforts by some U.S. and foreign historians, such as the Project on Internationalizing the Study of American History, to escape American exceptionalism, that nationalist framework continues to influence historical writing. That exceptionalist bias, which characterized the Progressive Era, still shapes historical scholarship on U.S. and world history during that era. This is a fundamental problem in Alan Dawley, *Changing the World: American Progressives in War and Revolution* (Princeton, NJ, 2003), despite his attempt to relate American progressivism to world history and his advocacy of a new "world consciousness." He ignored even the most outstanding scholarship by foreign historians (such as Klaus Schwabe, Jan Willem Schulte Nordholt, and John A. Thompson) on Woodrow Wilson, "the preeminent progressive." See my review of Dawley's book in *Peace and Change* 30 (July 2005): 412–16.

[38] Akira Iriye, *The Cambridge History of American Foreign Relations, Vol. III: The Globalizing of America, 1913–1945* (Cambridge, 1993), 72.

[39] Akira Iriye, *Global Community: The Role of International Organizations in the Making of the Contemporary World* (Berkeley, CA, 2002).

[40] Tony Smith, *America's Mission: The United States and the Worldwide Struggle for Democracy in the Twentieth Century* (Princeton, NJ, 1994).

[41] Frank Ninkovich, *The Wilsonian Century: U.S. Foreign Relations since 1900* (Chicago, 1999).

challengers. In that contest over power and ideology, Wilson's legacy of "making the world safe for democracy" triumphed over the alternatives of Fascism and Communism.[42]

This triumph of Wilsonian liberal internationalism appeared to social philosopher Francis Fukuyama to mark the "end of history."[43] What Wilson had heralded during World War I had finally become the reality at the end of the Cold War. Political scientist Michael Mandelbaum agreed, affirming that liberal democracy and capitalism had now prevailed in the world and provided the foundation for its peace. History could not progress any further, having reached its zenith. Wilsonian ideas of peace, democracy, and free markets, he concluded, were "the ideas that conquered the world."[44] All these scholars offered triumphalist interpretations of America's contribution to world history, and praised Wilson for defining the essential elements of U.S. foreign policy in the twentieth century.

The conventional explanation of the treaty fight in the United States, which had exalted Wilson the internationalist over Lodge the isolationist, also continued to echo throughout recent scholarship in the form of praise for the president's multilateralism in contrast to unilateralism, usually identified with the Republican leader. In this lingering version of the dualistic internationalist-versus-isolationist interpretation, Wilson's contribution to building a world community and establishing international institutions placed him in the vanguard of modernity and globalization, while his critics such as Lodge still appeared as reactionary nationalists. Political scientist John Gerard Ruggie gave a nuanced version of this viewpoint, linking Wilson's advocacy of the League of Nations with the kind of multilateral diplomacy that Ruggie urged for "winning the peace" after the Cold War.[45] Former secretary of defense Robert S. McNamara and political scientist James G. Blight gave a less sophisticated version. They thought "Wilson's ghost" – like Jacob Marley's in Charles Dickens's *A Christmas Carol* – was calling out to them with a message for reducing the risk of conflict, killing, and catastrophe in the twenty-first century. "The message of Wilson's ghost is this," McNamara and Blight

[42] Amos Perlmutter, *Making the World Safe for Democracy: A Century of Wilsonianism and Its Totalitarian Challengers* (Chapel Hill, NC, 1997).

[43] Francis Fukuyama, *The End of History and the Last Man* (New York, 1992).

[44] Michael Mandlebaum, *The Ideas That Conquered the World: Peace, Democracy, and Free Markets in the Twenty-first Century* (New York, 2002).

[45] John Gerard Ruggie, *Winning the Peace: America and World Order in the New Era* (New York, 1996).

claimed: "Beware of the blindness and folly that led Europe's leaders into the First World War, a disaster theretofore without compare in world history; and beware of the temptation to believe that sustainable peace will be maintained simply by plotting to achieve an alleged 'balance of power' without a strong international organization to enforce it."[46] Wilson's legacy of multilateralism, they all agreed, provided the best means for peacemaking and peacekeeping in the post–Cold War era. They neglected, however, his equally strong commitment to unilateralism. The League of Nations, as Wilson had conceived it, combined both approaches to world affairs, but they identified him only with multilateralism.

Americans, including scholars, who have embraced Wilsonianism as the ideal vision for the world's future have often neglected its worst characteristics or limitations. They have almost completely overlooked Wilson's racism and his other shortcomings regarding human rights. Despite his promise to make the world safe for democracy, he continued to believe in white supremacy and offered no solution to the modern tragedy of genocide. His League of Nations did not address these terrible problems.

Wilson's own racism shaped his approach to international relations. Those who have lauded his legacy have usually not focused on this feature of Wilson's ideology and statecraft. His idea of democracy did not affirm racial equality. On the contrary, this first southern president since the American Civil War believed in white supremacy. His attitude toward African Americans, whom he wanted to keep separate with the Jim Crow system of racial segregation at home, had its counterpart in his foreign policy. He used the hierarchy of race to define the stages of development that would characterize the various types of League mandates (A, B, and C) for the former empires of the defeated Central Powers. In his judgment, peoples in Europe were ready for self-government, but others were not. In Wilson's mind, Africans were at the lowest stage of development. In the Near East, whose peoples were regarded as fairly advanced, "A" mandates would be established for some nations arising from the former Ottoman Empire. "B" and "C" mandates would be created for the so-called less-developed peoples of Germany's former African and Pacific-island colonies. His conception of League mandates allowed Wilson to accommodate traditional European colonialism in the new guise of international trusteeships. Despite his advocacy of the principle of national

---

[46] Robert S. McNamara and James G. Blight, *Wilson's Ghost: Reducing the Risk of Conflict, Killing, and Catastrophe in the 21st Century* (New York, 2001), 3.

self-determination, he limited its application to Europe. During the drafting
of the League Covenant, he also rejected the Japanese amendment to
affirm the equality of all races or nations. Wilson expressed his white
racism in his liberal internationalism.⁴⁷

Wilson's vision of the League of Nations did not guarantee universal
human rights. The Armenian genocide of 1915 illustrated this limitation.
Although he clearly understood that the Armenian people were suffering from genocide, he restricted his actions on their behalf both during
and after the war. They were white Christians, and therefore high on
his racial hierarchy, but he still did not think the United States could or
should intervene with military force to protect them against the Turks or
later the Bolsheviks. He did not want the United States to bear this burden. Despite bipartisan support from both Republicans and Democrats
for U.S. involvement and efforts by the Allies to convince him that the
United States should accept a League mandate for this Caucasian nation,
Wilson declined. While touting the League as the defender of all nations
against external aggression, he eschewed this responsibility by the United
States for the Armenians. Military intervention in Armenia would have
been too costly, he feared, making a realistic assessment that contradicted
his apparently universal promise. Wilson therefore made the unilateral
decision not to involve the United States, despite his idealistic rhetoric
that ostensibly promised self-determination and collective security for
all nations. Committing U.S. troops for that purpose looked too much
like an entangling alliance in the old world. The unhappy episode of
Armenian genocide clearly revealed the limits of Wilsonian ideology and
of American power to transform or redeem the old world.⁴⁸

Limitations such as these notwithstanding, Wilsonianism has continued
to shape the way many Americans view the world in the twenty-first century. After the terrorist attacks of September 11, 2001, President George
W. Bush used Wilson's legacy to justify his global war on terrorism.⁴⁹

⁴⁷ Ambrosius, *Wilsonianism*, 21–29; Joseph A. Fry, *Dixie Looks Abroad: The South and U.S. Foreign Relations, 1789–1973* (Baton Rouge, LA, 2002), 139–74; Margaret MacMillan, *Paris 1919: Six Months That Changed the World* (New York, 2001), 98–106, 306–21.
⁴⁸ Lloyd E. Ambrosius, "Wilsonian Diplomacy and Armenia: The Limits of Power and Ideology," *America and the Armenian Genocide of 1915*, ed. Jay Winter (Cambridge, 2003), 113–45; Samantha Power, *"A Problem from Hell": America and the Age of Genocide* (New York, 2002), 1–16; Peter Balakian, *The Burning Tigris: The Armenian Genocide and America's Response* (New York, 2003).
⁴⁹ Ambrosius, *Wilsonianism*, 14–18; David M. Kennedy, "What 'W' Owes to WW," *The Atlantic* 295 (March 2005): 36–40.

Calling for a new crusade to defend civilization against this barbaric terrorist danger and to create a new world order of democracy and peace, he demanded that other nations join the United States in this multilateral effort. But he also insisted on unilateral decision-making, assigning to the United Nations the role he expected it to play. When other great powers refused to accept their assignments, he organized a new coalition outside the United Nations to launch the war against Iraq. He was not willing to be bound by any international organization or entangling alliance.[50]

Bush defined the goals of his global war on terrorism in the ideological terms of what I would call neoconservative Wilsonianism. Although his foreign policy was a radical departure from the American diplomatic tradition, it appeared more traditional.[51] Bush's rhetoric echoed the triumphalist themes and interpretations of Wilson's legacy in the post–Cold War years. The goals sounded familiar, although the means were quite different. The ongoing debate among historians, political scientists, and others over Wilson and his vision of America's redemptive role in world history continued to be vitally important. This debate involved key questions about whether the United States should, in conducting its foreign relations to deal with contemporary challenges, adopt a multilateral approach through the United Nations – the successor to Wilson's League of Nations – or through the North Atlantic Treaty Organization – the military alliance that was the closest equivalent to the French security treaties after World War I – or instead adopt a unilateral approach outside of these international institutions. These were not just academic questions. Different interpretations of Woodrow Wilson and his legacy were still contested in public discourse as well as among scholars, demonstrating his continuing relevance as a point of reference. For better or worse, Wilsonianism still helped define the choices for the future in the twenty-first century, as it had during the Great War in the Progressive Era.

[50] Stefan Halper, *America Alone: The Neo-Conservatives and the Global Order* (Cambridge, 2004); James Mann, *Rise of the Vulcans: The History of Bush's War Cabinet* (New York, 2004).

[51] John B. Judis, *The Folly of Empire: What George W. Bush Could Learn from Theodore Roosevelt and Woodrow Wilson* (New York, 2004), criticized President Bush for his pursuit of an American empire, comparing him unfavorably with TR and Wilson, who had learned "the folly of empire." Contrary to Judis, John Lewis Gaddis, *Surprise, Security, and the American Experience* (Cambridge, MA, 2004), emphasized continuity in U.S. foreign relations from the nineteenth and twentieth centuries to the Bush Doctrine.

CONCLUSIONS

What conclusions might be drawn from this analysis? First, by making a sharp distinction between entangling alliances and the League of Nations, Wilson missed the opportunity to find common ground with the European Allies and the U.S. Senate. Like the British and French governments, Lodge and other Republican leaders wanted the United States to make a firm commitment to defend Western Europe against future German aggression, and therefore favored the Franco-American and Anglo-French security treaties. Wilson, however, preferred the vague, universal commitment of Article 10 of the League Covenant. He sought the Senate's acceptance of the Versailles Treaty without any amendments or even reservations. Subordinating the French security treaty to the League, he sacrificed the possibility of winning the Senate's approval for either. While pursuing the ideal of a new world order, in which the League would be the centerpiece, the president missed the opportunity to create another form of multilateral cooperation to preserve peace after World War I.

Second, as the consequence of this failure, the United States would not play the kind of constructive role in peacemaking after World War I that the United Kingdom had undertaken after the Napoleonic Wars and that the United States would assume after World War II. As G. John Ikenberry argued persuasively, the lack of viable international institutions made the settlement of 1919 fundamentally different from those of 1815 or 1945. Alliances aimed at preserving the new international order, and that reflected the existing balance of power in Europe, were critical to the preservation of peace in those other two cases. While pursuing his ideal of the League of Nations, Wilson eschewed the entanglement of an alliance. Without American membership, the new League could not function effectively as a substitute for an alliance. By failing to work with the European Allies to institutionalize the peace settlement with a powerful League or an alliance, the United States under Wilson's leadership missed the best opportunity to construct a durable new order of international relations after 1919. Neither liberal institutions nor peace survived for long in postwar Europe.

Third, recognition of Wilson's responsibility for these failures to find common ground between the European Allies and the United States, and thus for constructing a durable and peaceful international order after World War I, has been obscured by confusion over the definition of multilateralism and unilateralism. Political scientists and others who have adopted these terms have typically assumed that these were mutually exclusive approaches to international relations, and therefore that state-craft would reflect one or the other. Accordingly, they have depicted Wilson as a multilateralist and Lodge as a unilateralist. Historians had traditionally made this same distinction by labeling Wilson as an inter-nationalist and Lodge as an isolationist. John Gerard Ruggie rightly noted that internationalism can take the form of either multilateralism or unilateralism, and therefore that the term "isolationism" is not very appropriate for the United States in the twentieth century. But he over-looked the possibility that the same person, such as Wilson, might adopt multilateralist and unilateralist approaches to America's involvement in world affairs, even at the same time. He viewed Wilson as a prime exam-ple of multilateralism, but not also of unilateralism. Ruggie looked back to him as a symbol of the right approach to "winning the peace" in the post–Cold War era. Defining the categories as he did, however, prevented Ruggie from recognizing the negative consequences of Wilson's unilater-alism. He was not alone. Robert S. McNamera and James G. Blight, and other scholars who have exalted Wilson and his legacy of Wilsonianism, have made the same mistake.[52]

Fourth, this confusion over the definition of terminology was not just a semantic problem. It has obscured the negative side of Wilson's ideol-ogy and statecraft. Once he has been lifted up as the example or sym-bol of multilateral American involvement in international relations, it is difficult for scholars or others to recognize the unattractive features of his leadership, such as his racism and his indifference to human rights as understood in the post–Cold War era. Outstanding historians such as Akira Iriye and Frank Ninkovich and political scientists such as Tony Smith and Amos Perlmutter, while heralding Wilson and his legacy of Wilsonianism as the foundation for America's role in the modern world of the twentieth century, ignored both his racist policies at home and abroad and his handling of the Armenian genocide. These negative fea-tures did not fit well in their triumphalist accounts of "the Wilsonian century" or their definition of "America's mission" in the world. Others, such as Francis Fukuyama and Michael Mandelbaum, also neglected these less-attractive aspects of Wilsonianism, while touting the triumph of Wilson's ideas of peace, liberal democracy, and capitalism in the post–Cold War world.

---

[52] In contrast, Niall Ferguson, *Colossus: The Price of America's Empire* (New York, 2004), 132–66, recognized the false dichotomy that some made between multilateralism and unilateralism, noting that these two approaches often went together in recent U.S. for-eign relations.

Fifth, underlying this confusion over terminology was the pervasive influence of American exceptionalism. Wilson and other Americans, including scholars, believed in the universal nature of their principles. Because these seemed self-evidently good for all peoples, Americans could not recognize that their ideals might not be universally acceptable as the ideological foundation for a new international order. Thus, while offering their progressive ideas for a better world, as Wilson did with his vision for the League of Nations, Americans have often not understood why other nations might not welcome their unilateral definition of a new form of multilateralism. They have not comprehended why others have seen unilateralism in U.S. statecraft while Americans were proclaiming multilateralism. Robert McNamara exemplified this cultural problem as secretary of defense during the 1960s, and again in his recent advice for the twenty-first century. In *Wilson's Ghost* (2001), he prescribed multi-lateralism – which he saw as Wilson's main legacy – as the key to peace, arguing that the United States should never make a unilateral decision for war. This appeared to be a fundamental change from his attitude during the Vietnam War. However, in both cases, he assumed that what was good for the United States was also good for the whole world, and therefore that other nations should accept his kind of American leadership – by which he actually meant American hegemony – in international relations. This flawed assumption, which reflected his underlying belief in American exceptionalism, allowed him to prescribe multilateral decision-making while he still expected never to sacrifice any U.S. interests. Like his hero Wilson, McNamara could not distinguish between American and universal interests. Terminology that, by definition, precluded the same person from practicing both multilateralism and unilateralism also prevented McNamara from seeing this combination in Wilson or in himself. He was not alone, for these distinctions also escaped the attention of many prominent scholars who have used Wilson's own categories for interpreting his ideology and statecraft and his legacy in U.S. foreign relations.[53]

Sixth, Wilson's legacy still seemed relevant to subsequent generations of U.S. scholars and policy-makers. Within the framework of American exceptionalism, it readily followed that the Senate's rejection of the Versailles Treaty had resulted in "breaking the heart of the world," or that the twentieth century was actually "the Wilsonian century," or that the Wilsonian triad of peace, liberal democracy, and capitalism were "the

[53] Ambrosius, *Wilsonianism*, 157–73.

ideas that conquered the world." Outside of this Wilsonian framework, however, world history had proceeded in other directions. September 11, 2001 demonstrated that reality. Nevertheless, when President George W. Bush defined his response to those terrorist attacks, he embraced Wilson's legacy, promising to make the world safe for freedom and democracy. The Bush Doctrine, as John Lewis Gaddis argued, was deeply rooted in the American experience of the nineteenth and twentieth centuries. But that begged the more important question as to whether this tradition, which included Wilsonianism, was relevant to the twenty-first century. Wilson had proclaimed a new world order that would hopefully create the kingdom of God on earth, but this redemptive task had proved to be beyond the power of the United States during the Great War. In view of that experience, wisdom might suggest the importance of pursuing peace without false expectations of eradicating evil throughout the world. Yet that earlier failure did not stop Bush from adopting a similar approach in his global war on terrorism. He too exalted moral principles over international law, presuming, of course, that American ideals were universally applicable in this latest "war for righteousness." For him, as for earlier progressive warriors, American exceptionalism seemed to assure the universal character of U.S. goals in this perennial pursuit of a new world order. Despite Wilson's failure after World War I, his legacy has continued to influence public discourse over America's role in war and peace. Understanding Wilsonianism is therefore crucial not only in the historiography of the Progressive Era but also in the ongoing debate over U.S. foreign relations in the twenty-first century.

7

Wilsonian Diplomacy and Armenia

The Limits of Power and Ideology

Armenia emerged as a new nation during World War I, joining the world order that was taking shape in the wake of collapsing empires. President Woodrow Wilson, in his wartime addresses, proclaimed the principles that should guide the peacemaking for this new world. His decision to attend the 1919 Paris Peace Conference increased the expectations that all peoples, including the Armenians, would have a better future. Wilsonian ideology promised peace and justice for all nations, both old and new. American power, greater than that of any other empire, would presumably enable the United States to help others fulfill Wilson's ideals in the postwar world. Contrary to these hopes, however, Armenia failed as a new nation, revealing not only its own limits but also those of Wilsonianism. The realities of international politics prevented the Armenian people, who had suffered so much in the past, from achieving the Wilsonian promise after the Great War. The limits of American power and ideology resulted in an outcome very different from what the Armenians wanted and what the U.S. president had heralded.

AMERICANS AND ARMENIA DURING THE
GREAT WAR

Armenia possessed assets that made it attractive to American leaders. Its people were white – literally Caucasian – and Christian, at least culturally as a result of the Armenian Orthodox Church's role since the fourth century AD in shaping and preserving national traditions.[1] It

---

[1] Ronald Grigor Suny, *Looking Toward Aurat: Armenia in the Modern World* (Bloomington, IN, 1993).

also enjoyed bipartisan support from the American political elite. Not only the Democratic president but also the Republican leader, Senator Henry Cabot Lodge of Massachusetts, favored the new nation. Lodge joined the American Committee for the Independence of Armenia, which Wilson's former ambassador to Germany, James W. Gerard, organized in 1918. This lobby, including a broad range of prominent Americans from Democrats William Jennings Bryan and Cleveland H. Dodge to Republicans Charles Evans Hughes and Elihu Root, worked closely with both the Wilson administration and the Republican-controlled Congress to promote the Armenian cause.[2]

With this broad range of bipartisan support, Armenia apparently enjoyed a real advantage in the peacemaking after World War I. No other new nation could claim such a prominent lobby in the United States. Moreover, the Armenian cause ranked second only to that of French security against renewed German aggression in the willingness of leading Republicans such as Lodge and Root to approve long-term commitments by the United States in the old world.[3] The question for pro-Armenian Americans was how to translate this amorphous bipartisan support into effective action that would actually assist Armenia. The answer would depend not only on the pro-Armenian inclinations of President Wilson and Congress, or the State Department and U.S. diplomats, but also on the capability of the United States to project its influence into the crossroads region of the Near East under the prevailing wartime and postwar conditions. This would test the limits of U.S. power and ideology.

Among the Americans most actively promoting U.S. support for Armenia were two former ambassadors: James W. Gerard and Henry Morgenthau. Gerard organized and led the American Committee for the Independence of Armenia. Morgenthau, who had represented the United States at Constantinople from 1913 to 1916, exposed the Ottoman Empire's connections with Imperial Germany and its cruel treatment of the Armenians. He informed not only the Wilson administration but also the American people about the Armenian genocide. After returning home, he published a potent account of his years in Turkey, *Ambassador Morgenthau's Story* (1918).[4]

[2] Richard G. Hovannisian, *The Republic of Armenia: The First Years, 1918–1919* (Berkeley, CA, 1971), 1: 261–65, 293–95, 309–12.
[3] Lloyd E. Ambrosius, "Wilson, Republicans, and French Security after World War I," *Journal of American History* 59 (September 1972): 341–52.
[4] Henry Morgenthau, *Ambassador Morgenthau's Story* (Garden City, NY, 1918). For Morgenthau's reports to Lansing in 1915, see U.S. Department of State, *Papers Relating to*

Morgenthau wanted to expose the anti-Armenian behavior of the Young Turks and their ally, Imperial Germany. In his book he reported that "the Turkish Government was determined to keep the news, as long as possible, from the outside world. It was clearly the intention that Europe and America should hear of the annihilation of the Armenian race only after the annihilation had been accomplished."[5] The former ambassador sought, contrary to Turkey's preference, to disclose Armenia's plight and Germany's involvement in it. In 1918, before the book appeared, he published the chapters of *Ambassador Morgenthau's Story* as articles in *World's Work*. Sending the first three installments to Wilson, he sought the president's opinion about the idea of turning the book into a motion picture. Playing up Germany's alliance with Turkey, and thus its complicity with the Armenian massacres, seemed to Morgenthau's publishers an ideal way to disseminate "anti-German propaganda" in the United States. "I myself think," he told Wilson, "that nothing could so completely bring before the American people the true nature of the German aggression as a picture showing the Armenian massacres and the responsibility of Germany for them."[6]

Wilson opposed Morgenthau's idea. The president noted that he was "very much distressed" that Gerard had allowed his book, *My Four Years in Germany* (1917), to be turned into a motion picture. "Movies I have seen recently," Wilson explained, "have portrayed so many horrors that I think their effect is far from stimulating, and that it does not, as a matter of fact, suggest the right attitude of mind or the right national action. There is nothing practical that we can do for the time being in the matter of the Armenian massacres, for example, and the attitude of the country toward Turkey is already fixed."[7] Recognizing the limits of American power to assist Armenia, Wilson did not welcome Morgenthau's proposal for more anti-German and anti-Turkish propaganda.

This response was consistent with Wilson's decision not to recommend an American declaration of war against the Ottoman Empire. In December 1917, he had asked Congress to declare war against the Habsburg Empire, but not against Turkey or Bulgaria. The president had observed that "the government of Austria-Hungary is not acting upon its

the *Foreign Relations of the United States: The Lansing Papers, 1914–1920* (Washington, DC, 1939), 1: 762–75.

[5] Morgenthau, *Ambassador Morgenthau's Story*, 326.

[6] Morgenthau to Wilson, June 11, 1918, *The Papers of Woodrow Wilson* [hereafter *PWW*], ed. Arthur S. Link (Princeton, NJ, 1985), 48: 284.

[7] Wilson to Morgenthau, June 14, 1918, *PWW*, 48: 311.

own initiative or in response to the wishes and feelings of its own peoples but as the instrument of another nation. We must meet its force with our own and regard the Central Powers as but one." He acknowledged that "the same logic would lead also to a declaration of war against Turkey and Bulgaria. They also are the tools of Germany." But for practical reasons, Wilson did not call upon Congress to declare war against them, noting that "they are mere tools and do not yet stand in the direct path of our necessary action. We shall go wherever the necessities of this war carry us, but it seems to me that we should go only where immediate and practical considerations lead us and not heed any others."[8]

Congress, while accepting Wilson's recommendation and voting for war against the Austro-Hungarian Empire, wanted clarification of the president's reluctance to take the same action against Bulgaria and Turkey. Secretary of State Robert Lansing gave the Senate Foreign Relations Committee a list of practical reasons for this decision. He acknowledged that the United States did not have a military force to commit on the eastern front. It would instead concentrate on fighting the war on the western front in 1918. Lansing emphasized, moreover, that a declaration of war against Turkey would jeopardize American missionary and educational interests in that country and would likely provoke the Turks into retaliation with new massacres of Christians and Jews.[9] In short, the limits of American power in this region made it prudent for the United States to ignore ideological consistency in favor of practical considerations. It was more realistic not to declare war against Turkey, or even Bulgaria.

Wilson's analysis of Germany's global threat provided the framework in which U.S. diplomats, particularly Felix Willoughby Smith in Tiflis, endeavored to assist the Armenians. As an obstacle to the German bid for hegemony from Berlin to Bagdad, Armenia became strategically significant for the United States during the last year of the Great War. Although rejecting open warfare against Germany or Turkey on the eastern front, Wilson and Lansing sanctioned covert operations designed to defeat the German-Turkish alliance and, incidentally, to support the Armenians. As U.S. consul, Smith spearheaded this activity in the Transcaucasian region of the disintegrating Russian Empire.[10]

---

[8] Woodrow Wilson, *The Public Papers of Woodrow Wilson* [hereafter *PPWW*], eds. Ray Stannard Baker and William E. Dodd (New York, 1927), 5: 135–36.

[9] Laurence Evans, *United States Policy and the Partition of Turkey, 1914–1924* (Baltimore, MD, 1965), 32–42.

[10] Hovannisian, *Republic of Armenia*, 1: 179.

Following the Russian Revolution in March 1917, Smith had urged the Wilson administration to resist the combined efforts by Germany and Turkey to gain control over Transcaucasia. Aware of the inadequacies of Russia's Provisional Government, he urged the State Department to encourage the various nationalities in the region to continue the war against the Central Powers. Smith wanted to exploit the separate national identities of the Caucasian peoples to reinforce their war effort against the German-Turkish alliance. He advocated, for example, the transfer of Armenian and Georgian troops from the collapsing eastern front to their homelands, where they could continue fighting against the Central Powers.

Since July 1917, Smith had lost confidence in the Provisional Government's capability, although he still favored a united and democratic Russia. "There seems to be a total lack of patriotism and national spirit towards this country as a whole," Smith reported to Lansing in October. He complained that

the Provisional Government has heretofore tended to discourage the local national spirit, considering it as a disruptive force, but recent events have shown that practically the only hope of union and peace lies in the encouragement of this racial or national spirit and the utilization of this force towards the formation of units which in turn would inevitably unite in the formation of a Russian federation.... These racial feelings if encouraged and wisely guided would save Russia and would be of particular and lasting benefit to this district.[11]

Smith's eagerness to encourage nationalist sentiments in Transcaucasia as a way of mobilizing its peoples against Germany and Turkey worried Lansing. After receiving the consul's repeated requests for assistance to Armenians and others, the secretary of state demanded an explanation of how "the financial support you propose will not tend to encourage sectionalism or disruption of Russia or civil war." He stressed that the "Department cannot encourage tendencies in any of these directions."[12] Lansing's concerns about too much national self-determination reflected Wilson's as well. The president, having long ago adopted a pro-Union interpretation of the American Civil War, did not favor the breakup of existing nation-states. He saw Russia as

---

[11] Smith to Lansing, Oct. 19, 1917, U.S. Department of State, *Papers Relating to the Foreign Relations of the United States, 1918: Russia* [hereafter *FRUS: Russia*] (Washington, DC, 1932), 2: 578–80.

[12] Smith to Lansing, Nov. 23, 1917, Lansing to Smith, Nov. 26. 1917, *FRUS: Russia*, 2: 582.

a whole nation, and thus hesitated to endorse any action that might foster secession by any section.[13]

Lansing informed Edward M. House, Wilson's personal envoy in Paris for a meeting with Allied leaders, that the State Department would not allow Smith to recognize any separatist nation in Transcaucasia. In late November 1917, the secretary of state explained that Smith "will not be given authority to recognize *de facto* government until it is evident that such action will not tend to foster sectionalism or disruption of Russia or civil war."[14] By this time the Bolsheviks had seized power in Petrograd and Moscow. Nevertheless, U.S. policy continued to favor a united and democratic Russia as foreseen by the Provisional Government. This enduring commitment to Russia not only prevented the United States from recognizing the new Soviet government but also restricted the ways it might sustain the Armenians and other Caucasian peoples.[15]

The Wilson administration worked with the Allies, particularly the British and the French, to channel financial assistance to these separate peoples within the former Russian Empire. This form of indirect assistance was Lansing's alternative to Smith's earlier proposal for direct U.S. aid to the Armenians and others in Transcaucasia. In December 1917, after the Bolsheviks concluded an armistice with Germany, Wilson approved the covert plan that the State Department then arranged with the Allies.[16]

Multiple purposes shaped American involvement in Transcaucasia. Wilson and Lansing pursued anti-Bolshevik as well as anti-German purposes. However, U.S. aid, albeit indirect, was also anti-Turkish and pro-Armenian.[17] This was a key aspect of Smith's proposal for financial assistance. In response to Lansing's concerns about fostering sectionalism

[13] Lloyd E. Ambrosius, "Dilemmas of National Self-Determination: Woodrow Wilson's Legacy," in Christian Baechler and Carole Fink, eds., *The Establishment of European Frontiers after the Two World Wars* (Bern, 1996), 25; Thomas J. Pressly, *Americans Interpret Their Civil War* (New York, 1962), 196–226.

[14] Lansing to Sharp, Nov. 28, 1917, *FRUS: Russia*, 2: 582–83.

[15] Lansing to Wilson, Jan. 10, 1918, U.S. Department of State, *FRUS: Lansing Papers* (Washington, DC, 1940), 2: 349–51.

[16] Lansing to Wilson, Dec. 10 and 12, 1917, *FRUS: Lansing Papers*, 2: 343–46; Page to Lansing, Dec. 18, 1917, Sharp to Lansing, Dec. 23 and 27, 1917, *FRUS: Russia*, 2: 591–92, 596–600; Wilson to Lansing, Jan. 1, 1918, *PWW*, 45: 417–19.

[17] Other scholars have neglected anti-Turkish or pro-Armenian dimensions, while focusing on anti-German or anti-Bolshevik features of U.S. intervention in the Russian civil war. See, for example, George F. Kennan, *Soviet-American Relations, 1917–1920: Russia Leaves the War* (Princeton, NJ, 1956), 1: 167–88, and David S. Fogelsong, *America's Secret War Against Bolshevism: U.S. Intervention in the Russian Civil War* (Chapel Hill, NC, 1995), 76–105.

and disrupting Russia, Smith noted the importance of Armenia, while assuring him that "the Allies would be supporting both Russian union and democracy against absolute dependence of Russia on Germany." If, however, they failed to provide critical financial assistance to Transcaucasia, "this would involve [the] loss of Armenia and render most likely the concentration of Turkish-German forces against [the] British in Baghdad."[18] Lansing and Wilson agreed. Because the United States lacked the means to deliver substantial quantities of direct aid to Armenia or elsewhere in the Caucasus region, expediency led them to adopt a collaborative plan with the Allies. Accordingly, Lansing instructed Smith to cooperate with British and French representatives in the region and to keep the State Department informed.[19]

Before the Bolshevik seizure of power in November 1917, Smith had begun to advocate U.S. help for the Caucasian peoples as the most effective way to protect them from Germany and Turkey, and thus to help defeat the Central Powers. This timing indicated that anti-Bolshevism was not Smith's primary motivation at the outset. The anti-German strategic rationale for assisting Armenians, Smith's initial priority, ended with the German armistice on November 11, 1918. Humanitarian concern for protecting Armenians against the Turks, also important to Smith, persisted into the postwar era. Pro-Armenian and anti-Turkish considerations, not merely anti-Bolshevism, remained important factors in the U.S. involvement in Transcaucasia after Germany's defeat. In the mixture of strategic, humanitarian, and ethnic agendas in this region, the Wilson administration pursued a complex foreign policy in the Near East.[20]

In Washington, neither Wilson nor Lansing, nor any other American leader, was willing to make costly commitments to the Armenians. Even while authorizing some covert assistance via the Allies to the region, the president did not plan to recognize Armenia or any other new nation in Transcaucasia. In his Fourteen Points on January 8, 1918, he called for preserving Russia's territorial integrity and respecting its right of self-determination. Accordingly, he did not favor independence for Russian Armenia. Nor did he favor independence for Turkish Armenia. Wilson's peace plan would leave Turkish portions of the Ottoman Empire under Turkish sovereignty, but he thought that "the other nationalities which are now under Turkish rule should be assured an undoubted security of life

[18] Smith to Lansing, Dec. 4, 1917, *FRUS: Russia*, 2: 584.
[19] Lansing to Smith, Dec. 28, 1917, *FRUS: Russia*, 2: 600–01.
[20] For the Armenian dimension, see especially Richard G. Hovannisian, *Armenia on the Road to Independence, 1918* (Berkeley, CA, 1967), 80–82, 117–19.

and an absolutely unmolested opportunity of autonomous development, and the Dardanelles should be permanently opened as a free passage to the ships and commerce of all nations under international guarantees."[21] Wilson had given some consideration to making point 12, which dealt with the Ottoman Empire, more specific by naming Armenia and other nationalities, but acquiesced in House's advice not to bother.[22] Thus he cautiously applied his principles, calling for the Open Door and collective security in the Turkish Straits and for national self-determination in the Russian and Turkish territories.

After Germany imposed the Treaty of Brest-Litovsk on the Bolshevik government on March 3, 1918, forcing the Soviets to cede some of Russian Armenia to Turkey, the plight of Armenians worsened.[23] Nevertheless, Wilson still ruled out both U.S. and Allied military intervention in this region. In late March and early April, Lord Reading, the British ambassador to the United States, presented the Allied case for military intervention in Russia. Among other arguments, he noted that "it is in the East that the German Government are now taking steps to overcome the effects of the blockade, to upset the security of British India, and to carry the war down to Afghanistan and Persia, incidentally giving the Turks a free hand in Armenia." Wilson was not convinced by Reading's case. "I must say," he informed Lansing, "that none of these memoranda has anything in it that is at all persuasive with me."[24] The president wanted no further American or Allied involvement in the Russian civil war regardless of the consequences for Armenia.

During the spring of 1918, Smith continued to inform the State Department about Armenia's worsening situation and urged more assistance. He reported that the Turks were still advancing, placing the "Armenians in real danger of extermination." He requested more British assistance to the Armenians, noting that they "possess great potential military force." Given "the inactivity of the Allies," the Armenians were not achieving their full potential. They were, however, generally able to hold their villages against the "armed Moslems." In early April, Smith warned that the Turks might occupy even more Caucasian territory unless the Armenians and Georgians received instant financial aid and future British

---

[21] An Address to a Joint Session of Congress, Jan. 8, 1918, *PWW* (Princeton, NJ, 1984), 45: 537–38; Address of the President, Jan. 8, 1918, *FRUS, 1918: The World War* (Washington, DC, 1933), 1: 15–16.
[22] Diary of Colonel House, Jan. 9, 1918, *PWW*, 45: 553.
[23] Summers to Lansing, Apr. 22, 1918, *FRUS: Russia* (Washington, DC, 1931), 1: 471–75.
[24] Wilson to Lansing, Apr. 4, 1918, *PWW* (Princeton, NJ, 1984), 47: 241–46.

military assistance. Turkish conquest of Armenia, he forecast, would mean the "massacre of Armenians." He hoped the State Department would arrange with London to transfer money to Tiflis "to provide for safety of [the] Armenian people and prevent [their] total extermination."[25]

Lansing relayed Smith's concerns to the U.S. ambassador in London, Walter Hines Page, seeking clarification from the British government. However, neither Washington nor London ever provided as much financial and military assistance as Smith requested. Only later, during the summer of 1918, did Wilson finally approve American and Allied military intervention in Russia, which resulted in the sending of some British troops to Armenia. Despite the consul's best efforts, the Armenians received only minimal help during the Great War.[26]

Caught in the midst of the many conflicts that overwhelmed their homelands during World War I, the Armenians sought to survive. By the end of May 1918, all efforts by the Caucasian peoples to work together against their common external enemies had ended in failure. The Germans and the Turks extended their dominance over much of formerly Russian Transcaucasia. In collaboration with these Central Powers, the Georgians and the Azerbaijanis established independent republics. The Armenians, left with no other alternative, also proclaimed their own separate republic in Russian Armenia on May 28. They did not, however, use the word "independence" to describe it. They kept open the possibility of federation with either a White or Soviet Russia, which might help protect them against the Turks.[27]

For the moment, the Wilson administration saw no way to give more assistance to the Armenians. It did not grant even de facto diplomatic recognition to the Armenian Republic. Nor did the United States declare war against Turkey, although the Allies had recommended this action.[28] Looking beyond the war, however, the president pledged to be more helpful to Armenia at the future peace conference. On July 4, 1918, he uttered this promise to Miran Sevasly, chairman of the Armenian National Union of America, who published it in an Armenian journal in Boston. Wilson later recounted that "I did express my own resolution to do all that I could to

[25] Lansing to Page, Apr. 3, 1918, *FRUS: Russia*, 2: 623–25.
[26] Lansing to Wilson, March 15, 1918, *PWW*, 47: 44–45. For the plight of Armenians in 1917–1918 and the inadequacies of American and Allied support, see Hovannisian, *Armenia on the Road to Independence*, 94–185.
[27] Hovannisian, *Armenia on the Road to Independence*, 157–215; Hovannisian, *Republic of Armenia*, 1: 1–38.
[28] Lansing to Wilson, May 20, 1918, *PPW*, 48: 79–80.

see that the hopes of the Armenians were satisfied and that no question of essential justice involved in the present European situation should be left unsettled in the general reckoning after the war."[29] The president wanted to help the Armenians, but eschewed more U.S. involvement at that time.

For both the United States and the Allies, Armenia in 1918 was an important interest, although not the highest priority. In response to a State Department inquiry, General Tasker H. Bliss, who represented the United States at the Allied Supreme War Council in Paris, summarized the American stakes in the Caucasus region, particularly in Armenia. He noted the traditional concern for "the moral and educational welfare of the Christians" in the Ottoman Empire. The Turkish massacres of Armenians since 1915 had made this humanitarian interest even more urgent for the United States. Bliss also emphasized the strategic importance of supporting Armenia in order to curb Germany's drive from Berlin to Baghdad. "After the Russian Revolution," he observed, "Germany improved her position first in European Russia, then in Transcaucasia." The Germans had helped the Turks recapture Turkish Armenia and also parts of Russian Armenia, which the Treaty of Brest-Litovsk granted to Turkey. Beyond these territorial gains, the German-Turkish alliance threatened to invade Persia.

General Bliss clearly understood that Consul Smith's efforts on behalf of the Transcaucasian nationalities had been designed to serve American and Allied strategic interests in the Great War, although the results might incidentally assist these peoples for their own sake. He explained that

Smith's aim, however, was not solely to help the Georgians and Armenians. He was anxious to warn the Allies of the danger in the Near East, and to induce them, in the interest of the Entente itself, to utilize these Christian peoples and their potential military force by properly leading and financing them in order to prevent the Central Powers from further improving their position in the Near East and in Asia.

When Acting Secretary of State Frank L. Polk forwarded the Bliss report to London, he instructed Ambassador Page to ask the British government for its assessment of the state of affairs in the Caucasus and the measures "to preserve the cooperation of the Armenians in the Allied cause."[30] U.S. officials thus viewed the Armenians more as an asset in winning the war than as a people worthy of support for their own sake.

---

[29] Wilson to Tumulty, c. July 19, 1918, *PWW* (Princeton, NJ, 1985), 49: 20.
[30] Polk to Page, July 31, 1918, *FRUS: World War*, 1: 891–93.

THE UNITED STATES AND ARMENIA AT THE PARIS
PEACE CONFERENCE OF 1919

Wilson continued to express sympathy for Armenians after the United States and the Allies finally defeated the Central Powers in the autumn of 1918, although Armenia lost its strategic value for the United States. Germany's drive for hegemony from Berlin to Baghdad had failed. Pope Benedict XV asked the president to help small and oppressed Christian nationalities, particularly the Armenians, at the peace conference. On the day before Christmas 1918, after arriving in Paris, Wilson assured the Catholic pope that "I am speaking not only for myself but also I am sure for the whole body of the American people when I say that the sufferings of no other people have appealed to them more deeply than those of the Armenians. It will certainly be one of my most cherished desires to play any part that I can in securing for that wronged and distressed people the protection of right and the complete deliverance from unjust subjection."[31] Whether Wilson and U.S. diplomats could achieve more for Armenia at the Paris Peace Conference than they had during the war would become the next challenge for Wilsonianism. Peacemaking in 1919 would again test the limits of American power and ideology.

While expressing a favorable attitude toward Armenia, Wilson avoided any specific commitments. Various advocates of the Armenian cause wanted the United States to take on a larger responsibility. Shortly before the president's departure for Europe, Lansing forwarded an appeal to him from some Americans with missionary interests in Turkey. They urged him to support the merger of Turkish Armenia and Russian Armenia into an independent new nation.[32] In London before the opening of the peace conference, evangelical church leaders, including Baptists and Methodists, told Wilson about both their support for the League of Nations and their concern for Armenian Christians. He gave them no promises, but did reveal his own anxiety about the immense task ahead. He affirmed the importance of religion for himself "in these times of perplexity with matters so large to settle that no man can feel that his mind can compass them." Professing his dependence on God, the president said: "I think one would go crazy if he did not believe in Providence. It

---

[31] Diary of Dr. Grayson, Dec. 18, 1918, Wilson to Benedict XV, Dec. 24, 1918, *PWW* (Princeton, NJ, 1986), 53: 420, 489.

[32] Lansing to Tumulty, Nov. 22, 1918, *PWW,* 53: 180.

would be a maze without a clue. Unless there were some supreme guidance we would despair of the results of human counsel."[33]

More down to earth, British prime minister David Lloyd George encouraged Wilson to accept a mandate for Armenia, and possibly for Constantinople, under the League of Nations, which they both hoped to create at the peace conference. Rather than depending on divine intercession, he thought U.S. troops might be more useful. This would obviously allow the British to shift the burden of assisting Armenians to the Americans. Wilson, however, was reluctant to entangle the United States in territorial questions in the old world, fearing that such intervention would tarnish America's reputation as a disinterested outsider.[34]

At the peace conference the British prime minister and the American president vied with each other to place the burden of assisting Armenia on someone else. Lloyd George wanted the victors to proceed with the assignment of future mandates under the League of Nations. The peacemakers anticipated the end of Turkish control in Armenia, Syria, Mesopotamia, Palestine, and Arabia. Although Lloyd George favored British mandates for vast areas of the former Ottoman Empire, he continued to look for a way to withdraw from Armenia. He did not want British troops to stay in Russian Armenia or move into Turkish Armenia. Wilson, noting that the United States had not declared war against the Ottoman Empire, thought the Allies should agree among themselves about which of them would keep troops in those parts of the former empire that the Turks should no longer control. He did not absolutely rule out an Armenian mandate for the United States, but wanted at least to postpone this question.[35]

Armenians looked to the peace conference from the outside. American and Allied leaders refused to seat Armenian delegates, in contrast to those from several other new nations. Neither of the two Armenian delegations, one headed by Avetis Aharonian representing the Armenian Republic and the other by Boghos Nubar representing Turkish Armenians, gained official recognition in Paris. Wilson explained to Nubar that the peace conference could not accept any delegation from Armenia because it had not yet joined the family of nations as a recognized state. He insisted, however, that "this will not mean the slightest neglect of the interests of Armenia."[36]

[33] Remarks to Free Church Leaders, Dec. 28, 1918, *PWW*, 53: 530.
[34] Memorandum [Dec. 30, 1918], *PWW*, 53: 561–62.
[35] Meetings of Council of Ten, Jan. 28 and 30, 1919, *PWW*, 53: 329–30, 369–71.
[36] Wilson to Nubar, Jan. 23, 1919, *PWW*, 53: 226.

Wilson quickly learned what Armenians wanted from the peace con-ference. Reminding him of their status as Christian martyrs who had suffered greatly from Turkish misrule, Nubar requested liberation for all the Armenian provinces of the former Ottoman Empire. He defined this territory generously to include a vast area from Mount Ararat to the Mediterranean, including historically Armenian Cilicia on the coast. He advocated union between these liberated areas of Turkish Armenia and the Armenian Republic to create a new nation. Before it became a fully independent democracy, he wanted the League of Nations to give a tem-porary mandate for the new Armenian state to one of the great powers. Appealing to Wilson, Nubar told him that "the great American democ-racy, by granting her assistance to our new State, can of all Nations, by her disinterestedness, give confidence to the Armenians about the future of their Motherland. That would be an act worthy of the great American people who joined this War for the sake of their ideals."[37] Aharonian and Nubar later presented their joint requests on behalf of Armenia to the peace conference.[38]

During the drafting of the League of Nations Covenant early in 1919, Wilson began to give more serious consideration to accepting greater U.S. responsibility for Armenia. He asked Secretary of War Newton D. Baker about the legality and wisdom of sending American troops to Constantinople and Armenia. Noting the U.S. interest in Robert College in Constantinople and "the pitiful fortunes of the Armenians," the pres-ident expected the American people to approve the sending of a small force, which presumably would be welcomed in the occupied areas.[39] Baker discouraged this idea. As an alternative, he suggested that the United States might relieve Great Britain of some of its duties on the western front so that British troops could go to Turkey. If Wilson decided to send U.S. troops, however, Baker wanted to restrict their mission to Turkey and Armenia, where they might protect Christians, a mission that American public opinion would most likely approve. Revealing his ignorance about the harsh conditions in those countries, especially in the mountains of Armenia, the secretary added that "they would have a pleasanter climate than is possible in the winter and spring months in France."[40]

---

[37] Nubar to Wilson, Jan. 29 and Feb. 6, 1919, *PWW*, 53: 346, 516–18.
[38] Council of Ten Minutes, Feb. 26, 1919, *FRUS: The Paris Peace Conference, 1919* (Washington, DC, 1943), 4: 147–57.
[39] Wilson to Baker, Feb. 8, 1919, *PWW* (Princeton, NJ, 1986), 55: 27–28.
[40] Baker to Wilson, Feb. 11, 1919, *PWW*, 55: 81–82.

Both Republicans and Democrats in the United States urged Wilson to support Armenia in Paris. On behalf of the American Committee for the Independence of Armenia, James Gerard and Senators Henry Cabot Lodge and John Sharp Williams sent him a resolution adopted at a New York meeting after hearing Charles Evans Hughes and William Jennings Bryan voice their concerns for the welfare of Armenia. The resolution called for "a separate and independent state" encompassing not only Russian Armenia and all of Turkish Armenia, including Cilicia, but also Persian Armenia. The resolution did not, however, indicate what means beyond diplomacy the United States should employ on Armenia's behalf. Aware of the potential costs and the difficulties involved, Wilson hesitated to make any specific American commitment to Armenia in Paris.[41]

After returning home in late February 1919, Wilson increased his rhetorical support for Armenia. Upon his arrival in Boston, he advocated the League of Nations Covenant, which he and Allied leaders had just finished drafting in Paris. He defended this new plan for collective security to preserve world peace. Alluding to Armenians, the president told his audience: "You poured out your money to help succor Armenians after they suffered. Now set up your strength so that they shall never suffer again." The League of Nations, he announced, should protect new nations such as Armenia. "Arrangements of the present peace cannot stand a generation unless they are guaranteed by the united forces of the civilized world."[42] Wilson repeated this view at a White House meeting with the Senate and House committees responsible for dealing with foreign relations.[43] Thus he used the Armenian cause to win approval for the League. He was also signaling his inclination to make a greater U.S. commitment to postwar Armenia.

In even more explicit terms Wilson shared his emerging views about American involvement in the former Ottoman Empire at a meeting with the Democratic National Committee. He noted that the German, Austro-Hungarian, and Turkish empires had disintegrated at the end of the war. Because not all peoples in the German colonies or in the Habsburg and Ottoman empires were ready for self-rule, he expected the League of Nations to become the "trustee for these great areas of dismembered empires." The president now believed that the United States

---

[41] Gerard, Lodge and Williams to Wilson [c. Feb. 10, 1919], Dodge to Wilson, Feb. 25, 1919, Gerard to Wilson [March 5, 1919], *PWW*, 55: 65–66, 265, 446.

[42] Address in Boston, Feb. 24, 1919, *PWW*, 55: 238–45.

[43] News Report [Feb. 26, 1919], *PWW*, 55: 268–76.

should accept its share of responsibility as a mandatory for Armenia and possibly Constantinople. "The whole heart of America has been engaged for Armenia," he observed. Referring to fellow Americans, he stated that "they know more about Armenia and its sufferings than they know about any other European area; we have colleges out there; we have great missionary enterprises, just as we have had Robert College in Constantinople. That is a part of the world where already American influence extends – a saving influence and an educating and an uplifting influence." Given this historic American interest, Wilson concluded that "I am not without hope that the people of the United States would find it acceptable to go in and be the trustees of the interests of the Armenian people and see to it that the unspeakable Turk and the almost equally difficult Kurd had their necks sat on long enough to teach them manners and give the industrious and earnest people of Armenia time to develop a country which is naturally rich with possibilities."[44]

After returning to the peace conference in Paris, Wilson faced the question of mandates for Armenia and other parts of the former Ottoman Empire. Bryan, identifying himself as a member of the American Committee for the Independence of Armenia, appealed to the president to fight for justice for the Christian Armenians. Bryan thought that Armenia should encompass Cilicia, which would give the new state access to the Mediterranean. Wilson agreed, immediately responding that "my interest in Armenia is identical with your own."[45] This kind of affirmation increased the expectations that the United States would substantially assist the new nation. So, too, did House's statement to French premier Georges Clemenceau and British prime minister Lloyd George while sitting in for the president at the peace conference. Shortly before Wilson's return, House had affirmed his belief that the United States would accept mandates for Armenia and Constantinople.[46]

Wilson and Allied leaders agreed that much of the former Ottoman Empire should be severed from Turkey and placed under mandates, but found it more difficult to divide those areas among themselves. He told the Allies that he would attempt to get the American people to accept mandates for Armenia and Constantinople. But before proceeding with the division of territory and assignment of mandates, he wanted to send an inter-allied commission to the Near East "to find the most scientific

[44] Remarks to Democratic Committee, Feb. 28, 1919, *PWW*, 55: 309–24.
[45] Bryan to Wilson, March 19, 1919, Wilson to Bryan, March 19, 1919, *PWW* (Princeton, NJ, 1987), 56: 95–96.
[46] House to Wilson [March 7, 1919], *PWW*, 55: 458–59.

basis possible for a settlement." Neither the British nor the French wanted this commission. They welcomed the prospect that the United States might become the mandatory for Armenia, and perhaps for other areas of Turkey, but did not want to jeopardize their own claims in the former Ottoman Empire.[47]

Clemenceau, seeking to preserve cooperation among the three great powers against postwar Germany, showed his willingness to make concessions on the Armenian mandate and other issues. On April 14, he informed House that France would accept the compromise regarding the Rhineland occupation and the Anglo-American guarantee of French security. The peacemakers had negotiated this deal over the past month since Wilson had returned to Paris. In the same conversation Clemenceau also told House that if the United States became the mandatory for Armenia, France would give up its claim to Cilicia, allowing it to be included in the Armenian mandate. Clemenceau offered this concession to the United States, although earlier Anglo-French agreements, which had provided for British and French spheres of influence in the Ottoman Empire, had promised Cilicia to France as part of Syria in exchange for British dominance in Mesopotamia, Palestine, and Arabia.[48] His top priority was to involve the United States in maintaining the peace settlement, whether in Europe as the guarantor of French security against Germany or in the Near East as the mandatory for Armenia.

Negotiations in Paris delayed assistance for Armenia either from the United States or the Allies. In May 1919, while the peacemakers discussed sending an inter-allied commission to the Near East, they postponed the establishment of mandates. Lloyd George urged Wilson meanwhile to send U.S. troops into Turkish Armenia and Constantinople. The president declined, observing that "the British troops were the only ones accustomed to this kind of business, although the French had some experience. United States officers would be quite unaccustomed to it." He doubted whether any American troops were available for the assignment.[49] Even as he was anticipating U.S. acceptance of the Armenian mandate, Wilson did not plan for costly involvement in the Near East either now or in the

[47] Diary of Dr. Grayson, March 20, 1919, Meeting of Council of Four, March 20, 1919, Diary of Vance McCormick, March 22, 1919, Memorandum of Arthur James Balfour, March 23, 1919, Memorandum, March 25, 1919, *PWW*, 56: 102–03, 116–18, 180, 203–04, 272–75.

[48] Diary of Colonel House, Apr. 14, 1919, *PWW* (Princeton, NJ, 1987), 57: 334–35.

[49] Meeting of Council of Four, May 5, 1919, *PWW* (Princeton, NJ, 1987), 58: 436–38.

future. His reluctance to send a military force to Armenia revealed the limits of American power and ideology in the peacemaking.

Despite his own reservations, Wilson expected the U.S. Senate to approve and the Turks to acquiesce in the eventual role that the United States might play in the former Ottoman Empire. He assured Clemenceau that the Senate would accept new responsibility for the United States as the mandatory for Armenia. He also thought the Turks would submit to guidance even in Turkey itself. He expressed the opinion that the Turks were "really docile people. They were all right so long as they were not put in authority. Under the guidance of a friendly power, they might prove a docile people." Clemenceau tried to warn him to anticipate a difficult task in Armenia. The president acknowledged that reports from Armenia were so appalling that he found it hard to read them. "At this very moment," he said, "the Turks are interning a great number of Armenians, many of whom are dying of hunger. I have been given some horrible details." Lloyd George urged him to publish these reports to shape American public opinion in favor of accepting the Armenian mandate. Despite Wilson's attempts to reassure them, Allied leaders obviously doubted whether the United States would undertake this potentially costly mandate, or even whether Wilson understood postwar realities in Armenia.[50]

While refusing to send U.S. troops to Armenia and postponing a decision on the establishment of mandates, the president attempted to assure the Armenians of his good intentions. "In common with all thoughtful and humane persons," he wrote to Avetis Aharonian on May 13,

I have learned of the sufferings of the Armenian people with the most poignant distress, and beg to assure you that if any practicable means of assisting them in their distress presented themselves at the moment, I for one would rejoice to make use of them. It adds to the tragical distress of the whole situation that for the present there seems to be no way which is not already being as far as possible followed in which to relieve the suffering which is exciting the sympathy of the whole world. I can only hope that as the processes of peace are hastened and a settlement is arrived at which can be insisted upon, that an opportunity may then promptly arise for taking effective steps to better the conditions and eventually assure the security of the people of Armenia.[51]

Wilson apparently hoped to convince the head of the Armenian Republic's delegation in Paris that he genuinely cared for the Armenian people, but

---

[50] Meeting of Council of Four, May 13, 1919, *PWW* (Princeton, NJ, 1988), 59: 87–103; Paul Mantoux, *The Deliberations of the Council of Four (March 24-June 28, 1919)*, ed. Arthur S. Link with Manfred F. Boemeke (Princeton, NJ, 1992), 2: 49–60.

[51] Wilson to Aharonian, May 13, 1919, *PWW*, 59: 103–04.

that there were no "practicable means" to give them any assistance now. At most he held out a vague hope for the future after reaching a peace settlement. Unless the president was being totally disingenuous in his assessment, he was recognizing the inability of the United States to fulfill the Wilsonian promise. By acknowledging these limits of American power in Armenia, he also revealed the irrelevance of Wilsonianism in that country. Wilson could find no way to transform his principles into reality for that new nation during the peace conference. In this instance his ideology was inadequate for the new world order that was emerging after the Great War. Wilsonianism was not a universal solution for the world's problems.

As the American and Allied leaders considered the disposition of the former Ottoman Empire, Wilson made a qualified commitment to Armenia. On May 14, 1919, at a meeting of the Council of Four, he agreed to accept League of Nations mandates for Armenia and Constantinople, subject to approval by the Senate. He also joined with Lloyd George and Clemenceau in a tentative agreement giving the Smyrna region of Asia Minor to Greece and placing the remainder of Turkish Anatolia under mandates assigned to Italy and France. The boundaries were not yet drawn for any of these mandates. Pending that division of territory, Lloyd George and Clemenceau agreed to determine the respective British and French spheres of military occupation in the former Ottoman Empire. They assigned this task to two subordinates, Sir Henry Wilson and Andre Tardieu.[52]

Within a week, even these provisional understandings among the peacemakers collapsed. Anglo-French tensions erupted in the Council of Four on May 21. Lloyd George now proposed that the mandate for Turkish Anatolia should go to the United States, not to Italy and France. Arguing that postwar Turkey should not be divided among several great powers, he proposed that the mandate for all of Turkey, including Constantinople, be given to the United States, as well as the one for Armenia. This British attempt to use the United States as a wedge to reduce French influence in the Near East evoked a strong response from Clemenceau. Wilson, too, rejected the idea. Although he agreed with Lloyd George that it would be best to place Turkey under a single mandate, the president did not want it. "I must say without further delay," he asserted, "that it will be very

---

[52] Council of Four Minutes, May 14, 1919, *FRUS: The Paris Peace Conference, 1919* (Washington, DC, 1944), 5: 614–23; Hankey's and Mantoux's Notes, May 14, 1919, *PWW*, 59: 136–47; Mantoux, *Deliberations*, 2: 60–73.

difficult for the United States to assume the mission which you propose
to it. It has no direct interests in Anatolia; it has not invested capital there.
We could only accept the role that you offer us as a burden and against
bitter opposition from American opinion. We desire absolutely nothing
in Asia Minor. We desire only two things: agreement among the great
powers and the peace of the world."[53]

Wilson eschewed additional involvement in the Near East. Apparently
more aware of the potential costs of trying to control the "docile" Turks,
he preferred not to place Turkey under a mandate than to accept this
responsibility for the United States. Yet he reaffirmed his commitment to
the Armenian mandate, which he regarded as a humanitarian mission.
"Americans," he explained, "have already sent missionaries, money, and
relief societies to Armenia. American opinion is interested in Armenia."
While Congress might approve the Armenian mandate, he doubted
that it would approve one for Turkish Anatolia. Henry White, the only
Republican in the American Commission to Negotiate Peace in Paris,
afterward reinforced this point, warning him that Congress would probably reject a mandate for Turkey, and perhaps even for Constantinople.[54]

Lloyd George's willingness to sacrifice French interests, contrary to
his own previous commitments, prevented any agreement at this time.
Clemenceau felt betrayed not only over mandates for Turkey but also over
spheres for British and French military occupation. The Tardieu-Wilson
negotiations had failed to resolve this issue. Tardieu had attempted to get
the British troops to withdraw from Syria, so that French troops could
replace them, but Henry Wilson had endeavored first to alter the earlier
Anglo-French division of the Ottoman Empire. The British wanted to
reduce the French area of Syria and to enlarge their own mandate for
Mesopotamia and Palestine. Tardieu refused to negotiate boundaries,
which he regarded as the prerogative of the peace conference. An angry
Clemenceau brought this issue back to the Council of Four. "My constant
policy," he said, "has been to preserve the union of France with Great
Britain and with America. In order to do that I have made greater concessions than I first would have thought possible." But the French premier
resisted any more compromises with Lloyd George. President Wilson
sought to deal with this territorial dispute by relegating it to the inter-
allied commission that he had earlier proposed. Under the circumstances,

---

[53] Mantoux's Notes, May 21, 1919, *PWW*, 59: 345; Mantoux, *Deliberations*, 2: 137.
[54] Mantoux's Notes, May 21, 1919, White to Wilson, May 22, 1919, *PWW*, 59: 345, 395–
96; Mantoux, *Deliberations*, 2: 137.

Clemenceau refused to appoint French representatives to the commission. Lloyd George also declined. The president nevertheless decided to send American representatives, Henry C. King and Charles R. Crane, on their own to the Near East. Wilson's decision to proceed with the King-Crane commission, along with the Anglo-French impasse, again postponed peacemaking for the former Ottoman Empire, and consequently for Armenia.[55]

Shortly before Wilson left Paris, he and Allied leaders briefly discussed the future peace treaty for Turkey and the fate of Armenia. In the Council of Four on June 25, he told them that the remaining U.S. delegates could deal with these questions. He had given his views to Lansing, House, Bliss, and White. The president wanted to sever from Turkey the parts of the Ottoman Empire that would be placed under League of Nations mandates, while leaving the Turks their sovereignty in Anatolia. The treaty could require Turkey to surrender all other areas of the former Ottoman Empire. He expected Armenia, which should include part of Cilicia, to become a separate state. Having not yet recognized the Armenian Republic, Wilson remained noncommittal on the question of whether Russian Armenia should join Turkish Armenia in a single new nation. Nor did he know where the boundaries should be drawn between Armenia and Turkey. Despite Wilson's expressed desire to avoid long delay, all these unresolved issues would postpone the peace treaty for Turkey.[56]

As the United States and the Allies failed to resolve their own differences regarding the former Ottoman Empire, the future of Armenia remained problematic. Just before returning home from Paris, Wilson told newspaper correspondents that he personally favored American mandatories for Armenia and Constantinople. But he emphasized that Congress must decide whether to accept these new responsibilities. He explained that he had promised only to present this decision to the American people and Congress.[57]

[55] Meeting of Council of Four, May 21, 1919, Diary of Edith Benham, May 21, 1919, Diary of Dr. Grayson, May 22, 1919, Diary of William Linn Westermann, May 22, 1919, *PWW*, 59: 326–46, 369–72, 374–76; Council of Four Minutes, May 21 and 22, 1919, *FRUS: Paris Peace Conference*, 5: 756–71, 807–12; Mantoux, *Deliberations*, 2: 128–40.

[56] Close to Lansing, June 24, 1919, Meeting of Council of Four, June 25, 1919, *PWW* (Princeton, NJ, 1989), 61: 127–29, 156–57; Council of Four Minutes, June 25, 1919, *FRUS: The Paris Peace Conference, 1919* (Washington, DC, 1946), 6: 675–77; Mantoux, *Deliberations*, 2: 552–54.

[57] Diary of Dr. Grayson, June 27, 1919, Notes of Walter Weyl, June 27, 1919, Report by Charles Thompson, June 27, 1919, Diary of Ray Stannard Baker, June 27, 1919, *PWW*, 61: 238, 240, 246, 253.

WILSON, THE LEAGUE OF NATIONS,
AND AN ARMENIAN MANDATE

After arriving in the United States, Wilson revealed his own decision to postpone the Armenian mandate. On July 10, 1919, the day he presented the Versailles Treaty to the Senate, he held a press conference. One reporter asked him: "Do you expect to ask that the United States act as mandatory for Armenia?" The president answered: "Let us not go too fast. Let's get the treaty first."[58] Until the Senate approved the Versailles Treaty, including the League of Nations Covenant, he did not intend to proceed with the Armenian mandate. Thus he made acceptance of this mandate conditional upon the outcome of the treaty fight. Meanwhile, Armenians could expect little assistance from the United States.

Wilson's decision to postpone consideration of the Armenian mandate, making it dependent on the Senate's approval of the League of Nations, created a potential political problem for him. Oddly enough, he was not certain whether he could restrain the public demands for immediate U.S. assistance to Armenia. Gerard and others in the American Committee for the Independence of Armenia urged him to take quick action to stop Turkish aggression against Armenia. Wilson assured Senator John Sharp Williams, a Mississippi Democrat who had joined Gerard in expressing his concern, that he would transmit their request to the peace conference. However, the president sent a very different message to Paris. Confessing his anxiety, Wilson told Lansing: "I fear that it would be most unwise to put before Congress just at this stage of its discussion of the Covenant either a proposal to promise to assume the Mandate for Armenia or a proposal to send American troops there to replace the British and assume the temporary protection of the population; and yet will our own public opinion tolerate our doing, at least our attempting, nothing?"[59] Despite pressures to act quickly, Wilson rejected U.S. military intervention to protect the Armenians from the Turks at this time. Pending ratification of the Versailles Treaty, he left them to their own fate.

As Wilson considered what to do about Armenia, he adopted an increasingly negative view of international politics. His pessimism reflected his sensitivity to the limits of power and ideology. It was easier to proclaim principles than to implement them. While advocating American membership in the League of Nations in the future, Wilson privately expressed his

[58] Report of a Press Conference, July 10, 1919, *PWW*, 61: 424.
[59] Wilson to Williams, Aug. 2, 1919, Wilson to Lansing, Aug. 4, 1919, *PWW* (Princeton, NJ, 1990), 62: 116, 149.

growing doubts about involving the United States in any arrangement for collective security in the old world. His reluctance to help Armenia was part of his larger reconsideration of American foreign relations. He questioned whether the United States should ever risk entanglement abroad either through the League of Nations or the French security treaty. He liked the idea of collective security better than the practice.

Wilson expressed his new doubts about American involvement in international politics with reference to the formation of League of Nations mandates. House, who represented the United States in London on the Commission on Mandates, reported to him and Lansing that the French had refused to proceed with the establishment of mandates. Although aimed at the British because of the Anglo-French impasse over the division of the former Ottoman Empire into mandates, Wilson reacted negatively against what he perceived to be a French attack on the League itself and on the new world order that it symbolized. Rather than blaming the British, he condemned the French and other Europeans who were apparently resorting to traditional diplomacy. "I will tolerate no such suggestion as this message conveys," Wilson informed Lansing with reference to House's telegram. "I will withdraw the French treaty rather than consent to see the Turkish Empire divided as spoils!" He threatened, moreover, to jettison the Versailles Treaty unless Clemenceau changed his position. "I shall not press the treaty with Germany upon the Senate if this is to be the course pursued about the other treaties. The United States will certainly not enter the League of Nations to guarantee any such settlements, or any such intolerable bargains as the Greeks and Italians seem to be attempting."[60]

Wilson vented his anger primarily against France over the breakdown in the peacemaking, but other nations such as Armenia would also suffer as a consequence. Frustrated by the limits of American power and ideology, he gyrated between the extremes of advocating the principles of Wilsonianism and withdrawing the United States from the old world. He sought either to control or to abandon international politics. Wilson did not like the compromises or the costs inherent in relations among nations. He ordered Lansing to instruct Frank L. Polk, who now headed the U.S. delegation in Paris, to threaten Clemenceau with American rejection of the entire peace settlement unless he agreed to proceed with the creation of mandates. The president also informed House of this

[60] House to Wilson and Lansing, Aug. 6, 1919, Wilson to Lansing, Aug. 8, 1919, *PWW*, 62: 187–89, 235.

important decision. When Polk raised the issue in Paris, the French premier immediately offered to comply with Wilson's request to continue with the consideration of mandates, carefully explaining that his previous action had been directed at the British, not the Americans.[61] This resolved the immediate crisis, but not the underlying problems of sorting out the competing interests in the Near East.

While Wilson was attempting to win votes in the Senate for the Versailles Treaty, which embodied his principles for the new world order, he told Lansing that he was not at all certain he wanted the United States to be involved. Wilsonianism in theory and in practice were two altogether different things. In view of the continuing conflicts in Europe and the Near East, the president vehemently denounced the old world in a statement to the secretary of state on August 20, 1919. "When I see such conduct as this," he asserted, "when I learn of the secret treaty of Great Britain with Persia, when I find Italy and Greece arranging between themselves as to the division of western Asia Minor, and when I think of the greed and utter selfishness of it all, I am almost inclined to refuse to permit this country to be a member of the League of Nations when it is composed of such intriguers and robbers. I am disposed to throw up the whole business and get out." Lansing noted that the president expressed these words with "considerable heat" and that "he never before spoke so emphatically."[62] Wilson was obviously frustrated by the ongoing practice of traditional politics. Experiencing the limits of American power and ideology to create a new world order, he now sensed failure. If Wilsonianism could not transform international relations, as he had promised, he seriously considered escaping from the ordeal of peacemaking.

Wilson's route of escape led him increasingly to emphasize ideals over reality. He reiterated his concern for Armenia, but rejected any type of costly U.S. involvement in the country. The British were preparing to withdraw their troops from Transcaucasia, starting in mid-August 1919, making the question of American help a matter of urgency. He knew that the only effective way to protect the Armenians was to send U.S. troop to the region, even before formally accepting the mandate. Yet he refused to consider that option. "In the present situation of things out there," Wilson explained to Senator Williams, "it does look as if the only effectual assistance would be the assistance of an armed force to subdue those

[61] Wilson to Lansing, Aug. 8, 1919, Lansing to Polk, Aug. 9, 1919, Wilson to Lansing and House, Aug. 11, 1919, Polk to Wilson and Lansing, Aug. 11, 1919, *PWW*, 62: 235, 242, 256–58.

[62] Memorandum by Robert Lansing, Aug. 20, 1919, *PWW*, 62: 428–29.

who are committing outrages more terrible, I believe, than history ever before witnessed, so heartbreaking indeed that I have found it impossible to hold my spirits steady enough to read the accounts of them. I wish with all my heart that Congress and the country could assent to our assuming the trusteeship for Armenia and going to the help of those suffering people in an effective way."[63] The president expressed his hope that Congress might approve a significant U.S. role in Armenia, but he had not recommended any such action. Nor was he intending to do so now. He held to his earlier decision to postpone the Armenian mandate until after the Senate approved the Versailles Treaty, which he knew was problematic.[64] Pending that unlikely outcome, he refused to consider dispatching U.S. troops to Armenia.

Wilson sought to shift responsibility for inaction to the Congress and the British, knowing that new Armenian massacres might follow the withdrawal of British troops. "It is manifestly impossible for us," he told his old friend Cleveland Dodge, a prominent member of the American Committee for the Independence of Armenia, "at any rate in the present temper of Congress, to send American troops there, much as I should like to do so, and I am making every effort, both at London and at Paris, to induce the British to change their military plans in that quarter, but I must say the outlook is not hopeful, and we are at our wits' ends what to do."[65] This misleading statement vastly overstated the minimal efforts that Wilson and Lansing were actually making to keep British troops in Transcaucasia where they might help protect Armenians pending the establishment of an American mandatory for Armenia. They did not want even to pay the British to stay temporarily, much less to take on any direct U.S. military role. The secretary, moreover, privately encouraged the president never to accept the Armenian mandate, suggesting the possibility of attaching it to some other profitable mandate in the region.[66] They were obviously more concerned about shifting the responsibility for protecting Armenia to the Allies, and blaming Congress for inaction, than with actually helping the Armenians.

Going through the motions of appearing to advocate immediate action to protect the Armenians, Wilson continued to postpone any U.S. involvement that might exact a price. When the King-Crane

---

[63] Wilson to Williams, Aug. 12, 1919, *PWW*, 62: 259–60.
[64] For the struggle over the League of Nations, see Lloyd E. Ambrosius, *Woodrow Wilson and the American Diplomatic Tradition: The Treaty Fight in Perspective* (Cambridge, 1987).
[65] Wilson to Dodge, Aug. 14, 1919, *PWW*, 62: 285–86.
[66] Desk Diary of Robert Lansing, Aug. 21, 1919, *PWW*, 62: 453–54.

commission completed its trip through the Near East and submitted its report in late August, he did not use its recommendations as the occasion for any diplomatic initiative. While in Paris, he had postponed peacemaking for the former Ottoman Empire to await the return of the King-Crane commission, but did not now attach any urgency to its report.[67]

Wilson did encourage Senator Williams to seek authorization from Congress for U.S. troops to be sent to Armenia, but this was a charade. The president instructed Assistant Secretary of State William Phillips to contact the senator about passage of such a resolution, but refrained from a formal request to Congress. Despite Wilson's informal intervention, Williams deleted from his draft resolution the provision approving the use of U.S. armed forces in Armenia. He did so, the senator explained, because the Senate Foreign Relations Committee was reluctant to authorize this deployment, especially since the French seemed ready to send their own troops to Armenia. In fact, the French were not preparing to dispatch their troops to Russian Armenia, from which the British were evacuating. On September 23, Wilson expressed his disappointment to Phillips that "Senator Williams has concluded to omit the authorization for sending troops to Armenia. I believe that it is of the immediate humane necessity to take energetic action and that the very existence of the Armenian people depends upon it. I would greatly appreciate his urgent assistance in this matter."[68] This request was exceedingly disingenuous within the context of Wilson's earlier decision not to deploy U.S. troops to Armenia until the Senate had approved both the Versailles Treaty and the Armenia mandate, and of his public statements, including his speech on that very day.

On his western tour, Wilson pointed to Armenia as a prime example of the reason for the League of Nations. He endeavored to exploit pro-Armenian sympathy to secure the Senate's approval of the Versailles Treaty. On September 6, he explained what the peacemakers in Paris had attempted to accomplish. "We wanted to see that helpless peoples were nowhere in the world put at the mercy of unscrupulous enemies and masters," the president said. "There is one pitiful example which is in the hearts of all of us. I mean the example of Armenia. There was a Christian

[67] Crane to Wilson, Aug. 31, 1919, *PWW*, 62: 607–09; Report by Crane and King, Aug. 28, 1919, *FRUS: The Paris Peace Conference, 1919* (Washington, DC, 1947), 12: 751–863. See also Richard G. Hovannisian, *The Republic of Armenia: From Versailles to London, 1919–1920* (Berkeley, CA, 1982), 2: 322–34.
[68] Wilson to Phillips, Sept. 16 and 23, 1919, Phillips to Wilson, Sept. 20 and 23, 1919, *PWW* (Princeton, NJ, 1990), 63: 304–05, 423, 464.

people, helpless, at the mercy of a Turkish government which thought it the service of God to destroy them. And at this moment, my fellow citizens, it is an open question whether the Armenian people will not, while we sit here and debate, be absolutely destroyed.... When shall we wake up to the moral responsibility of this great occasion?" While sounding this note of urgency, Wilson qualified his own commitment to Armenia. He reiterated that "these unspeakable things [in Armenia] ... cannot be handled until the debate is over" and the United States had ratified the peace treaty.[69] At best, this would postpone any U.S. action to defend the Armenians to the distant future.

During his western tour, Wilson elaborated the principle of collective security, emphasizing his expectation that U.S. involvement in the League of Nations would not be costly. In Salt Lake City on September 23, he emphatically rejected reservations to the Versailles Treaty, and particularly one that would qualify the mutual obligation of League members under Article 10 of the Covenant to defend each other against external aggression. Wilson's uncompromising stance against reservations would actually guarantee the treaty's eventual defeat in the Senate. Even if that had not been the outcome of the treaty fight, he emphasized that the United States would not be obliged by Article 10 or any other provision in the Covenant to defend other nations in the old world. "If you want to put out a fire in Utah," the president assured his audience, "you don't send to Oklahoma for the fire engine. If you want to put out a fire in the Balkans, if you want to stamp out the smoldering flames in some part of Central Europe, you don't send to the United States for troops. The Council of the League selects the powers which are most ready, most available, most suitable, and selects them at their own consent, so that the United States would in no such circumstance conceivable be drawn in unless the flames spread to the world." Wilson closed his Salt Lake City address, moreover, with the assurance that the United States could participate in the League of Nations to liberate foreign nations from the dangers of external aggression without the costs of bloodshed. "Are you willing to go into the great adventure of liberating hundreds of millions of human beings from a threat of foreign power?" he asked. "If you are timid, I can assure you [that] you can do it without a drop of human blood. If you are squeamish about fighting, I will tell you that you won't have to fight." Wilson's public statements, which expressed at once his own growing reluctance to involve the United States in the old world and

[69] Address in Kansas City, Sept. 6, 1919, *PWW*, 63: 71; Wilson, *PPWW*, 6: 7–8.

184   *Woodrow Wilson and American Internationalism*

his global promise of collective security without sacrifice, clearly belied his private message to Williams on this same day. Although the president publicly described the plight of Armenians as an example of the importance of ratifying the peace treaty and joining the League, his Salt Lake City address called into question the sincerity of his meager private efforts to encourage Congress to initiate a resolution authorizing the use of U.S. troops in Armenia.[70] For Wilson by now, the ideal of collective security was better than the reality.

WILSON AND THE POLITICS OF ESCAPE

No longer engaged in serious peacemaking, Wilson was practicing the politics of escape. Still championing the League in theory, he avoided immediate or costly U.S. military involvement in the Near East. Even before his major stroke a few days later, he had already sacrificed any real possibility of assisting Armenia. He did not act on his own presidential authority. Nor did he attempt to reach bipartisan agreement with Republicans that might have enabled the United States to help the Armenians. Except for France, Armenia offered better prospects for bipartisan consensus than any other nation. Several Republican leaders, including Senator Lodge, had shown genuine interest in guaranteeing French security against German aggression. They also favored Armenia. Wilson, however, had steadfastly refused to seek agreement with them on behalf of either nation, subordinating specific U.S. commitments to France or Armenia to his ideal League. Until the Republican-controlled Senate accepted the Versailles Treaty exactly as he had negotiated it, he delayed consideration of both the French security treaty and the Armenian mandate. He postponed and thereby destroyed any real prospect for U.S. action to defend either France or Armenia. He liked the idea of global collective security better than the practice.

Wilsonianism offered the universal promise of a new world order, but the president could not deliver it to Armenia. On November 19, 1919, the Senate rejected the Versailles Treaty, thereby keeping the United States from joining the League of Nations. Anticipating that outcome, Lansing understood that an American mandatory for Armenia was also dead. "As for assuming a mandate over anything or anybody," he informed Polk, "the present state of the public mind makes the idea almost out of the question."[71] The time for effective U.S. action had long since passed.

---

[70] Address in Salt Lake City, Sept. 23, 1919, *PWW*, 63: 449–63; Wilson, *PPWW*, 6: 346–65.
[71] Lansing to Polk, Nov. 17, 1919, *PWW* (Princeton, NJ, 1991), 64: 54–57.

Wilson's failure to win the Senate's approval for the Versailles Treaty, along with his poor health following his major stroke in early October, removed the United States from active participation in the peacemaking. The Allies proceeded on their own with the peace treaty for Turkey. At conferences in London and San Remo from February through April 1920, Allied premiers and foreign ministers negotiated the conditions of peace for the former Ottoman Empire. Meanwhile, Turkish Nationalists under Mustafa Kemal created a counter-government in Ankara, asserting their dominance in Anatolia and challenging the established Turkish government, the neighboring countries, and the Allies. This resurgence of Turkish nationalism threatened the Armenians, who now experienced more massacres, and demonstrated that the Allies could not easily impose their terms on Turkey. In this context, British prime minister Lloyd George and French premier Alexandre Millerand, who had replaced Clemenceau, sought to reduce their nations' obligations toward Armenia. They did not want the Armenian mandate. Nor did they want to extend the border of Turkish Armenia so far into Anatolia that the Turks would never accept it, thereby jeopardizing the new Armenian state's very existence from the outset. If the Allies could induce the United States to accept the Armenian mandate and guarantee the new Armenian-Turkish boundary, this would be the ideal solution for them as well as the Armenians.[72]

Wilson monitored the peacemaking from the sidelines, occasionally injecting himself into the process. Acting Secretary of State Frank L. Polk, who had recently returned from Paris, informed him about the London conference. He noted that U.S. experts agreed with the Europeans that Armenia should receive less territory than its delegates had previously claimed. None of them wanted to include Cilicia in the new nation. Even within more restricted boundaries, Armenia could not protect itself from the Tartars, Kurds, and Turks. "The various races are so mixed up in North Eastern Asia Minor," Polk observed, "that it was the unanimous opinion of the experts that without an international police there would be no peace in that part of the world." If the United States were to accept the Armenian mandate, this would require a large military force. "It is obvious that the British and French cannot and will not supply the troops necessary to maintain order, and I fear there is no hope of our people feeling this obligation so strongly as to compel Congress to consent to a mandate,

---

[72] Richard G. Hovannisian, *The Republic of Armenia: From London to Sevres, February–August, 1920* (Berkeley, CA, 1996), 3: 20–112.

and appropriate the necessary money."[73] In other words, given the problems and the costs, Polk acknowledged the difficulty of fulfilling the Wilsonian promise of collective security and national self-determination for Armenia.

In March 1920, notwithstanding the complications, Wilson reaffirmed his belief that the United States should accept the Armenian mandate. He authorized Polk to convey this message to Paris. The president did not want either Great Britain or France to become the mandatory for Armenia, or France to hold Cilicia. Instead, he asserted, "it is our clear duty to assume that mandate and I want to be left as free as possible to urge such an assumption of responsibility at the opportune time." He was not actually planning to make this request to Congress at this time, but wanted to keep open the possibility in the future.[74]

Wilson's apparent openness to accepting the Armenian mandate gave the Allies a way to resolve their difficulties at San Remo. In late April, seeking to shift the burden for protecting Armenia from themselves, they formally requested the United States to accept the Armenian mandate. The Allies also wanted Wilson to arbitrate the western boundaries of Armenia with Turkey. In effect, the president could determine the extent of territory that he wanted the United States to protect as the mandatory for Armenia. A month later Wilson finally took action on these requests. Secretary of State Bainbridge Colby, who had replaced Lansing, advised Wilson to ask Congress to approve the Armenian mandate. He noted that the Russian Bolsheviks and the Turkish Nationalists were cooperating together against the Armenians. "At the present time," Colby stressed, "when the Allied Powers admit their inability to render any assistance and solemnly appeal to us, a refusal on our part might involve further bloodshed, the ruin of the present Armenian Republic, and the opening of the way to further Bolshevism, pan-Touranianism and pan-Islamism in Turkey and in Asia."[75]

Before Wilson acted in late May, James Gerard pleaded with him to help Armenia directly. The Bolsheviks were threatening the Armenian Republic, Gerard emphasized, creating the "most grave crisis in Armenian history." Without prompt U.S. assistance for Armenia, he warned, "she will be wiped out by massacre and starvation." More was needed than the de facto diplomatic recognition that the United States had extended

---

[73] Polk to Wilson, Feb. 21, 1920, *PWW*, 64: 448–50.
[74] Polk to Wilson, March 6, 10 and 22, 1920, Wilson to Polk, March 8 and 17, 1920, *PWW* (Princeton, NJ, 1992), 65: 64–65, 72–77, 91, 111–15.
[75] Swen to Colby, May 20, 1920, Colby to Wilson, May 20, 1920, *PWW*, 65: 299, 305–12.

to the Armenian Republic on April 23, 1920. Gerard reminded Wilson, moreover, that in August 1919 several leading Republicans, including Senator Lodge, Elihu Root, and Charles Evans Hughes, had informed him that he had the authority as president to send U.S. armed forces to Armenia. He could help Armenia without awaiting congressional approval of a mandate.[76]

Republicans took the initiative to register their concern for Armenia. Senator Warren G. Harding, as chairman of a subcommittee of the Senate Foreign Relations Committee, prepared a resolution that the Senate passed on May 13. This resolution expressed the hope that the Armenians would fully realize their national aspirations for freedom, endorsed the president's decision to recognize the Armenian Republic, and requested him to dispatch a warship with marines to the port of Batum for the purpose of protecting American lives and property. It articulated the Republican senators' approval for limited American commitments overseas.[77]

When Wilson finally submitted the Armenian mandate to Congress on May 24, it was already too late. He made an eloquent appeal on behalf of Armenia, but no one expected it to affect the outcome. He saw it as "providential" that the Senate was expressing its concern for Armenia in the Harding resolution at about the same time that the San Remo conference was asking the United States to accept the Armenian mandate. "The sympathy for Armenia among our people," the president said, "has sprung from untainted conscience, pure Christian faith, and an earnest desire to see Christian people everywhere succored in their time of suffering, and lifted from their abject subjection and distress and enabled to stand upon their feet and take their place among the free nations of the world. Our recognition of the independence of Armenia will mean genuine liberty and assured happiness for her people, if we fearlessly undertake the duties of guidance and assistance in the functions of a mandatory."[78]

Wilson succeeded only in shifting the blame for inaction to Congress. On March 19, 1920, the Senate had again defeated the Versailles Treaty, keeping the United States out of the League of Nations. There was no prospect that the Republican-controlled Senate would now accept a League mandate, not even for Armenia. In the politics of escape, the Allies had transferred the responsibility for protecting Armenia to the United States, and the president now shifted the burden to Congress. Senator Philander

[76] Gerard to Wilson, May 14 and 18, 1920, *PWW*, 65: 287–88, 298.
[77] Ambrosius, *Woodrow Wilson and the American Diplomatic Tradition*, 257–58.
[78] Message, May 24, 1920, *PWW*, 65: 320–23; Wilson, *PPWW*, 6: 487–91.

C. Knox prepared a resolution for the Foreign Relations Committee, which declined to accept a mandate. On June 1, the Senate passed this resolution. Eleven Democrats joined all the Republicans to provide a decisive margin of 52 to 23 votes for the resolution. They rejected the mandate as too costly and too entangling, despite their avowed desire to assist Armenia. This was the expected outcome in the charade of Wilsonian peacemaking.[79]

Wilson left the delineation of the Armenian-Turkish boundary to the experts whom Secretary Colby appointed for the task, but their actions made no difference in reality. William Westermann, who had worked in 1919 as the Western Asia specialist in the American Commission to Negotiate Peace under Isaiah Bowman's direction in Paris, headed the group of experts to draw the lines. Westermann submitted their report to the State Department on September 28, 1920, outlining the proposed boundaries of "Wilsonian Armenia." On November 22, Wilson belatedly approved the report and submitted it to the Allies in Paris. By this time, however, it changed nothing because Mustafa Kemal's Nationalists had conquered nearly all of Turkish Armenia.[80]

Wilson's position on the Armenian-Russian boundary had also given no real support to Armenia. On August 9, 1920, Colby submitted his famous note summarizing U.S. policy toward the Russian Revolution. In it he reaffirmed that the Wilson administration would not recognize the Bolshevik regime. Pending the creation of a democratic government, the United States declined to approve the dismemberment of Russia. For this reason, unlike the Allies, it had refrained from recognizing the republics of Georgia and Azerbaijan. "Finally," Colby added, "while gladly giving recognition to the independence of Armenia, the Government of the United States has taken the position that the final determination of its boundaries must not be made without Russia's cooperation and agreement. Not only is Russia concerned because a considerable part of the territory of the new State of Armenia, when it shall be defined, formerly belonged to the Russian Empire: equally important is the fact that Armenia must have the good will and the protective friendship of

[79] Ambrosius, *Woodrow Wilson and the American Diplomatic Tradition*, 258; Richard G. Hovannisian, *The Republic of Armenia: Between Crescent and Sickle: Partition and Sovietization* (Berkeley, CA, 1996), 4: 10–28.
[80] Wilson to Davis, July 4, 1920, Colby to Wilson, July 20, 1920, *PWW*, 65: 496–97, 532; Colby to Wilson, Aug. 26 and Nov. 11, 1920, Wilson to Colby, Sept. 10 and Nov. 13, 1920, *PWW* (Princeton, NJ, 1992), 66: 65, 110, 349–50, 357. See also Hovannisian, *Republic of Armenia*, 4: 28–44.

Russia if it is to remain independent and free."[81] The Russian Bolsheviks, however, were no more friendly toward Russian Armenia than the Turkish Nationalists were toward Turkish Armenia.

At this late stage in the peacemaking, U.S. diplomats could do nothing more for Armenia than to participate in the politics of escape. The Allies wanted to place the burden on the United States, while Wilson sought to shift it either back to them or to Congress. On November 22, the League of Nations Assembly adopted a resolution, which Paul Hymans, president of the League Council, sent to the State Department, requesting the United States to undertake the humanitarian task of stopping the hostilities in Armenia. Concerned that total inaction would leave Wilson vulnerable to criticism, Colby advised him to offer the good offices of mediation by a personal representative. "The situation comes upon the Western nations at a time when they are distracted and almost helpless in the post-war reaction," Colby explained. "The possibilities of organizing an effective force are almost nil, and unless you exercise your moral authority it would almost seem that there is no way to avert the fate that hangs over the Armenians." The secretary of state recommended the appointment of Henry Morgenthau as the president's personal representative. Colby was obviously more interested in appearances than results. "You might be rebuffed, and your representative might fail, but I think it would be an action on your part which the world would welcome and history approve." Wilson agreed, naming Morgenthau for this role and informing Hymans of the decision.[82]

This charade of Wilsonian peacemaking made no difference in Armenia. By the end of 1920, all of Armenia had fallen under foreign control. The Turkish Nationalists had conquered "Wilsonian Armenia" and the Russian Bolsheviks had established their dominance in the Armenian Republic. Armenia's enemies were not at all interested in Wilson's mediation when it was clear that diplomacy would not be backed by military force. When the Allies in the League once more requested U.S. intervention, the Wilson administration again practiced the politics of escape, believing that "the responsibility and blame should be thrown back on them." Wilson's official response, on January 18, 1921, reiterated his willingness to instruct Morgenthau to proceed with his mission, but only if the Allies helped create favorable conditions for success. The message admitted that "the President

---

[81] Colby to Wilson, Aug. 9, 1920, *PWW*, 66: 19–25.
[82] Colby to Wilson, Nov. 26, 27, 28, and 29, 1920, Davis to Wilson, Dec. 6, 1920, Davis to Hymans, Dec. 15, 1920, *PWW*, 66: 421–23, 426–28, 436–37, 443–44, 480, 517–18.

has no control, and any measures which he might take or recommend in this direction would be dependent upon the hearty cooperation and support of the Allied Powers." Wilson acknowledged, moreover, a fundamental problem with the concept of collective security: "The great impediment to peaceful reconstruction in these troubled border territories, the imminent danger of new hostilities, is caused by the utter confusion between offense and defense. Unless this distinction can be clearly defined, there is not only small hope of peace, but no hope of a clear perception of who is responsible for new wars." These words were crafted as a public exoneration for Wilson's inability to help the Armenians.[83] Armenia was beyond the control of the United States, revealing the limits of American power and ideology. Wilsonianism had failed.

THE LIMITS OF WILSONIANISM

Arnold J. Toynbee placed this failure in the larger context of international affairs after the Great War with particular reference to Armenia, Georgia, and Azerbaijan. "In writing the epitaph of these short-lived 'successor states' of the Russian Empire in the Middle East," he observed,

> it would not be wholly correct to describe the cause of death as either suicide or murder.... In this part of the world the Supreme Council in Paris ... were not in a position to exercise effective power, and by attempting nevertheless to make a show of authority they committed both a moral and a political blunder. By supporting the 'Whites' against the 'Reds' in Russia and the Greeks against the Turkish Nationalists in Anatolia, they aroused a fury of opposition which they could not control; and by encouraging the inexperienced and unorganized Transcaucasian Republics to look to them for a guidance and a protection which they had no intention of giving at any sacrifice to themselves, they deterred them from coming to terms before it was too late with the two locally dominant Powers, and merely exposed them to reprisals as satellites of Turkey's and Russia's most dangerous enemies.[84]

Felix Willoughby Smith had recognized this crucial point. Although deeply involved in seeking to convince the Wilson administration to give more help to the Armenians and other peoples in Transcaucasia during the war, he also understood that meager assistance would not suffice and might actually convey the wrong message. On January 7, 1918, the U.S. consul in Tiflis had candidly advised officials in the State Department: "If we are not to give aid to the Caucasus, we should clear out, giving local

---

[83] Davis to Wilson, Jan. 15 and 21, 1920, *PWW* (Princeton, NJ, 1992), 67: 63–67, 79.
[84] Arnold J. Toynbee, *Survey of International Affairs, 1920–1923* (London, 1925), 373–74.

Christians notice, so that they can come to an understanding with the Ottomans."[85]

Richard G. Hovannisian appreciated this insight, notwithstanding the virtual impossibility for the Armenians to pursue the unthinkable alternative to dependence on the Allies and the United States – that is, accommodation with Turkey. "In retrospect," he concluded,

it is clear that Armenia should have probed every available avenue for an understanding with her bruised neighbor to the west; but in reality the obstacles were too many and too great. Not only was the Turk despised as the historic oppressor and of late the butcher of half the nation, but on a more objective plane, the Armenian question had become an international issue, its solution seemingly dependent more on decisions reached in Europe than in either Constantinople or Erevan.[86]

Tragically, Armenia was caught between its nearby enemies who were intent on destroying it and its distant friends who were equally intent on avoiding the costs of defending it.

Scholars who have touted Wilsonianism as the universal ideology for a new world order have missed this important point about the limits of American power. It is perhaps significant that Tony Smith, Amos Perlmutter, and Frank Ninkovich[87] left Armenia out of their triumphalist accounts of the Wilsonian century, for it would not fit well. The Armenian experience after World War I offers a different perspective on power and ideology in American diplomatic history, questioning the triumphalism of some recent interpretations. Wilson's inability to implement his own principles in Armenia suggests that Wilsonianism cannot provide the universal foundation for a new world order. With limited power, the United States cannot fulfill the Wilsonian promise everywhere.

---

[85] Hovannisian, *Armenia on the Road to Independence*, 118.

[86] Honannisian, *Republic of Armenia*, 1: 417.

[87] Tony Smith, *America's Mission: The United States and the Worldwide Struggle for Democracy in the Twentieth Century* (Princeton, NJ, 1994); Amos Perlmutter, *Making the World Safe for Democracy: A Century of Wilsonianism and Its Totalitarian Challengers* (Chapel Hill, NC, 1997); Frank Ninkovich, *The Wilsonian Century: U.S. Foreign Policy since 1900* (Chicago, 1999).

8

Woodrow Wilson and George W. Bush

Historical Comparisons of Ends and Means in Their Foreign Policies

Presidents Woodrow Wilson and George W. Bush appealed to historic American ideals to justify their new foreign policies. During World War I and after September 11, 2001, they both led the nation into war for the avowed purpose of protecting traditional values and institutions at home and of expanding these throughout the world, promising to make freedom and democracy the foundation for peace. They assigned a redemptive role to the United States, fighting evil to create a new international order. Various commentators have recognized these parallels between Wilson and Bush. Often focusing on their common ideology, they have neglected the disparity between ends and means in the foreign policies of these two presidents. Historians who have placed Bush in the mainstream of the American diplomatic tradition, moreover, have exaggerated historical continuity by ignoring his willingness to use unprecedented means of preemptive war to achieve traditional Wilsonian goals.

HISTORICAL RATIONALE FOR THE BUSH DOCTRINE

Pundits and scholars have offered various arguments to explain or justify the Bush Doctrine. Some, agreeing with Bush, have endorsed his global war on terrorism by arguing that September 11 marked the beginning of a radically new era in world history. Novel threats, they claimed, required a new national security strategy, which justified America's preventive war in Iraq as well as its retaliatory war in Afghanistan. Others, also concurring with Bush, have exalted America's providential mission to transform the world, and thus to secure its peace. In combination, these two arguments gave Bush a rationale for his new national security doctrine: Given the radically new dangers confronting the United States and its unique (or providential) opportunity as the world's preeminent superpower, it needed to take a proactive stance toward potential rivals and terrorists. While not necessarily rejecting either of these two arguments, some historians have noted pre-9/11 precedents for the president's national security strategy. They have sought to give legitimacy to the Bush Doctrine by identifying it with well-established American traditions. Placing Bush's foreign policy in the mainstream of U.S. history, they have exaggerated historical continuity and overlooked significant differences between him and previous presidents. In doing so they have offered questionable historical interpretations as well as dubious foreign policy advice.

Using Wilson as an important point of reference, this essay analyzes the debate over Bush's global war on terrorism and its place in U.S. diplomatic history. Rather than dealing with all comparisons between the two presidents, it evaluates only some of the most important recent books and articles that highlight similarities and differences between their historic roles in U.S. foreign relations. It does not focus on other aspects of their lives and statecraft such as common roots in the American South, race and religion as factors in their private identities and public policies, and contrasts between their so-called progressive or conservative views on the government's role in the political economy and society. Nor does it examine all facets of their respective foreign policies. These merit further attention, but will not be covered here except to the extent that authors of the cited works have alluded to them.

Focusing on ideology, Stanford University historian David M. Kennedy stressed historical continuity from Wilson to Bush. In *The Atlantic* (March 2005), he attested that Bush owed his foreign policy principles to Wilson, whether he knew it or not. Kennedy identified Bush not only with Wilson and his legacy but also with an earlier American heritage from which Wilsonianism had emerged. "Many critics have berated Bush," Kennedy remarked, "accusing him of jettisoning two centuries of tradition and abandoning the high ground from which Americans have historically waged war with stouthearted moral confidence. But although this criticism is valid in many ways, Bush's approach also reaffirms what may well be America's only consistent tradition in foreign policy." Wilsonian ideals guided Bush's thinking, Kennedy avowed, although his doctrine of preemption marked a radical departure in American diplomacy. According to Kennedy, Bush's approach to the global war on terrorism conformed

to historic American goals, but his willingness to attack first was unprecedented. "George W. Bush's 2002 National Security Strategy proclaimed
a new American right to wage preventive war," noted Kennedy, who
observed this novel assertion but did not question it. "Following the cat-
astrophic events of September 11, 2001, Bush declared, it was simply
too risky <u>not</u> to act pre-emptively. Whatever the merits, this doctrine is a
radical departure for American diplomacy."[1]

Kennedy correctly identified that the Bush Doctrine both adhered to
and departed from the American diplomatic tradition, but, focusing on
ends rather than means, he neglected to explain this dual characteristic.
Only in one brief reference to 1775, 1861, and 1941 did he deal with the
actual conduct of Americans at the start of war as compared with the
American ideals that were used to justify war, noting that "at Concord
Bridge, Fort Sumter, and Pearl Harbor it was America's adversaries who
fired the first shot."[2] Throughout the remainder of the article Kennedy
disregarded the differences between the two presidents in practice. He
concentrated on ideology rather than the actual conduct of American
diplomacy, on ends rather than means, emphasizing ideological continuity from Wilson to Bush. As a consequence, his predominant message was
that Bush's global war on terrorism conformed to, rather than departed
from, the American diplomatic tradition. History was apparently on the
forty-third president's side.

Kennedy stressed the Bush Doctrine's proclamation of "the values of
freedom" and "the hope of democracy, development, free markets, and
free trade" for "every corner of the world." He observed: "Those idealistic – some would say hubristic – words uncannily echo Woodrow
Wilson's rationale for American participation in World War I." Whether
Bush acknowledged his debt to Wilson, Kennedy argued, "Wilson would
recognize George W. Bush as his natural successor." Bush's strategy for
fighting the global war on terrorism adhered to the tenets of Wilsonianism.
Both presidents believed they were pursuing the only way to create the
kind of world in which they wanted to live. Kennedy emphasized, moreover, that "Wilson did not think that what came to be known, and often
derided, as 'Wilsonianism' was just a policy selected from a palette of
possible choices. Rather, he saw it as the sole approach to international
relations that his countrymen would embrace as consistent with their
past and their principles. Wilson did not so much invent American foreign

---

[1] David M. Kennedy, "What 'W' Owes to 'WW,'" *The Atlantic* 295 (March 2005): 36.
[2] Kennedy, *The Atlantic*, 36.

policy as discover it." He rejected both traditional isolationism and "the timeless precepts of diplomatic realism, or realpolitik" in his response to the Great War in Europe. As Kennedy further noted, "two assumptions underlay Wilson's thinking: [1] that the circumstances of the modern era were utterly novel, and [2] that providence had entrusted America with a mandate to carry out a singular mission in the world." Bush shared these two assumptions, which guided his response to September 11. "Wilson's ideas continue to dominate American foreign policy in the twenty-first century," Kennedy concluded. "In the aftermath of 9/11 they have, if anything, taken on even greater vitality."[3]

Like Kennedy, University of Virginia historian Melvyn P. Leffler also placed the Bush Doctrine in the mainstream of the American diplomatic tradition. "My argument," he affirmed in *Diplomatic History* (June 2005), "is that there is more continuity than change in the policies of the Bush administration. Bush's rhetoric and actions have deep roots in the history of American foreign policy." Yet there were also "important changes," he added. Leffler stressed the importance of "good judgment." At times of crisis, he argued, Americans have tended to focus on their ideals – or their belief in the nation's universal mission – to mobilize their power to deal with the perceived threats. Their redefinition of interests would emerge from this assertion of values in response to new dangers. After 9/11, the Bush Doctrine exemplified this pattern. In Leffler's view, its most important characteristic was its "overriding goal" of promoting an international order favorable to freedom. That goal was more significant than the doctrine's widely criticized features of preemption, unilateralism, and hegemony. Thus, like Kennedy, Leffler stressed the ideological continuity in Bush's foreign policy. He placed it in the historic tradition of the Open Door, Wilson's Fourteen Points, the Atlantic Charter, and the Truman Doctrine.[4]

Going beyond Kennedy, Leffler argued that the Bush Doctrine's features of preemption, unilateralism, and hegemony were also not as new as critics alleged. He found precedents for all these in twentieth-century presidencies from Theodore Roosevelt to Bill Clinton, especially during the Cold War. Thus, he concluded, Bush's dismissal of deterrence, containment, military alliances, and multilateralism in his global war on

---

[3] Kennedy, *The Atlantic*, 36–40.

[4] Melvyn P. Leffler, "9/11 and American Foreign Policy," *Diplomatic History* 29 (June 2005): 395–96. See also Melvyn P. Leffler, "9/11 and the Past and Future of American Foreign Policy," *International Affairs* 79 (October 2003): 1045–63.

terrorism fell short of a "revolutionary" departure from the established pattern of American foreign relations. In his analysis of the Bush Doctrine, however, Leffler exaggerated the significance of so-called precedents. For instance, he cited Clinton's approval of preemptive action in his June 1995 Presidential Decision Directive 95 as an antecedent of the Bush Doctrine. To protect American citizens and their facilities at home and abroad from terrorism, Clinton directed that "the U.S. shall pursue vigorously efforts to deter and preempt, apprehend and prosecute, or assist other governments to prosecute, individuals who perpetrate or plan to perpetrate such attacks."[5] Identifying Clinton's directive as a precedent for Bush's so-called preemptive war against Iraq, Leffler overlooked the magnitude of difference between Clinton's authorization of preemptive action against "individuals" and Bush's full-scale war against a foreign nation. Although they shared the common goal of stopping terrorism, Bush's preventive war against Iraq marked a radical departure from Clinton's far more cautious and limited approach to counterterrorism.[6]

Leffler's focus on common ideological commitments to promote freedom and democracy obscured the substantial difference between Bush and twentieth-century presidents in practice and the concomitant disparity between ends and means in his foreign policy. Leffler concluded that: "There has been no revolution in American foreign policy; there has been a frightening recalibration of the relationships between ideals and interests in the face of 'existential' threats."[7] This argument is not persuasive. A realistic approach to counterterrorism would have asked not just what goals (whether defined as ideals or interests) the United States should pursue after 9/11 but also what methods it might legitimately adopt within the limits of its power to achieve the desired aims. It would have reassessed ends and means together. Except for recognizing the need for good judgment, Leffler neglected the very serious disparity between Bush's proclaimed goals and the actual practices of his administration, especially its unrealistic belief in war as the preferred way to make the world safe for democracy. As James Mann, writer-in-residence at the Center for Strategic and International Affairs, observed, "The ideals of Woodrow Wilson were to be revived, this time linked hand in hand with America's unprecedented military

---

[5] Leffler, *Diplomatic History*, 404.
[6] See also Richard A. Clarke, *Against All Enemies: Inside America's War on Terror* (New York, 2004).
[7] Leffler, *Diplomatic History*, 413.

power."[8] Under the influence of neoconservatives, the president missed the opportunity to define a more realistic foreign policy.[9]

Lafayette College historian Arnold A. Offner criticized both the ends and means of Bush's new foreign policy. He understood that the United States needed more than good judgment in the implementation of the Bush Doctrine. Because it jeopardized both American ideals and interests, he denounced this redefinition of the U.S. role in world affairs. Accordingly, he rejected Leffler's conclusion that "George W. Bush's national security strategy (NSS) of 2002 is not revolutionary doctrine but largely consistent with America's long-held sense of universal mission and commitment to Wilsonian liberalism, and that presidents from TR to Bill Clinton have engaged in preemptive action." To the contrary, Offner rightly asserted, Bush's new policy was "an extremely radical and dangerous departure from accepted norms." Thus he questioned "both the means and ends of the Bush administration."[10]

JOHN B. JUDIS AND AMERICAN EXCEPTIONALISM

In contrast to Kennedy and Leffler, John B. Judis, senior editor of *The New Republic*, argued that Wilson would not have recognized Bush as his legitimate successor. The Bush Doctrine marked a radical departure from Wilsonianism. In *The Folly of Empire* (2004), Judis criticized Bush for ignoring the lessons that TR and Wilson had derived from the American imperial experience a century earlier. Having learned from that so-called aberration in the American diplomatic tradition at the turn of the twentieth century, those Progressive presidents had exemplified a prudence that was lacking in Bush's reckless and relentless pursuit of an American empire. This was a terrible sacrifice, Judis believed. "The end of the Cold War," he thought, "created the conditions for finally realizing the promise of Wilson's foreign policy." Presidents George H. W. Bush and Bill Clinton pursued that promise of peace and

[8] James Mann, *Rise of the Vulcans: The History of Bush's War Cabinet* (New York, 2004), 329.
[9] See also Richard N. Haass, *The Opportunity: America's Moment to Alter History's Course* (New York, 2005).
[10] Arnold A. Offner, "Rogue President, Rogue Nation: Bush and U.S. National Security," *Diplomatic History* 29 (June 2005): 433–35. See also Clyde Prestowitz, *Rogue Nation: American Unilateralism and the Failure of Good Intentions* (New York, 2003); Andrew J. Bacevich, *The New American Militarism: How Americans Are Seduced by War* (New York, 2005); Lloyd C. Gardner and Marilyn Blatt Young, eds., *The New American Empire: A 21st Century Teach-In on U.S. Foreign Policy* (New York, 2005).

prosperity in a new world order with a system of collective security among nations and an "open door" global economy. They understood that the United States benefited from international cooperation or multilateralism. "These years represented a triumph of Wilsonianism and of the lessons that America had learned from the Spanish-American War, two world wars, and the Vietnam War. But these lessons were entirely lost on the administration of George W. Bush that took office in January 2001." Again seeking to build a new American empire, Bush and the neoconservatives who now controlled U.S. foreign policy ignored the lessons that Progressive presidents had learned a century earlier. "Under Theodore Roosevelt and Woodrow Wilson," whom Judis contrasted with Bush, "and later under a succession of presidents from Franklin Roosevelt to Bill Clinton, these experiences convinced Americans to change their attitude toward imperial conquests and toward nationalism in countries like the Philippines and Iraq."[11] Unfortunately, Judis concluded, Bush had reverted to the Republican imperialism that had led to American occupation and annexation of the Philippines after the Spanish-American War of 1898.

As a liberal, Judis used an exceptionalist interpretation of American history to criticize Bush. Ironically, some historians who defended the Bush administration appealed to this same tradition, which affirmed America's unique role in world history. Neoconservatives also shared this historically liberal perspective. Judis identified Wilsonianism with anti-imperialism. Except for the momentary aberration after the Spanish-American War, he believed the United States had not created an empire. It had shunned colonialism, making America's experience quite different from Europe's. Its territorial expansion across North America, he thought, was not equivalent to European imperialism. He did not interpret this westward movement as founding a continental empire. The emergence of the United States as the world's preeminent power by the end of the twentieth century also did not appear to Judis as evidence that this nation had become a global empire.[12] Nor did he recognize what British historian Niall Ferguson, himself an advocate of a liberal American empire, called "the imperialism of anti-imperialism."[13] Bush's pursuit of an American

[11] John B. Judis, *The Folly of Empire: What George W. Bush Could Learn from Theodore Roosevelt and Woodrow Wilson* (New York, 2004), 7–9; John B. Judis, "What Woodrow Wilson Can Teach Today's Imperialists," *The New Republic* 228 (June 9, 2003): 19–23.

[12] For a more persuasive interpretation, see Andrew J. Bacevich, *American Empire: The Realities & Consequences of U.S. Diplomacy* (Cambridge, MA, 2002).

[13] Niall Ferguson, *Colossus: The Price of America's Empire* (New York, 2004), 61–104.

empire thus looked to Judis like a radical departure from what he perceived as the nation's essential tradition of anti-imperialism.

For half a century, however, leading historians of U.S. foreign relations have rejected this exceptionalist interpretation of American history, which Judis still affirmed and which had found its classic statement in historian Frederick Jackson Turner's frontier thesis. In *Empire on the Pacific* (1955), Norman A. Graebner challenged Turner's explanation of progressive westward expansion across the North American continent. In the 1840s, he argued, President James K. Polk defined his imperial ambitions with reference to the natural harbors on the Pacific coast, which were important for international commerce. The future American ports at Seattle, San Francisco, and San Diego were more important in Polk's thinking than the settlement of farmers and the development of democratic institutions on the western frontier. Moreover, by using the word "empire," Graebner avoided the euphemism of westward expansion, which advocates of Turner's frontier thesis used in their denial of American imperialism.[14] Richard W. Van Alstyne likewise recognized in *The Rising American Empire* (1960) that, beginning with the Revolution, the United States had sought to create and expand its own new empire in competition with the old world's great powers. The title of his book came from George Washington's vision in 1783 of a "rising empire" in the new world.[15] Thomas Jefferson reaffirmed this imperial future for the United States, which he called an "empire of liberty."[16] By the end of the nineteenth century, however, Americans had redefined their concept of empire, restricting it to colonialism, so that their westward expansion across North America did not appear to them as imperialism. They embraced Turner's frontier thesis, which affirmed a unique American national identity in contrast to the old world. Although the European great powers were now engaged in imperialism, the United States adhered to its presumably anti-imperial tradition, except for its temporary aberration after the Spanish-American War. Along with Graebner and Van Alstyne, other leading historians long ago rejected this self-serving version of the American past and recognized the United States as the "imperial democracy" or "the new empire."[17]

---

[14] Norman A. Graebner, *Empire on the Pacific* (New York, 1955).

[15] R. W. Van Alstyne, *The Rising American Empire* (Oxford, 1960).

[16] Robert W. Tucker and David C. Hendrickson, *Empire of Liberty: The Statecraft of Thomas Jefferson* (New York, 1990).

[17] Ernest R. May, *Imperial Democracy: The Emergence of America as a Great Power* (New York, 1961); Walter LaFeber, *The New Empire: An Interpretation of American Expansion, 1860–1898* (Ithaca, NY, 1963).

In *The Myth of the West* (1995), Dutch historian Jan Willem Schulte Nordholt brilliantly analyzed the exceptionalist interpretation of American history, which Turner affirmed in his frontier thesis and Wilson proclaimed in his foreign policy. America, according to this mythology, was the "last empire" or the culmination of world history. Paradoxically, this vision of the new world originated from biblical and classical roots in the old world. It enabled Americans, as the successors of this European intellectual heritage, to convince themselves that their "last empire" was not really like those of other great powers. Although other empires had risen and declined, the myth of the West assured Americans of their nation's (or empire's) progressive future. Time and place had come together in America, making this new land the "city on a hill" or "last frontier" or "end of history."[18] In his biography of *Woodrow Wilson* (1991), Schulte Nordholt showed the influence of this mythical exceptionalism on the president's "life for world peace."[19] It continued in his legacy of Wilsonianism throughout the twentieth century and then in the Bush Doctrine after 9/11.[20]

In Judis's view, however, Americans never engaged in building an empire, with a few exceptions particularly at the turn of the twentieth century. Their conduct of foreign relations manifested the nation's exceptionalism. They identified themselves as a "chosen people" with a moral or religious mission to redeem the world, but not through imperial conquest. Early American settlers had acquired a millennial, progressive view of history from the Protestant Reformation. Nineteenth-century Americans combined this linear understanding of history with the Enlightenment theory of stages of development from barbarism to civilization to justify their continental expansion. Out of this mixture came their rationale for Indian removal and their concept of "manifest destiny" to vindicate territorial conquest across North America to the Pacific. Until the "imperial moment" after 1898, however, they had resisted the temptation to acquire a colonial empire.[21]

---

[18] Jan Willem Schulte Nordholt, *The Myth of the West: America as the Last Empire* (Grand Rapids, MI, 1995). See also C. Vann Woodward, *The Old World's New World* (New York, 1991).

[19] Jan Willem Schulte Nordholt, *Woodrow Wilson: A Life for World Peace* (Berkeley, CA, 1991).

[20] Lloyd E. Ambrosius, *Wilsonianism: Woodrow Wilson and His Legacy in American Foreign Relations* (New York, 2002); Walter LaFeber, "The Bush Doctrine," *Diplomatic History* 26 (Fall 2002): 543–58.

[21] Judis, *The Folly of Empire*, 11–29.

According to Judis, a few Americans at the turn of the century, with illusions of omnipotence, endeavored to create a new empire. Prominent Republicans such as William McKinley, Henry Cabot Lodge, John Hay, Brooks Adams, and Theodore Roosevelt favored the acquisition of the Philippines even at the cost of war against the Filipinos who fought for their independence. Some Democrats, including Woodrow Wilson, also supported this new imperialism. Christianity, Anglo-Saxon or Teutonic racial theories, America's frontier experience, and the idea of democratic peace, Judis recounted, were all used to explain why the United States needed to establish an overseas empire. In an 1899 essay on "Expansion and Peace," Roosevelt expressed beliefs that resembled later justifications for the Bush Doctrine. "On the border between civilization and barbarism," TR wrote, "war is generally normal because it must be under the conditions of barbarism," given that "civilized man finds he can keep the peace only by subduing his barbarian neighbor." In an early version of democratic peace theory, TR added: "Fundamentally, the cause of expansion is the cause of peace. With civilized powers there is but little danger of getting into war.... In North America, as elsewhere throughout the entire world, the expansion of a civilized nation has invariably meant the growth of the area in which peace is normal throughout the world."[22] Anti-imperialists criticized this new imperialism, but without success at first.

Eventually, however, the problem of control – or the limits of American power to conquer and remake the Philippines easily and cheaply – challenged TR's imperial illusions and brought him to recognize the folly of empire. Increasingly aware of other foreign dangers, he gained greater appreciation for a balance of power in international politics. "Roosevelt's newfound fear of war in Europe and Asia," observed Judis, "led him to take positions that would be familiar to later American administrations but were at odds with his own stance at the end of the nineteenth century. In that burst of millennial enthusiasm, Roosevelt had imagined America playing a transformative role in creating a new-world imperial order; however, by the end of his presidency, he had reverted to more classic European balance-of-power conceptions."[23]

Wilson also recognized the folly of empire, Judis believed. Although he maintained a millennial view of history, this progressive president envisioned a new world order with national self-determination and

---

[22] Judis, *The Folly of Empire*, 63. See also Warren Zimmermann, *First Great Triumph: How Five Americans Made Their Country a World Power* (New York, 2002).
[23] Judis, *The Folly of Empire*, 72.

collective security. His new League of Nations promised to dismantle the old international system of imperialism. "Wilson's contribution to American foreign policy," Judis argued, "can be expressed in religious terms. He attempted to transform the world in America's image by transporting the original Puritan covenant between God and the American settlers into a covenant for the entire world that would exchange peace and democracy for obedience to the League's laws. He would talk of creating a 'conscience for the world.' "[24] Although the president called for a radical transformation of international politics to make the world safe for democracy, Judis did not identify this search for global hegemony – or what Wilson's contemporaries called "international social control" – with the pursuit of an American empire.[25]

Judis praised Wilson for recognizing the roots of instability in the international system that generated World War I. These included the old balance of power in Europe's diplomacy, the commercial rivalry over colonies, the philosophy that might is right, and the autocratic regimes that resorted to war against their democratic neighbors. Ending imperialism and promoting democracy were his solutions. Wilson's Fourteen Points outlined his vision of a new world order to replace the old international system. In 1919, he succeeded at the Paris Peace Conference in creating the League of Nations, but failed to implement his principles in other parts of the Versailles Treaty. The president also suffered defeat at home when the Senate rejected this treaty and prevented the United States from joining the League. Nevertheless, in Judis's view, he had proposed the correct remedy. "While Wilson's attempt to reformulate America's foreign policy would fail to win the assent of his own country or of Europeans in 1919 and 1920," Judis concluded, "it would be revived during World War II and the Cold War. And to the extent that Americans would follow Wilson's approach – addressing the structural causes of war, including colonialism and protectionism – they would enjoy remarkable success over the remainder of the century." Above all, Wilson had fully discredited imperialism for all great powers, and especially the United States. Judis emphasized: "Americans would differ over the next decades as to how zealously they should attempt to dismantle other nations' empires, but no president for the remainder of the twentieth century would advocate the

[24] Judis, The Folly of Empire, 79–80.
[25] For a different interpretation, see Lloyd E. Ambrosius, Woodrow Wilson and the American Diplomatic Tradition: The Treaty Fight in Perspective (Cambridge, 1987); Lloyd E. Ambrosius, "Woodrow Wilson, Alliances, and the League of Nations," The Journal of the Gilded Age and Progressive Era 5 (April 2006): 139–65.

growth of an American empire. Wilson had finally laid that alternative to rest. Wilson also redefined the American millennium." He established the ideal of "a world of democracies."[26]

Judis praised the prudence of twentieth-century American presidents in generally resisting the temptations of imperialism. This required self-restraint, which was difficult when military intervention seemed to offer advantages. Even Wilson, who denounced Dollar Diplomacy, did not always adhere strictly to his principles. He intervened twice in Mexico, and took control over Haiti and the Dominican Republic. These experiences, however, made him more cautious. He did not rush into World War I against Germany. Nor did he succumb to the Allies' appeal for extensive intervention against revolutionary Bolshevism in Russia. Applying the wisdom he had learned from his experience with the Mexican Revolution, Judis noted, Wilson asserted that: "My policy regarding Russia is very similar to my Mexican policy. I believe in letting them work out their own salvation, even though they wallow in anarchy for a while."[27] FDR followed this model of prudence, even as he too affirmed Wilsonian principles during World War II. Judis emphasized that "Roosevelt defined the war as a struggle between good and evil – 'between those who believe in mankind and those who do not' – but like Wilson, he did not allow this vision of Armageddon to cloud his understanding of the underlying causes of war and of what was necessary to prevent future wars."[28] FDR's Four Freedoms reaffirmed Wilsonian ideals, but his statecraft demonstrated a realistic understanding of the limits of power. This same pattern continued during the Cold War. As Judis noted, "Roosevelt's successors would not abandon Wilson's approach to foreign policy, but they would have to adapt it to a divided world."[29]

Americans were sometimes tempted to abandon Wilson's legacy of anti-imperialism, Judis acknowledged. He cited only a few instances, however, given his identification of an empire with overseas colonies. The United States succumbed in Vietnam during the 1960s, he charged. Under President Lyndon B. Johnson's leadership, it "put itself squarely on the side of imperialism and colonialism. It was practicing an informal kind of imperialism. It also failed to take heed of what Wilson had learned in Mexico in 1914: that the United States, acting alone, could not transform countries overnight into models of democracy and freedom."[30] Oil

---

[26] Judis, *The Folly of Empire*, 116–17.
[27] Judis, *The Folly of Empire*, 107.
[28] Judis, *The Folly of Empire*, 124.
[29] Judis, *The Folly of Empire*, 132.
[30] Judis, *The Folly of Empire*, 140.

and Israel also tested America's adherence to the Wilsonian principle of self-determination, Judis argued, particularly referring to U.S. support for the shah in Iran and for Israel against the Palestinian people. "The U.S. policy in the Mideast represented another instance where the Cold War clouded America's commitment to dismantling imperialism," he concluded. In the long run, however, Wilsonianism prevailed throughout the Cold War and at its end. President Ronald Reagan served as "the millennial harbinger" of democratic transformation worldwide. In his Westminster Speech to the British Parliament, he heralded this crusade for freedom. Yet, Judis noted, "Reagan, like Woodrow Wilson, would transcend the seeming limits of his own rhetoric and his religious background. Reagan would uncover the possibility of peace and of an end to the Cold War."[31] His statecraft evidenced prudence, not the reckless pursuit of ideological goals or imperialism.

Wilsonianism triumphed during the post–Cold War presidencies of George H. W. Bush and Bill Clinton, but the younger Bush soon discarded that heritage, according to Judis. "In the 1990s, with the Cold War's end, the ideal of collective security, rooted in a century of bitter experience and an integrated world economy, had finally become capable of realization. Yet as a new century dawned, George W. Bush's administration abandoned this Wilsonian foreign policy for a toxic mixture of nationalism and neoconservatism."[32] Suffering from the illusion of omnipotence, it succumbed to the temptations of imperialism. Unfortunately, Judis argued, "America's new imperialism and unilateralism" sacrificed its twentieth-century commitment to multilateralism, ignoring the lesson that "the key to America's long-standing leadership has been its willingness to subordinate its singular will to that of international organizations and alliances."[33] Bush affirmed only Wilson's goals, not his methods. He and the neoconservatives who guided his conduct of U.S. foreign relations had espoused the Wilsonian vision of global democracy, but they sought to achieve it through unilateral means. In so doing they unwisely and dangerously resorted to the folly of empire.

Judis presented an idealized version of Wilson as a counterpoint to Bush, but even so he made one fundamental point. Wilson's rhetoric might soar through the clouds as he outlined his global vision of making

---

[31] Judis, *The Folly of Empire*, 143.
[32] Judis, *The Folly of Empire*, 201.
[33] Judis, *The Folly of Empire*, 207. For a similar argument, see G. John Ikenberry, *After Victory: Institutions, Strategic Restraint, and the Rebuilding of Order after Major Wars* (Princeton, NJ, 2001).

the world safe for democracy, but he was far more prudent in practice. He offered his ideals as universal principles, but he also exercised caution and self-restraint. His brother-in-law Stockton Axson recognized this feature in Wilson, attributing it to his Scottish and Scotch-Irish lineage: "[T]here was in him a kernel of tough common sense. He was an idealist with a strong realization of the practical."[34] Both idealistic and practical, Wilson proclaimed universal principles while he also limited his actions, as Judis noted in reference to his restraint in using military intervention against Bolshevism in Russia. In theory, the president promised to make the world safe for democracy and to guarantee collective security for all nations. In practice, however, he never intended for the United States to take on this responsibility throughout the world. This contrast between theory and practice generated postwar disillusionment. He failed to live up to the hopes of various peoples, who believed that he betrayed his promise by not helping them fulfill their own expectations. Although not cited by Judis, the tragedy of the Armenian genocide exemplified this problem. Both during and after the Great War, Wilson refused to send U.S. troops into the Middle East to protect the Armenians from the Turks and later the Bolsheviks, leaving them at the mercy of their enemies. His rhetoric was universal, but his actions were circumscribed, reflecting the limits of American power and also of his ideology that promised more than he could deliver.[35] Wilson's unwillingness to intervene in the Middle East even to help the Armenians, a white Christian people, was hardly a legitimate precedent for Bush's later pursuit of democratic transformation throughout the entire region. In comparing these two presidents, Judis correctly distinguished between ends and means in U.S. foreign policy. Bush reaffirmed Wilsonian principles, but his statecraft lacked Wilson's characteristic prudence.

JOHN LEWIS GADDIS AND THE BUSH DOCTRINE

In contrast to Judis, Yale University historian John Lewis Gaddis identified Bush with Wilson and the diplomatic legacy of the United States

---

[34] Stockton Axson, *"Brother Woodrow": A Memoir of Woodrow Wilson*, ed. Arthur S. Link (Princeton, NJ, 1993), 4.

[35] Lloyd E. Ambrosius, "Wilsonian Diplomacy and Armenia: The Limits of Power and Ideology," *America and the Armenian Genocide of 1915*, ed. Jay Winter (Cambridge, 2003), 113–45; Samantha Power, *"A Problem from Hell": America and the Age of Genocide* (New York, 2002), 1–16; Peter Balakian, *The Burning Tigris: The Armenian Genocide and America's Response* (New York, 2003).

from the nineteenth and twentieth centuries. In *Surprise, Security, and the American Experience* (2004), he traced this tradition from John Quincy Adams, Andrew Jackson, and Polk, through McKinley, TR, William H. Taft, and Wilson, to FDR, and on to George W. Bush. Although somewhat critical of Bush, Gaddis generally praised his definition of a national security strategy as the culmination of the American diplomatic tradition. This praise won for the historian a rare invitation to the White House to discuss his book with the president.[36]

In *Foreign Affairs* (January–February 2005), Gaddis offered his suggestions for fine-tuning Bush's grand strategy in his second term. He claimed that it offered the basis for a new bipartisan consensus in the aftermath of 9/11 and of Bush's war against Saddam Hussein's Iraq. "A conservative Republican administration responded by embracing a liberal Democratic ideal – making the world safe for democracy – as a national security imperative," concluded Gaddis. "If that does not provide the basis for a renewed grand strategic bipartisanship, similar to the one that followed Pearl Harbor so long ago, then one has to wonder what ever would."[37] Although he recognized that the Bush administration had conflated prevention with preemption, Gaddis approved its "first act of pre-emption for preventive purposes: the invasion of Iraq." He praised the administration for attempting to win multilateral endorsement for this new war in 2003. He recognized, but then discounted, widespread foreign criticism of unilateral U.S. decision-making. "President Bush's decision to invade Iraq anyway provoked complaints that great power was being wielded without great responsibility, followed by an unprecedented collapse of support for the United States abroad. From nearly universal sympathy in the weeks after September 11, Americans within a year and a half found their country widely regarded as an international pariah."[38] Despite this negative global reaction and the difficulty in winning the peace after quickly winning an apparent victory in the war, Gaddis insisted that "Iraq is not Vietnam." These unintended consequences and unforeseen obstacles notwithstanding, he thought "there is still time, then, to defeat the insurgency – even though the insurgents are no doubt also learning from their own mistakes."[39] He believed the Iraq

[36] John Lewis Gaddis, *Surprise, Security, and the American Experience* (Cambridge, MA, 2004); John F. Dickerson, "What the President Reads," *Time* 165 (January 17, 2005): 45.
[37] John Lewis Gaddis, "Grand Strategy in the Second Term," *Foreign Affairs* 84 (January–February 2005): 14.
[38] Gaddis, *Foreign Affairs*, 5–6.
[39] Gaddis, *Foreign Affairs*, 8–9.

war could still help achieve the larger goal of promoting freedom, noting that "President Bush has insisted that the world will not be safe from terrorists until the Middle East is safe for democracy."[40]

Like Kennedy, Gaddis focused on ends rather than means, praising Bush's definition of the purpose while discounting the costs and the gap between expectations and results. His suggestions for fixing the president's grand strategy, like the Bush Doctrine itself, did not include specific methods to achieve the general goals. He simply recommended that the administration might benefit from asking: What would Bismarck do? "The most skillful practitioner ever of shock and awe, Otto von Bismarck, shattered the post-1815 European settlement in order to unify Germany in 1871," Gaddis recalled. "Having done so, however, he did not assume that the pieces would simply fall into place as he wished them to: he made sure that they did through the careful, patient construction of a new European order that offered benefits to all who were included within it. Bismarck's system survived for almost half a century."[41] To suggest that Bush should emulate Bismarck's statecraft, as Gaddis did, was not very helpful. He did not explain what he thought Bismarck would have done. Moreover, if Bush were to take this advice seriously, he would have to jettison his own Wilsonian ideology, which Gaddis also recommended as the basis for national consensus. Wilson and Bush proclaimed the same American ideals to justify their wars, as both Kennedy and Gaddis affirmed. In this regard, the Bush Doctrine did resemble Wilson's vision of a new world order.[42] However, Bush's grand strategy, even as Gaddis sought to fix it, failed to connect Wilsonian goals with specific policies to make the world safe for democracy.[43] In this regard, too, Bush followed Wilson's legacy of failure to unite ends and means.

In his book, Gaddis developed the thesis that Bush's global war on terrorism adhered to well-established traditions in U.S. diplomacy. He traced the key ideas in the Bush Doctrine back through the American experience. He noted that in the nineteenth century, as Frederick Jackson Turner and C. Vann Woodward had observed, Americans benefited from the availability of both free land and free security. During the War of 1812, the British army attacked the national capitol in Washington,

[40] Gaddis, *Foreign Affairs*, 12.
[41] Gaddis, *Foreign Affairs*, 15.
[42] See also Ambrosius, *Wilsonianism*, 16–18.
[43] On this failure in Iraq, see Larry Diamond, "What Went Wrong in Iraq," *Foreign Affairs* 83 (September–October 2004): 34–56; Larry Diamond, *Squandered Victory: The American Occupation and the Bungled Effort to Bring Democracy to Iraq* (New York, 2005).

DC, burning the Executive Mansion on August 24, 1814, from which President James Madison and his wife Dolley had just fled. After that humiliating defeat, Americans sought absolute security through expansion, as James Chace and Caleb Carr recounted in *America Invulnerable* (1988).[44] To secure their own freedom, Americans began to enlarge their area of predominance, hoping thereby to escape from foreign threats. Gaddis emphasized that "for the United States, *safety comes from enlarging, rather than from contracting, its sphere of responsibilities.*"[45]

Gaddis credited John Quincy Adams as the chief architect of this expansionist plan for national security. Before Adams served as President James Monroe's secretary of state and then as president, he was already an experienced diplomat. At Ghent he had helped negotiate the end of the War of 1812. Gaddis stressed that "it was Adams, more than anyone else, who worked out the methods by which expansion could be made to provide the security that C. Vann Woodward, over a century later, would write about. These sound surprisingly relevant in the aftermath of September 11th: they were preemption, unilateralism, and hegemony."[46]

Preemption became the American practice, Gaddis argued, in dealing with the continuing European presence in North America and also with Native Americans. Adams justified General Andrew Jackson's invasion of Florida in 1818 as a legitimate response to raids across the southern border by Creeks, Seminoles, and escaped slaves. In pursuit of "security through expansion," Adams and Jackson thought it was appropriate to move into the areas of these "non-state actors" in Florida and elsewhere on the advancing frontier. Later as president, Jackson continued this same approach. Gaddis observed that "Jackson's argument – that an expanding 'civilization' spread out along an insecure frontier had the right of preemption – was a predictable extension of Adams's own thinking, as well as a powerful justification for such dispossessions throughout the rest of the nineteenth century." In the 1840s, Polk used the preemptive approach to annex Texas and then conquer the Southwest to the Pacific by resorting to war with Mexico. This continental expansion enhanced national security and justified preemption.[47]

According to Gaddis, the United States extended preemption beyond North America at the end of the nineteenth century. After the sinking of

---

44 James Chace and Caleb Carr, *America Invulnerable: The Quest for Absolute Security from 1812 to Star Wars* (New York, 1988).
45 Gaddis, *Surprise, Security, and the American Experience*, 13.
46 Gaddis, *Surprise, Security, and the American Experience*, 15–16.
47 Gaddis, *Surprise, Security, and the American Experience*, 16–19.

the *U.S.S. Maine* in 1898, President McKinley led the nation into war against Spain over Cuba and then called for annexing the Philippines and other Spanish possessions. Presidents during the Progressive Era, Roosevelt, Taft, and Wilson, also launched "preemptive interventions" into Caribbean and Latin American countries where instability might tempt the European great powers, especially Imperial Germany. "Concerns about 'failed' or 'derelict' states, then," Gaddis concluded, "are nothing new in the history of United States foreign relations, nor are strategies of preemption in dealing with them. So when President George W. Bush warned, at West Point in June 2002, that Americans must 'be ready for preemptive action when necessary to defend our liberty and to defend our lives,' he was echoing an old tradition rather than establishing a new one. Adams, Jackson, Polk, McKinley, Roosevelt, Taft, and Wilson all have understood it perfectly well."[48]

Unilateralism also characterized the American practice in international relations, Gaddis argued. In his famous Farewell Address, President Washington had affirmed this stance, which later found expression in the Monroe Doctrine. As secretary of state, Adams played a key role in defining this doctrine. The United States sought its own security by separating the new world from the old. While Americans avoided entanglements in Europe, they expected Europeans to refrain from interfering in the Western Hemisphere. Sometimes labeled as isolationism, although the United States never actually isolated itself from the rest of the world, unilateralism shaped American foreign relations throughout the nineteenth and early twentieth centuries. America's standoffish involvement in World War I demonstrated its continuing influence. "The United States intervened decisively in World War I," Gaddis observed, "but only as an 'associated,' not an 'allied,' power; and when President Wilson proposed a peace to be enforced by a League of Nations obligated to act against future wars, his own country repudiated it." This rejection of multilateralism continued prior to World War II, he noted. "Unilateralism reached its apex during the 1920s and 1930s when, despite the power the United States now had to shape the course of events throughout the world, Americans refused to use that power lest it somehow compromise their own so rightly prized freedom of action."[49] The resurgence of unilateralism in post–Cold War American foreign policy, first in Clinton's administration and then even more in George W. Bush's, was therefore nothing new.

---

[48] Gaddis, *Surprise, Security, and the American Experience,* 19–22.
[49] Gaddis, *Surprise, Security, and the American Experience,* 25.

Hegemony was also a well-established tradition in U.S. foreign relations, Gaddis emphasized. It too went back to Adams, who had sought an American preponderance of power over the North American continent. This would prevent the Europeans from maintaining a balance of power in the new world. Adams did not want the European empires to restrict the United States. Once Americans had achieved hegemony in North America, and thereby precluded a new balance of power here, the United States could expand its influence into South America. This American experience appeared to Gaddis still relevant in the post–Cold War era: "Let me suggest here only that, for all of his concern about taking on monsters abroad, had John Quincy Adams lived to see the end of the Cold War, he would not have found the position of the United States within the international system an unfamiliar one." What Adams had prescribed for North America now seemed to be applicable worldwide. "Despite the difference between a continental and a global scale," Gaddis argued, "the American commitment to maintaining a predominance of power – as distinct from a balance of power – was much the same in the 1990s as it had been in his day. Nor would Adams have detected evidence of hypocrisy cloaking ambition in what President Bush announced at West Point in June 2002: that 'America has, and intends to keep, military strength beyond challenge.'" Once more Gaddis placed Bush squarely within the American diplomatic tradition that Adams had defined. This "grand strategy of John Quincy Adams," which had become deeply "embedded within our national consciousness," configured the Bush Doctrine after 9/11.[50]

In the early twentieth century, Gaddis observed, American presidents had wrestled with the question of how far to expand American predominance to protect national security. Wilson gave his answer during World War I. Gaddis claimed that "in Wilson's mind, at least, the issue of how far the American sphere of responsibility must extend to ensure American security had now been settled: it would extend everywhere." His global vision for a new international order would guarantee collective security for the whole world. "Wilson's concept of a League of Nations," Gaddis argued, "implied a commitment, from all of its members and certainly from the United States, to act collectively to resist future aggression wherever in the world it took place. The war had shown that security was a seamless web: if it came apart anywhere, the fabric could unravel everywhere. The international community must therefore prevent such threats

[50] Gaddis, *Surprise, Security, and the American Experience*, 30–31.

to peace from developing, and if necessary retaliate against whoever had broken the peace."[51] Affirming the wisdom of this global definition of American national security, Gaddis endorsed the perspective of St. John's University historian Frank Ninkovich, who had credited Wilson with originating the "domino theory" in U.S. foreign policy.[52] According to this theory, later applied in the Vietnam War, the United States could protect itself only by expanding its predominance to all parts of the world. It could not distinguish between primary and secondary interests in different regions. No limits or balances of power could be tolerated in this conception of America's grand strategy. Bush embraced this Wilsonian legacy, and Gaddis affirmed it too, both believing that the national security of the United States in the twenty-first century required American global hegemony.

During World War II and the Cold War, however, the United States had accepted limits to its power and had refrained from seeking absolute security. Gaddis recognized this self-restraint in Franklin D. Roosevelt, who embraced Wilson's global understanding of national security but was more realistic. Because FDR thought the United States could never be safe in a world that permitted military aggressors to profit from war, Gaddis concluded,

he was, in this sense, a Wilsonian, fully inclined to accept, as a principle, the seamless web metaphor for international security. He was also, however, a far more skillful leader than Wilson, for he never neglected, as Wilson did, the need to keep *proclaimed* interests from extending beyond *actual* capabilities. This was the great consistency that explained FDR's inconsistencies. It helps to account for the fact that his strategy brought two separate wars to almost simultaneous conclusions with the victor far stronger than at their beginnings.[53]

In other words, his victorious strategy took into account both ends and means. Moreover, while winning the war and planning the peace, FDR expanded American hegemony from the Western Hemisphere to the rest of the world. "Equally significant," Gaddis also noted, "is the fact that Roosevelt pulled off this expanded hegemony by scrapping rather than embracing the two other key components of Adams's strategy, unilateralism and preemption."[54] He awaited Japan's attack on Pearl Harbor before leading the United States into World War II and then he adopted a

[51] Gaddis, *Surprise, Security, and the American Experience*, 42.
[52] Frank Ninkovich, *Modernity and Power: A History of the Domino Theory in the Twentieth Century* (Chicago, 1994).
[53] Gaddis, *Surprise, Security, and the American Experience*, 47.
[54] Gaddis, *Surprise, Security, and the American Experience*, 48.

multilateral approach to the wartime alliance and to postwar peacemaking, seeking American predominance in a new United Nations to replace the discredited League of Nations.

Throughout the Cold War, Gaddis recognized, the United States followed the pattern that FDR had established. It sought hegemony or a preponderance of power, but mostly adhered to multilateralism while seeking to deter Soviet military aggression and contain the spread of Communism. "The history of American grand strategy during the Cold War," Gaddis noted, "is remarkable for the *infrequency* with which the United States acted unilaterally, as well as for top-level resistance to the idea of preemption and its related nuclear era concept, preventive war."[55] In practice, American leaders had accepted limits to their control of foreign affairs, accommodating themselves to a global balance of power. Other nations that feared Soviet or Communist threats joined the United States, forming alliances to implement deterrence and containment. These policies had enabled the United States and its allies to win the Cold War. Nevertheless, Gaddis now believed, statecraft that had won World War II and the Cold War was no longer relevant after 9/11. Earlier precedents seemed more useful. Unlike Leffler, who found evidence of preemption, unilateralism, and hegemony during the Cold War, Gaddis traced Bush's national security strategy back to the American experience in the nineteenth and early twentieth centuries. Both historians, however, focused on U.S. foreign policy traditions to explain the Bush Doctrine.[56]

After the Cold War and especially after 9/11, according to Gaddis as well as Bush, the United States needed a new grand strategy. Ironically, however, he did not develop the argument that novel threats in a radically new era in world history warranted the Bush Doctrine. He sought instead to legitimize it by emphasizing its well-established American historical roots. "What all of this implies, then," Gaddis asserted, "is a redefinition, for only the third time in American history, of what it will take to protect the nation from surprise attack. That requirement has expanded now from John Quincy Adams's vision of continental hegemony through Franklin D. Roosevelt's conception of a great power coalition aimed at containing, deterring, and if necessary defeating aggressor states to what is already being called the Bush Doctrine: that the United States will identify and eliminate terrorists wherever they are, together with regimes that sustain them. Respecting sovereignty is no longer sufficient because that

---

[55] Gaddis, *Surprise, Security, and the American Experience*, 58.
[56] Leffler, *Diplomatic History*, 395–413.

implies a game in which the players understand and respect the rules. In this new game there are no rules."[57] Embracing this rationale for transgressing the limits of international law, Gaddis disregarded the potentially dangerous consequence that the Bush Doctrine would set the tone at the bottom of the chain of command for American torture of Iraqi prisoners at Abu Ghraib and other violations of human rights.[58]

Gaddis did not explain why the threats after 9/11 were so novel as to require the scrapping of containment and deterrence. He did not make this case for Bush's radical departure from the World War II and Cold War experience. Instead, he stressed historical continuity with an earlier legacy. Gaddis argued that Bush followed well-established traditions in U.S. diplomacy. Adams had originated the key ideas in the Bush Doctrine, he claimed, and Wilson had expanded them worldwide. This contention missed the crucial point, however, that historical continuity could not justify a radically new grand strategy. That would have required a different argument about discontinuity between the past and the future, not the one that Gaddis made to legitimize Bush's wars. The underlying logic was deeply flawed, moreover, by his America-centric focus, although that probably explained why so many Americans, in contrast to foreigners, overlooked the Bush Doctrine's radical implications for the world's future.

Gaddis neglected the relevant history. He placed the Bush Doctrine within the historic traditions of the United States, and thereby explained its widespread appeal to Americans, but failed to assess its potential effects in the international context of the Middle East. He missed the fundamental point that Columbia University historian Rashid Khalidi made in *Resurrecting Empire* (2004). Khalidi observed that Americans typically lack interest in the history of other peoples, or even of their own past, because of their focus on the future. In contrast, Middle Eastern peoples have long memories of their encounters with the West. In its myopic vision, the Bush administration expected to remake the Middle East. It suffered from imperial hubris and ignorance of the realities in this region.[59] These self-inflicted limitations, Khalidi charged, "were grounded in willful ignorance and misinterpretation of the history,

---

[57] Gaddis, *Surprise, Security, and the American Experience,* 85–86.
[58] Seymour M. Hersh, *Chain of Command: The Road from 9/11 to Abu Ghraib* (New York, 2004).
[59] Rashid Khalidi, *Resurrecting Empire: Western Footprints and America's Perilous Path in the Middle East* (Boston, 2004), vi–ix. See also Douglas Little, *American Orientalism: The United States and the Middle East Since 1945* (Chapel Hill, NC, 2002); Anonymous [Michael Scheuer], *Imperial Hubris: Why the West Is Losing the War on Terror* (Washington, DC, 2004).

politics, and culture of the Middle East."[60] Moreover, this intentional misunderstanding or distortion prevented American policy-makers from recognizing or acknowledging the inherent contradiction in seeking to impose democracy on other peoples in the Middle East or elsewhere. By its very nature, American or British military occupation of Iraq denied self-rule to its people. It might serve foreign interests, but, to the extent that it imposed control from outside, it denied democracy within Iraq.[61] To gain a realistic assessment of the Middle East, Khalidi argued persuasively, Americans needed to escape their myopic version of world history – or what Schulte Nordholt called "the myth of the West." Unfortunately, Gaddis failed to do this. He kept his focus on the United States and embraced its exceptionalism. He was not alone.

At the end of the Cold War, it had appeared to other triumphal Americans that world history was moving toward fulfillment of Wilsonian ideals. Francis Fukuyama, who served as a State Department policy analyst and later became a Johns Hopkins University political economist, proclaimed the imminent "end of history." He affirmed that "the fact that there will be setbacks and disappointments in the process of democratization, or that not every market economy will prosper, should not distract us from the larger pattern that is emerging in world history." He claimed that the "choices that countries face in determining how they will organize themselves politically and economically [have] been *diminishing* over time." Although human history had witnessed various types of regimes in the past, he rejoiced that "the only form of government that has survived intact to the end of the twentieth century has been liberal democracy."[62] This was now the only viable option for all countries.

Johns Hopkins University political scientist Michael Mandelbaum fully agreed. Although Wilson himself had failed to create a new world order based on his ideas of peace, democracy, and free markets, this "Wilsonian triad" had become the global reality by the twenty-first century. These were, Mandelbaum proclaimed, "the ideas that conquered the world." He explained:

Wilson's ideas did not take hold [in 1918–19], another terrible war erupted two decades later, and his career came to be regarded as a failure, its details forgotten by all but historians. At the outset of the twenty-first century, however, these ideas

---

[60] Khalidi, *Resurrecting Empire*, 146.
[61] Khalidi, *Resurrecting Empire*, 164–65.
[62] Francis Fukuyama, *The End of History and the Last Man* (New York, 1992), 45; Francis Fukuyama, "Beyond Our Shores," *The Wall Street Journal* (December 24, 2002), Editorial Page <www.opinionjournal.com>.

had come to dominate the world. His prescription for organizing political and economic life and for conducting foreign policy are the keys to understanding the new world that emerged when the great global conflict of the second half of the twentieth century, the Cold War, came to an end.[63]

World history seemed to be progressing toward the triumph of Wilsonianism.

Less optimistic that Wilsonian ideals would continue to prevail after 9/11, Gaddis applauded Bush's decision to use aggressive military force to ensure their success in this hostile environment. "So the formula," he explained, "is Fukuyama plus force: the United States must finish the job that Woodrow Wilson started. The world, quite literally, is to be made safe for democracy, even those parts of it, like the Muslim Middle East, that have so far resisted that tendency. Terrorism – and by implication the authoritarianism that breeds it – must become as obsolete as slavery, piracy, or genocide: 'behavior that no respectable government can condone or support and that all must oppose.' Otherwise democracy, in this new age of vulnerability, will never be safe in the world."[64] Making the world safe for democracy thus required perpetual war.

Bush's unlimited pursuit of global hegemony resembled Kaiser Wilhelm II's *Weltpolitik* more than Bismarck's *Realpolitik*, although the president's avowed purpose was different. In 1914, after the assassination of Austria's archduke Franz Ferdinand in Sarajevo, Wilhelm II led Imperial Germany into a preventive war in Europe, justifying this aggressive military response as legitimate self-defense against the danger of state-supported terrorism. To retaliate against Serbia for its complicity in the assassination and thereby to protect the Austro-Hungarian and German empires against further attacks by terrorists or by regimes that supported them, he resorted to war, first in Europe and then beyond. Similarly, Bush led the United States into a global war on terrorism, rationalizing his use of military force with his new doctrine – a new *Weltpolitik*.

The Bush Doctrine extended the logic of Wilson's legacy far beyond anything that he had attempted, or that other U.S. presidents had regarded as necessary for national security. They had usually shown more prudence in keeping America's aims within the reach of its power. Gaddis acknowledged this radical departure. "It was one thing for a continental hegemon to threaten preemption within its own environs,

---

[63] Michael Mandelbaum, *The Ideas That Conquered the World: Peace, Democracy, and Free Markets in the Twenty-first Century* (New York, 2002), 6, 17.
[64] Gaddis, *Surprise, Security, and the American Experience*, 90.

as John Quincy Adams, Theodore Roosevelt, and Woodrow Wilson had all done," he admitted. "It was quite another thing for a global hegemon to threaten it wherever necessary, as George W. Bush appeared to be doing."[65] This radical shift in the conduct of U.S. foreign relations, most apparent in Bush's decision for war against Saddam Hussein's Iraq in 2003, produced undesirable consequences. "Among these," Gaddis allowed, "was the fact that, within a little more than a year and a half, the United States exchanged its long-established reputation as the principal *stabilizer* of the international system for one as its chief *destabilizer*."[66] The Bush administration convinced most Americans that its preventive war in Iraq was merely a legitimate extension of its global war on terrorism, but this new war did not look that way to foreign observers.[67] They did not think that Bush had learned what Bismarck – and also what other American presidents – had understood: the importance of a state's self-restraint in international relations. The Bush Doctrine did not define or prescribe such limits on the pursuit of Wilsonian ideals. Gaddis affirmed it nevertheless, despite his own suggestion that Americans might learn from Bismarck's example.

REALIST CRITIQUES OF THE BUSH DOCTRINE

Largely endorsing Bush's grand strategy for winning the global war on terrorism, Gaddis put forth some questionable interpretations of the American diplomatic tradition. In his review of *Surprise, Security, and the American Experience*, University of Virginia historian Norman A. Graebner identified several of these. He did not agree that Bush was following the precedents of John Quincy Adams. Although Adams had indeed approved Jackson's pursuit of Indians into Spanish Florida, this was quite different from Bush's policy of preemption to justify striking first in Iraq. Graebner noted that "Florida was contiguous territory, the threat was immediate, rendering the American response admissible under international law. There was no danger of Spanish retaliation, and Madrid recognized its responsibility. Adams's preemption of 1818 was no precedent for the U.S. invasion of Iraq."[68]

[65] Gaddis, *Surprise, Security, and the American Experience*, 100.
[66] Gaddis, *Surprise, Security, and the American Experience*, 101.
[67] Hans Leyendecker, *Die Lügen des Weißen Hauses: Warum Amerika einen Neuanfang braucht* (Hamburg, 2004).
[68] Norman A. Graebner, "Adamsian Unilateralism vs. The Bushian Imitation," *American Diplomacy* (December 2004), <www.americandiplomacy.org>.

Graebner also rejected Gaddis's claim that Bush's unilateralism followed Adams's precedent. At a time when American and European interests diverged and when the balance of power in Europe prevented its great empires from endangering U.S. security, there was no need for the United States to involve itself in European affairs. The Monroe Doctrine expressed this reality, promising U.S. self-restraint and expecting reciprocity from Europe. Adams opposed any kind of crusade to rescue Greece from Turkey or to liberate Latin America from Spain and Portugal. "Adams's unilateralism," Graebner argued, "was no greater precedent for American behavior following the 9/11 crisis."[69]

Likewise, Adams's pursuit of a continental empire was different. "His concept of American hegemony was equally limited," Graebner noted. "He claimed U.S. primacy on the North American continent, but he made no effort to acquire Canada, Texas, California, or Mexico. He opposed the Mexican War even as earlier he opposed the War of 1812. Adams's world was one of acute diplomacy, not war." He was not a wartime ideological crusader like Wilson and Bush. "Adams's concern with defending U.S. borders from pirates and Indians was hardly synonymous with Bush's determination to free the entire world of terrorists," Graebner concluded.[70] Unlike Gaddis, Graebner saw Adams as a diplomatist who understood the limits of power and sought to protect the United States without transforming the world through moral and military crusades. In other words, the ends and means in Adams's definition of U.S. foreign policy were coherent, in sharp contrast to Bush's rationale for his global war on terrorism.[71]

Graebner was not alone in questioning Gaddis's version of the American past. Princeton University historian James M. McPherson cautioned against the use of preventive war, noting that Americans had never started such wars with the exception of the South's attack on Fort Sumter. On April 12, 1861, the Confederate states launched a preemptive strike against the Union. Southern moderates, he observed, tried to warn their extremist colleagues against starting a war, preferring to await President Abraham Lincoln's actions. "Wait for an 'overt act' against southern rights before taking the drastic step of secession with its risk of civil war, they implored. But fire-eaters insisted that the South could not afford to wait

---

[69] Graebner, *American Diplomacy*, <www.americandiplomacy.org>.
[70] Graebner, *American Diplomacy*, <www.americandiplomacy.org>.
[71] See also Andrew J. Rotter, Mary Ann Heiss, Richard Immerman, Regina Gramer, and John Lewis Gaddis, "John Gaddis's *Surprise, Security, and the American Experience*: A Roundtable Critique," *Passport* 36 (August 2005): 4–16.

until the North loosed another John Brown or other weapons of mass destruction." Rather than wait, southern states seceded from the Union, formed the Confederacy, and launched a preventive war at Fort Sumter. This war did not turn out well for the southerners, however. "Less than four years later," McPherson reminded contemporary Americans, "the empire of this master race lay in ruins."[72] By implication, he suggested that Bush imperiled the United States by repeating the South's mistake.

WILSONIAN DEFENSE OF THE BUSH DOCTRINE

As both Gaddis and Judis noted, Wilson intervened frequently with U.S. military force in Caribbean and Latin American countries. Historians such as Frederick S. Calhoun have justified these actions, claiming that the president was promoting democracy.[73] Neoconservative military historian Max Boot agreed, emphasizing that "far from renouncing the interventionist policies of his Republican predecessors, Wilson expanded them. The stern Presbyterian professor believed that America had a duty to export democracy abroad, and he was prepared to act on it."[74] Viewing the president's actions as typical of "the savage wars of peace" that the United States fought throughout its history, Boot argued that these small wars contributed to America's rise as a world power. "While often portrayed as a soft, fuzzy doctrine," he explained, "Wilsonianism often requires the use of force."[75] Like Gaddis, Boot saw Wilson's military interventions in the Caribbean and Latin American countries as precedents for George W. Bush's preemptive war in the Middle East. This comparison, however, ignored Wilson's failure to establish democracy in any of the nearby nations that U.S. forces occupied and his great reluctance to send U.S. troops into distant regions. He was slow to take the United States into World War I and to approve military intervention in revolutionary Russia. Only after German submarines sank three American ships did the president ask Congress to declare war against Germany. Only after the European Allies had repeatedly requested military intervention in Russia did he finally agree. These were not

---

[72] James M. McPherson, "The Fruits of Preventive War," *Perspectives* 41 (May 2003): 5–6.

[73] Frederick S. Calhoun, *Power and Principle: Armed Intervention in Wilsonian Foreign Policy* (Kent, OH, 1986).

[74] Max Boot, *The Savage Wars of Peace: Small Wars and the Rise of American Power* (New York, 2002), 149.

[75] Max Boot, "George Wilson Bush," *The Wall Street Journal* (July 1, 2002), Editorial Page <www.opinionjournal.com>.

precedents for preventive war of the sort that Bush sought to justify with his doctrine of preemption. Moreover, these were not unilateral presidential actions. Wilson led the United States into World War I with the approval of Congress and he sent American troops into Russia at the request of the Allies. These actions demonstrated his cautious approach to the conduct of U.S. foreign relations, despite his rhetoric. Emphasizing his prudence, Judis made an essential point about a significant difference between Wilson and Bush that proponents of preemption, including Gaddis and Boot, missed when they identified the Bush Doctrine with Wilsonianism.

On the issue of multilateralism versus unilateralism, Judis and Gaddis were both partly right and partly wrong. Praising Wilson's multilateralism, Judis stressed his key role in creating the League of Nations, an international institution that was essential to his new world order. But Wilson also protected unilateral American decision-making during the drafting the Covenant at the Paris Peace Conference and in his plans for the new League's future proceedings. He insisted that all permanent members of the Council must have a veto over any recommendation it might make to fulfill the promise of collective security, thereby ensuring that it could never act without American approval if the United States joined the League. Judis discounted this protection for unilateral U.S. decision-making in the League, as did other proponents of multilateralism in the post–Cold War years.[76] This feature of the League, although not cited by Gaddis, supported his emphasis on Wilson's unilateralism. Yet the president also genuinely wanted the League as an institution for the practice of multilateral diplomacy. His enthusiasm for the new League was substantially different from Bush's disdain for its successor, the United Nations. When Gaddis placed Bush squarely in the Wilsonian tradition, he neglected this important difference. Wilson combined both unilateralism and multilateralism in his approach to international relations, but Bush preferred to act alone.[77]

More clearly than Judis, Gaddis recognized Wilson's quest for global hegemony. The president promoted the interests of an American empire,

---

[76] See, for example, John Gerard Ruggie, *Winning the Peace: America and World Order in the New Era* (New York, 1996); Robert S. McNamara and James G. Blight, *Wilson's Ghost: Reducing the Risk of Conflict, Killing, and Catastrophe in the 21st Century* (New York, 2001).

[77] Ivo H. Daalder and James M. Lindsay, *America Unbound: The Bush Revolution in Foreign Policy* (Washington, DC, 2003); Stefan Halper and Jonathan Clarke, *America Alone: The Neo-Conservatives and the Global Order* (Cambridge, 2004).

albeit different from European colonial empires and therefore not called an empire. Taking him at his word, Judis depicted an idealized Wilson who opposed imperialism and promoted democracy. Despite the president's denial of imperial ambitions, and Judis's failure to recognize these, his ideology justified American hegemony in world affairs at the expense of European empires. His contemporaries called it international social control. Wilsonianism rationalized the American empire's global expansion. Despite his critique of European imperialism, Wilson endeavored to make the United States into the world's leading nation (or empire) after World War I.

Bush identified himself with this hegemonic legacy. Addressing the National Endowment for Democracy on November 6, 2003, he placed himself in the tradition of Wilson, FDR, and Reagan. "The advance of freedom," Bush said, "is the calling of our time; it is the calling of our country. From the Fourteen Points to the Four Freedoms, to the Speech at Westminster, America has put our power at the service of principle. We believe that liberty is the design of nature; we believe that liberty is the direction of history."[78] When Judis claimed that Bush abandoned Wilsonianism, he neglected his ideological debt to Wilson, which Kennedy and Leffler rightly stressed. Focusing on means rather than ends, Judis emphasized Bush's reckless pursuit of an American empire in contrast to Wilson's more cautious statecraft. Reversing the focus, Gaddis recognized Bush's ideological link to Wilson and their common pursuit of American global hegemony that might well be called an empire.[79] But while affirming the Bush Doctrine as a grand strategy for national security in the historic tradition of Adams and Wilson, Gaddis ignored that Bush did not behave with the characteristic prudence of either Adams or Wilson. Nor was his statecraft like Bismarck's.

University of Texas historian Robert A. Divine understood the danger of focusing on ends while downplaying means in the conduct of U.S. foreign relations. He discerned that Americans, who have fought "perpetual war for perpetual peace," have found it difficult to end wars. "All too often," he observed, "U.S. leaders have failed to realize the close connection between the use of force in wartime and the political process of making peace." He cited Wilson's failure to write his idealistic principles into

[78] George W. Bush, "President Bush Discusses Freedom in Iraq and Middle East," November 6, 2003, <www.whitehouse.gov/news/releases/2003/11.html>.
[79] David P. Rapkin, "Empire and its Discontents," *New Political Economy* 10 (September 2005): 389–411.

the Versailles Treaty as an example of unintended consequences. Divine concluded that,

for the United States at least, war is a messy and unpredictable way to deal with international problems. Americans enter into conflicts convinced that they can create a better and more stable world once their enemies are defeated, only to meet with unexpected outcomes and a new set of challenges. Perhaps a more realistic view of war, one that does not raise so many hopes for a brighter future, would be the lesson we should draw from our twentieth-century experience with armed conflict.

Accordingly, Divine advised that "an understanding of the utopian nature of the Wilsonian quest for enduring peace may be the surest guide for dealing with these future international challenges."[80] It would enable Americans to avoid Wilson's mistakes.

The Bush administration ignored this sage advice. In pursuit of Wilsonian goals, it disregarded the likelihood of unintended consequences from U.S. military intervention and the difficulty of converting military victory into enduring peace. Lacking even Wilson's prudence in practice, which Judis stressed, Bush sought democratic transformation of the entire Middle East, beginning with Iraq. Gaddis, Divine's former student, also ignored his mentor's advice. He applauded Bush's grand strategy of preemption, unilateralism, and hegemony without explaining how the United States might spread democracy and restore peace in Iraq or anywhere else. A preemptive or preventive war, unilateral action, and hegemonic behavior would not automatically produce the desired results. Gaddis did not clarify what Bismarck would have done, or what Bush should do, to turn an apparent military victory in Iraq into a durable political settlement with either democracy or peace. Kennedy too failed to address the hard questions that Divine raised. Emphasizing what Bush owed Wilson, he kept his focus on their common ideology, ignoring the crucial but difficult tasks of postwar nation-building and peacemaking. Both Gaddis and Kennedy ignored the disparity between ends and means in the Bush Doctrine.

WALTER RUSSELL MEAD AND THE BUSH DOCTRINE

Walter Russell Mead, the Henry A. Kissinger senior fellow at the Council of Foreign Relations, also jumped onto the Bush bandwagon after September

[80] Robert A. Divine, *Perpetual War for Perpetual Peace* (College Station, TX, 2000), 85.

11, 2001. Like Gaddis and Kennedy, he identified the Bush Doctrine with Wilsonianism and the American diplomatic tradition. He praised Bush's grand strategy of preemption, unilateralism, and hegemony. Calling it "an American project – a grand strategic vision of what it is that the United States seeks to build in the world," Mead reinterpreted American history to find its origins. In *Power, Terror, Peace, and War* (2004), he claimed: "This project – to protect our own domestic security while building a peaceful world order of democratic states linked by common values and sharing a common prosperity – has deep roots in the American past." Like Gaddis, he focused on the American experience rather than novel threats in the world after 9/11. Explaining Bush's grand strategy for the twenty-first century, in his view, was essentially "a project of historical scholarship and deductive reasoning."[81]

Mead's recognition of the United States as a global hegemon was not new. He had acknowledged the existence of an American empire, however different it might be from others. In *Mortal Splendor* (1987), he traced the rise of this "liberal empire" as the twentieth-century successor of the British Empire. He noted that Wilson had outlined his vision of liberal internationalism during World War I, but the United States did not follow him. During World War II, however, Roosevelt succeeded. The liberalism of his New Deal at home created the foundation for America's liberal empire abroad. The United States fulfilled the vision of Wilson's Fourteen Points and FDR's Atlantic Charter and Four Freedoms during the Cold War. This liberal empire reached its zenith during the 1960s under Presidents John F. Kennedy and Lyndon B. Johnson. It lingered on under Presidents Richard Nixon and Jimmy Carter.

Defeat in the Vietnam War took its toll, but other factors also contributed to the relative worsening of America's place in world affairs. American hegemony, which had enabled the United States to establish its liberal empire after World War II, was no longer so influential in the 1980s. By that "Age of Decline" during Reagan's presidency, America's empire was clearly in transition. It could wane as well as wax, Mead now understood, as did Yale historian Paul Kennedy, who published *The Rise and Fall of the Great Powers* (1987) in the same year. A liberal empire in decline, Mead warned, might be tempted to abandon its democratic politics in favor of militarism. "Politics must offer hope, real hope, and in the long run this can be sustained only by real progress," Mead explained.

---

[81] Walter Russell Mead, *Power, Terror, Peace, and War: America's Grand Strategy in a World at Risk* (New York, 2004), 7, 19.

By politics, of course, we mean democratic politics. It is possible for military regimes like those throughout the U.S. sphere of influence to enforce a conservative vision with bayonets; perhaps this is the direction in which American conservatism has to travel if it wishes to retain power. If so, there will be no shortage of leaders willing to travel that road or of intellectuals willing to rationalize that decision, defending torture and dictatorship while preening themselves on their hardheaded realism and their affinity for the eternal values of Western civilization.[82]

In view of this prescient warning, it is ironic that Mead himself would later become one of those hardheaded intellectuals who rationalized the Bush Doctrine, identifying it with the militant nationalist heritage of Jacksonian realism.

In *Special Providence* (2002), Mead stressed how American foreign policy had changed the world, joining other triumphalists such as Francis Fukuyama and Michael Mandelbaum. This victory required the United States to create an empire and act as a global hegemon. "Call it empire, hegemony, world order, or globalization," he noted, "the question of global economic integration under British or American auspices and the political strategies that advance this great process have been at or near the center of both American and British foreign and domestic politics for centuries."[83] For the United States, economic globalization and democracy went together, both shaping its grand strategy. "Although the word *globalization* is new," Mead explained, "and although the process has accelerated and deepened in recent years, globalization has been the most important fact of world history during the entire history of the United States. Because of our geographical situation and the commercial enterprising nature of American society, globalization has been at the heart of American strategic thinking and policy making for virtually all of our history."[84] Moreover, democratic governments did not necessarily promote international peace. "The widespread view of our times that democracies don't get into aggressive wars was not accepted by our predecessors," he observed. "The growth of democracy in the United States and Europe went hand in hand with an enormous increase in bellicosity in international relations."[85] Globalization did not enhance the prospects for peace as liberals, such as Wilson, had

---

[82] Walter Russell Mead, *Mortal Splendor: The American Empire in Transition* (Boston, 1987), 185–86.

[83] Walter Russell Mead, *Special Providence: American Foreign Policy and How It Changed the World* (New York, 2002), 38.

[84] Mead, *Special Providence*, 80.

[85] Mead, *Special Providence*, 47.

hoped when they advocated the spread of democratic and capitalist values and institutions.

In *Special Providence*, Mead defined four schools in the American foreign policy tradition, each of which he identified with a prominent U.S. statesman. He associated Alexander Hamilton with promoting national capitalism and economic globalization, Woodrow Wilson with spreading democracy in a new world order of international law, human rights, and collective security, Thomas Jefferson with isolating the United States to avoid foreign entanglements and wars and to protect its own freedom and democracy, and Andrew Jackson with asserting national interests in a populist and militant way. His definitions of these schools were not precise, either theoretically or historically. Mead used "Wilsonian" as a label for more recent human rights agendas for people of color and women, although he acknowledged that Wilson had asserted the supremacy of white men in both American and international politics. His definition of democracy had marginalized women and people of color both at home and abroad. "Wilsonianism," Mead argued, "with all its virtues and defects, is a real thing. It is deeply, probably ineradicably, rooted in American culture and history, and those who hope to shape the country's foreign policy must come to terms with it one way or another."[86] Unlike Gaddis, Mead identified John Quincy Adams and the Monroe Doctrine with the less belligerent Jeffersonian school. Moreover, he recommended this approach as a beneficial corrective to the post–Cold War foreign policies of Presidents George H. W. Bush and Bill Clinton, who had combined the Hamiltonian and Wilsonian schools, and sometimes the Jacksonian way as well, in their vigorous and sometimes militant pursuit of both economic and political globalization during the 1990s.

Recognizing the nationalist appeal of the Jacksonian school, Mead identified it with unilateralism and preemptive war. Explaining their approach to international relations, he noted that Jacksonians believed that:

The United States must be vigilant, strongly armed. Our diplomacy must be cunning, forceful, and no more scrupulous than any other country's. At times we must fight preemptive wars. There is absolutely nothing wrong with subverting foreign governments or assassinating foreign leaders whose bad intentions are clear. Indeed, Jacksonians are more likely to tax political leaders with a failure to employ vigorous measures than to worry about the niceties of international law. Of all the major currents in American society, Jacksonians have the least regard for international law and international practice.[87]

[86] Mead, *Special Providence*, 173.
[87] Mead, *Special Providence*, 246.

In short, they traditionally behaved in unilateral and preemptive ways, resorting to war whenever they thought it would serve national interests. Like Max Boot, Mead acknowledged that Americans had been willing to use power in fairly ruthless ways. He observed: "The United States over its history has consistently summoned the will and the means to compel its enemies to yield to its demands. Attacks on civilian targets and the infliction of heavy casualties on enemy civilians have consistently played a vital part in American war strategies."[88] Mead argued that the United States should balance its Jacksonian nationalist belligerency and also its Wilsonian and Hamiltonian global impulses with Jeffersonian self-restraint. "There is no school whose perspectives we can afford to lose," he concluded, "but in looking at the tasks we now face, it seems to me that the voice of the Jeffersonian school is the one that currently needs to be heard."[89]

Yet Mead soon silenced the Jeffersonian voice in his own thinking about America's grand strategy. After 9/11, the Bush administration had embraced the militant Jacksonian approach, combining it with the Hamiltonian and Wilsonian traditions of economic globalization and worldwide promotion of democracy and freedom. Now Mead, like Gaddis, affirmed the "Fukuyama plus force" formula to finish what Wilson had begun. In *Power, Terror, Peace, and War*, he prescribed what he called the American Revival. He now identified the decline of America's liberal empire by the 1980s with the deterioration of its liberal political economy, which the Progressive presidents had promoted and FDR had established with his New Deal. This "kinder, gentler" capitalism, which Mead called Fordism, had flourished during the early Cold War, but was ebbing by the 1980s. Reagan began to replace Fordism with what Mead called "millennial capitalism."[90] Believing that this new post-Fordist political economy was both desirable and inevitable, Mead advocated the adoption of U.S. foreign policies that would aggressively promote it, labeling these as the American Revival. "The Revivalists are as ambitious in foreign policy as they are in domestic affairs," he noted. They reshaped the historic foreign policy schools into a new, aggressive approach to the world. "The American Revivalists aren't trying to establish a fifth party in American politics to contend against the other four; they are trying to take over all of the four older parties and remake them in the light of American Revival ideas."[91]

---

[88] Mead, *Special Providence*, 221.
[89] Mead, *Special Providence*, 331.
[90] Mead, *Power, Terror, Peace, and War*, 70–71.
[91] Mead, *Power, Terror, Peace, and War*, 84.

In this new era of globalization, which Mead welcomed, American Revivalists combined the Hamiltonian, Wilsonian, and Jacksonian approaches to international relations. He observed that Revival Hamiltonians urged "unfettered competitive capitalism" and Revival Wilsonians aggressively pursued their agenda of promoting democracy, especially in the Middle East. "Revival Wilsonians, whose ranks include the majority of neoconservative policy intellectuals who have played such an important role in Republican foreign policy debates in recent years, have radically restructured the Wilsonian agenda," he affirmed. "They put the first element – the linkage between idealism and security – on steroids, arguing, for example, in the case of the Middle East, that only a much more aggressive pursuit of American ideological values can deal with the security threats we now face." Uninterested in nation-building or international institutions, they nevertheless wanted to spread American ideology throughout the world. U.S. foreign policies should use the nation's exceptionalism as the model for global reform. Mead explained that "Revival Wilsonians believe that traditional American values are so compelling, so demonstrably superior, and so widely popular that they can sweep and reshape the world."[92] Rather than leaving this outcome to chance, however, they used military force to promote it.

The Bush administration, in Mead's view, adopted the American Revival's revolutionary ideology and applied it to Iraq. It employed Jacksonian means to fulfill Wilsonian purposes. He noted: "The neoconservative, Revival Wilsonian approach to the war shared some of this sense of [Jacksonian] military political realism, but added arguments that had less Jacksonian appeal. The neoconservatives saw the occupation of Iraq as the first stage in the reconstruction of the entire region. In this analysis, it was a war to make the world safe for democracy."[93] Revival Wilsonians believed that Wilson had been too naive in expecting world history to move progressively toward the fulfillment of American ideals. It would take a strong military shove from the United States to ensure this outcome. Thus the Bush administration needed to adopt the radically new doctrine of preemptive war and apply it with unilateral action. Yet after Mead embraced the Jacksonian features of the Bush Doctrine as the way to fulfill Wilsonian goals, he hoped that the costs might still be avoided. He suggested tactical adjustments and burden-sharing. "One can only hope," he concluded, "that in the remaining time in office, long or short, the Bush administration will keep its strategic vision, acquire more

[92] Mead, *Power, Terror, Peace, and War*, 88–89.
[93] Mead, *Power, Terror, Peace, and War*, 109–10, 117.

tactical skill, and build a broader national and international consensus for its policies. Without some improvement in execution and consensus building, history's judgment will likely be harsh."[94] While endorsing Bush's grand strategy, Mead hoped that minor changes in its implementation might produce a better historical conclusion. His advice was similar to Leffler's hope that good judgment could somehow compensate for the Bush Doctrine's inherent flaws.

Like Gaddis, who thought that Bush should learn from Bismarck, Mead failed to grasp that the Bush Doctrine committed the United States to a grand strategy that was incompatible with the tactical adjustments he now recommended. Bush's ideological pursuit of Wilsonian goals through preemption, unilateralism, and hegemony precluded any serious consideration of either Gaddis's or Mead's rather contradictory advice. Their suggestions were inconsistent with Bush's grand strategy, which they fully endorsed. Having joined the Bush bandwagon after 9/11, they could not effectively address the vitally important questions that critics were raising. Once they agreed that Bush's Wilsonian principles were the right goals and that his uses of military force unrestricted by international law or institutions were legitimate methods, they surrendered the possibility of challenging his foreign policy in any fundamental way. Mead abandoned his advocacy of Jeffersonian self-restraint as a beneficial corrective to Bush's relentless wielding of global power. The president's preventive war in Iraq appeared just as legitimate as his retaliatory war in Afghanistan. Identifying the Bush Doctrine with Wilsonianism and placing it in the mainstream of both American and world history, despite its radical or revolutionary features, Mead too became a hardheaded intellectual of the kind he had once criticized for being too willing to rationalize abuses of power in the name of "the eternal values of Western civilization."

IDEALISM AND REALISM

Historically, Americans have appealed to their highest ideals while pursuing their own wealth and power. As University of Pennsylvania historian Walter A. McDougall emphasized in *Freedom Just Around the Corner* (2004), they have been hustlers of the type that Herman Melville satirized in *The Confidence-Man* (1857). Both positive and negative, this historic American culture shaped the Progressive politics of Wilson's statecraft

---

[94] Mead, *Power, Terror, Peace, and War*, 162.

and his domestic and international legacy. "This three-fold American Dream of individual 'rags to riches' success, collective social progress, and national crusades overseas is usually associated with the Progressive Era around the turn of the twentieth century," noted McDougall. "But the trinity dated back to the creation of the American colonies, while its assumptions were challenged well before 1900."[95] Keenly aware of idealism's persuasive power in American history, especially in U.S. foreign relations, McDougall resisted the Bush bandwagon after 9/11. He did not believe that the United States should attempt to promote the utopia of a democratized Iraq. Balancing ends and means, it should instead pursue a more realistic goal within the scope of its more limited capability.[96] He did not subscribe to an American exceptionalist interpretation of world history.

Nor did other realists succumb to the ideological appeal of the Bush Doctrine. Colorado College political scientist David C. Hendrickson noted the irony that realists such as University of Chicago political scientist John J. Mearsheimer had joined the Peace Party, while liberals such as Michael Mandelbaum had joined the War Party, which called for "Wilsonianism in boots."[97] Like Gaddis and Mead, many Wilsonian liberals, including those who had become neoconservatives, joined Bush's new crusade to make the world safe for democracy, but skeptical realists cautioned against the dangers of the Bush Doctrine. They were concerned about the means that he used, not just the ends that he promised. They recognized the limits of American power to change the world. Realists thought that circumspection, not ideological crusades, should characterize American statecraft in international relations. Some Wilsonian liberals, such as Judis, also advised the practice of prudence and the avoidance of false hopes. Mindful of the costs of war and the likelihood of unintended consequences, these critics were unwilling to believe that the Bush administration could fulfill its renewed promise to make the world safe for democracy.

[95] Walter A. McDougall, *Freedom Just Around the Corner: A New American History, 1585–1828* (New York, 2004), 7.
[96] Walter A. McDougall, "What the U.S. Needs to Promote in Iraq," *American Diplomacy* (August 2003), <www.americandiplomacy.org>. See also Walter A. McDougall, *Promised Land, Crusader State: The American Encounter with the World Since 1776* (Boston, 1997).
[97] David C. Hendrickson, "The Lion and the Lamb: Realism and Liberalism Reconsidered," *World Policy Journal* 20 (Spring 2003), <www.ciaonet.org>, reviewing Mandelbaum, *The Ideas That Conquered the World* (New York, 2003) and John J. Mearsheimer, *The Tragedy of Great Power Politics* (New York, 2001).

Appealing to the old American hope of "freedom just around the corner," both Wilson and Bush proclaimed American ideals to justify their new foreign policies. Whether in 1917 or 2001 or 2003, they led the nation into war, promising to protect traditional values and institutions at home and to expand these abroad, thereby making freedom and democracy the foundation for world peace. They still affirmed "the myth of the West." They assigned a redemptive role to the United States, committing it to fight evil and create a new international order. After World War I, Wilson failed to make the world safe for democracy. His experience suggested that fighting wars to spread democracy and thereby attain perpetual peace was more likely to result in unanticipated costs and unintended consequences. These costs and consequences may, at least temporarily, be obscured by focusing public discourse on ideology rather than methods, on ends rather than means, as (I noted in 2006) the Bush administration has done.[98] Yet, like Wilson, Bush has not achieved his avowed purpose, and is unlikely to be more successful in the future. His presidency has suffered. A better understanding of both American and world history would have warned him against these potential failures. Sooner or later, historians will assess both the promises and the results of America's latest efforts to fulfill its global mission as earlier proclaimed by Woodrow Wilson and later trumpeted by George W. Bush.

---

[98] Belatedly acknowledging the folly of Bush's foreign policy, Francis Fukuyama, *America at the Crossroads: Democracy, Power, and the Neoconservative Legacy* (New Haven, CT, 2006), 9, concluded: "What we need, in other words, is a more realistic Wilsonianism that matches means to ends in dealing with other societies."

9

Legacy and Reputation

President Woodrow Wilson left an enduring legacy, which enhanced his lasting reputation, in both American and world history. Although the Republicans triumphed over the Democrats in the elections of 1920, they did not overturn all the progressive reforms he had achieved with his New Freedom at home. Nor did they succeed in killing his vision of America's new mission in international relations. With Republicans in charge of the White House and Congress during the 1920s, the nation turned away from Wilson's style of presidential leadership and his progressive domestic and foreign policies. But that reversal ended with the Great Depression of the 1930s and World War II of the 1940s. These new crises created the context for President Franklin D. Roosevelt to revive and expand Wilson's progressive agenda at home and abroad.

In its continuously revised forms, Wilson's legacy influenced American and world history throughout the remainder of the twentieth and into the twenty-first century. The Cold War consensus that most Americans embraced in the late 1940s and 1950s affirmed his modern liberalism. By the 1960s, partly in response to the expanded definition of liberalism, a new conservatism challenged the persisting liberal dominance in American politics. As the terms "liberalism" and "conservatism" acquired new meanings, the earlier liberal consensus gave way to greater ideological conflict over America's national character and its role in the world. The new conservatism questioned some but certainly not all of Wilson's legacy in this "age of fracture."[1] In the aftermath of the Cold War and of 9/11, the United States still affirmed many of his beliefs and policies

---

[1] Daniel T. Rogers, *Age of Fracture* (Cambridge, MA, 2011).

in its domestic affairs and its international relations. The ideological framework of Wilsonianism helped them explain America's place in contemporary history. His legacy and reputation were thus enduring.

PRESIDENTIAL RANKINGS

Various surveys of historians, other scholars, and the general public since World War II have shown that Wilson has consistently enjoyed a favorable ranking among U.S. presidents, but not in the first tier. Typically, George Washington, Abraham Lincoln, and Franklin D. Roosevelt were the top three, followed by Thomas Jefferson and Theodore Roosevelt. In almost all surveys, Wilson ranked in the second tier among the top ten along with Andrew Jackson, Harry Truman, Dwight Eisenhower, and various others such as John Adams, James Madison, James K. Polk, John F. Kennedy, and occasionally James Monroe, William McKinley, Lyndon B. Johnson, and Ronald Reagan. Wilson ranked as high as fourth in the earliest polls after World War II but fell as low as eleventh place in the twenty-first century. Recent polls of the general American public did not rank Wilson as high as scholars did. A Gallup poll in 2011 omitted Wilson from its list of the twenty greatest U.S. presidents.[2]

In line with his usual standing in surveys of historians and other scholars, Wilson came in eighth overall in the most recent Siena College rankings in 2010. The two Roosevelts, Lincoln, Washington, Jefferson, Madison, and Monroe outranked him, but he surpassed all the Cold War and post–Cold War presidents from Truman to Barack Obama. This poll of presidential scholars not only ranked presidents overall but also evaluated their traits and leadership. The scholars gave Wilson the highest scores for intelligence (fourth) and imagination (fifth) but graded him quite low for his ability to compromise (thirty-seventh) and avoid crucial mistakes (twenty-ninth); they saw his relationship with Congress (sixteenth) and luck (fifteenth) as also notably lower than his overall rank.[3]

In 2006, the Woodrow Wilson International Center for Scholars, in collaboration with the Woodrow Wilson House, hosted a symposium in

---

[2] "Historical Rankings of Presidents of the United States," Wikipedia, <https://en.wikipedia.org/wiki/Historical_rankings_of_Presidents_of_the_United_States>.

[3] "American Presidents: Greatest and Worst," Siena Research Institute, Siena College, <www.siena.edu/uploadedfiles/home/parents_and_community/community_page/sri/independent_research/Presidents%20Release_2010_final.pdf>; "Siena College Presidential Ranking, 2010," Siena Research Institute, Siena College, <www.siena.edu/uploadedfiles/home/parents_and_community/community_page/sri/independent_research/Presidents%202010%20Rank%20by%20Category.pdf>.

Washington, DC, on the 150th anniversary of Wilson's birthday. In an introduction to *Reconsidering Woodrow Wilson* (2008), which resulted from the symposium, historian John Milton Cooper, Jr., noted that *The Atlantic Monthly* recently ranked the former president tenth on its list of "The 100 Most Influential Americans of All Time." Only four presidents – Lincoln, Washington, Jefferson, and Franklin Roosevelt – outranked him. "In justifying Wilson's tenth-place ranking on its list of influential Americans," Cooper noted, "*The Atlantic* said of him, 'He made the world safe for U.S. intervention, if not for democracy.' Those twelve words nicely encapsulate essential elements of Wilson's historical reputation, if not of the man himself." The president's role in foreign affairs thus justified his inclusion on the list but also remained problematic. As Cooper observed, "Wilson has not become a figure of warm, generalized adulation. Rather, nine decades after his death, he still draws sharply conflicting estimates of his accomplishments and legacies; people still admire or revile him."[4] In short, Wilson's place in presidential rankings – or any evaluation of his legacy and reputation – depends on the historical memory or perspective of those who determine the rankings or make the evaluation.

WILSON'S NEW FREEDOM

Wilson's progressive agenda for reforming America, which he proclaimed in 1912 as the New Freedom, expressed his commitment to modern liberalism. He emphasized individual freedom within a democratic community. He valued liberty more than equality. For Americans, freedom had emerged from their colonial British experience. The American Revolution allowed them to establish their own self-government as a new nation. Wilson saw freedom and democracy as intertwined. Individual freedom guaranteed economic opportunities as well as civil liberties. Capitalism and democracy were the twin achievements of free Americans. His reforms, first as governor of New Jersey and then as U.S. president, did not threaten corporations, although he regulated them so that new entrepreneurs could gain access to the marketplace. Expanding liberal democracy and capitalism into new frontiers would fulfill his progressive vision for the United States and the world.

---

[4] John Milton Cooper, Jr., "Introduction: Wilson Revisited," *Reconsidering Woodrow Wilson: Progressivism, Internationalism, War, and Peace*, ed. John Milton Cooper, Jr. (Washington, DC and Baltimore, MD, 2008), 1.

Wilson's New Freedom addressed major problems of the political economy. He wanted three reforms to improve American capitalism. He called for a lower tariff, which would force industries to face foreign competition and become more efficient, thereby reducing prices. This would also help prevent corporations from becoming monopolistic. As he requested, Congress passed the Underwood Tariff in October 1913. To compensate for lost tariff revenue, this act established the graduated income tax, which the Sixteenth Amendment to the Constitution authorized. Next, Wilson advocated a new banking system to stabilize the flow of capital to industry and agriculture. Democrats and Republicans agreed that the nation's finances required fundamental changes but disagreed over how to reform the banks. As he proposed, the Federal Reserve Act in December 1913 created a Federal Reserve Board with twelve regional banks, combining the public and private sectors. It strengthened the banking system at home and placed the United States in a better international position during the Great War. Finally, Wilson strengthened antitrust laws to prevent monopolies from dominating the marketplace. The Clayton Antitrust Act in October 1914, along with the creation of the Federal Trade Commission a month earlier, empowered the federal government to regulate commerce. The president sought to benefit producers in industry and agriculture by reforming capitalism. His changes in the tariff, banking, and antitrust laws were the essence of the New Freedom.

Wilson changed priorities during World War I. Wartime mobilization led him to closer cooperation with corporate executives and bankers. He quit stressing the antimonopoly theme and embraced what he had once denounced as "dollar diplomacy." The administration intervened in economic affairs to promote greater production by both industry and agriculture, while also regulating them in unprecedented ways. Mediating between workers and employers, it sought to prevent strikes that would stop factories from producing the goods needed for war. Although always ambivalent toward unions, the president recognized the importance of the so-called labor question. He also expected those who profited from the war to help pay for it. The Revenue Acts of 1916 and 1918 made the income tax substantially more progressive. Wilson's wartime policies sought to mobilize the nation's capitalist economy.[5]

---

[5] W. Elliot Brownlee, "Wilson's Reform of Economic Structure: Progressive Liberalism and the Corporation," *Reconsidering Woodrow Wilson*, 57–89.

Wilson's New Freedom omitted reforms for expanding democracy to women or people of color. Until late in his presidency, he refused to support an amendment to the Constitution to extend voting rights to women. He wanted them at home, not in public affairs. He barred African Americans from political participation and economic opportunities. The Wilson administration brought the Jim Crow system of racial segregation into the federal government. The president empowered southerners in his cabinet to draw the color line in their departments. He did not champion civil liberties for all Americans. He wanted freedom for white Americans, not equality for people of color. His modern liberalism did not challenge the existing gender, race, and class divisions in the American nation. His vision of American democracy and capitalism focused on the rights of white men.[6]

Wilson's New Freedom left an enduring legacy. At its core, his progressive presidency championed an active role for the federal government to improve the nation's political economy. Once the war engulfed the United States, he projected his ideals onto other countries, calling for a new world order in line with America's liberal values and institutions. Although Republicans enacted higher tariffs during the 1920s, the United States began to lower them again in the 1930s and continued to do so even more after World War II. By the 1980s, conservative Republicans joined liberal Democrats in a bipartisan consensus favoring generally lower tariffs to promote world trade. That Wilsonian trend toward the globalization of commerce, with further tariff reductions to promote freer trade, accelerated after the Cold War. Moreover, the Federal Reserve System survived as a key financial institution. It exercised even more power over the increasingly globalized economy than it had at first during Wilson's presidency. The federal government also continued its crucial role in preserving an open marketplace. Although new conservatives, who expanded their political power during Ronald Reagan's presidency and in subsequent decades, denounced almost all forms of government regulation of economic activities, they too desired federal promotion of economic development and even approved some regulation of business activity to preserve free enterprise. The Justice Department enforced antitrust laws, while the Federal Trade Commission continued to operate. Wilson's New Freedom left an enduring legacy in the political economy at home and abroad.

[6] Gary Gerstle, "Race and Nation in the Thought and Politics of Woodrow Wilson," *Reconsidering Woodrow Wilson*, 93–162.

WILSON'S LIBERAL INTERNATIONALISM

Wilson's idealism left an even more significant legacy in international relations. Based on his modern liberalism, his vision for a new world order shaped his foreign policies, which later scholars called Wilsonianism. When he led the United States into World War I, he called for making the world safe for democracy. His liberal vision of postwar peace affirmed four tenets that expressed his understanding of America's national identity. He wanted to reform the world by creating an international community of liberal democracies with capitalist economies. He regarded nation-states as the key actors.

As his first tenet, Wilson advocated a new form of what would later be called collective security. During the war, he developed the idea for a postwar international organization that would preserve the peace by preventing external aggression. At the Paris Peace Conference of 1919, he gave top priority to the League of Nations. As he conceived it, the new League would join democratic nation-states together for their mutual defense. Deterring aggression across borders, it would guarantee international peace. This global community of nations would replace the old European order that had relied on balances of power and military alliances. The League, he believed, could provide national security for its members without requiring them to maintain large armies or navies to enforce binding commitments. Thus the United States could retain its unilateral freedom to decide its role in the world, yet also contribute to international peace.

As his second tenet, the president advocated national self-determination, affirming both state sovereignty and democracy. All nations, he thought, were entitled to self-government. Just as the United States had claimed this right during the American Revolution, new nations might emerge from the old Russian, German, Austro-Hungarian, and Ottoman empires in Europe and the Middle East after the war. Although he proclaimed national self-determination as a universal ideal, he did not believe that all peoples were ready for self-government. In his view, only mature nations that had reached a certain level of political development could govern themselves.

Wilson's vision of a liberal democratic world order favored Open Door international commerce and finance as well as travel and cultural exchange. In accordance with this third tenet of Wilsonianism, he wanted to guarantee freedom of the seas and remove international barriers to trade and investment. In theory, he also called for open diplomacy, despite his failure in practice to make his statecraft more transparent. Such a liberal world order would facilitate international capitalism, just as his New Freedom promoted it at home.

Undergirding Wilsonianism, as its fourth tenet, was the president's belief in progressive history. American and world history revealed a progressive pattern of development, he thought, as primitive peoples moved toward greater maturity over the generations. He saw this pattern in the history of the West from the ancient world to modern America. The idea of human progress in history seemed self-evident to him. Because the United States represented the culmination of progressive historical development, it offered the best model for other nations. In an era of war and revolution, Wilson formulated a global agenda, which he outlined in the Fourteen Points on January 8, 1918. "For American progressives," historian Alan Dawley observed, "there was no escaping these world-historical events, and from that time forward, the dual quest for improvement at home and abroad was at the heart of what it meant to be a progressive." As America's "preeminent progressive," the president called for "changing the world."[7]

Wilsonianism affirmed the ideology known as American exceptionalism. Wilson's vision of a new world order expressed his nationalism. Making the world safe for democracy required the global triumph of modern American liberalism. Ironically, while offering the United States as the best model for the world, he avowed its unique character. After the Great War, despite the difficulties he encountered in Paris while seeking to establish his new world order, he continued to affirm American exceptionalism in his interpretation of international relations. On his western tour in September 1919, he reaffirmed his belief that the United States should fulfill its God-given mission by joining the League of Nations. Wilson thought it would "make every nation a nobler instrument of Divine Providence – that is world politics." America's providential mission had now become the world's. In his perspective, there was no contradiction between nationalism and internationalism. "The greatest nationalist is the man who wants his nation to be the greatest nation, and the greatest nation is the nation which penetrates to the heart of its duty and mission among the nations of the world," he proclaimed.[8] Because that was

---

[7] Alan Dawley, *Changing the World: American Progressives in War and Revolution* (Princeton, NJ, 2003), 2, 8; Lloyd E. Ambrosius, "Democracy, Peace, and World Order," *Reconsidering Woodrow Wilson*, 225–49.

[8] Address, St. Louis, Sept. 5, 1919, Woodrow Wilson, *The Public Papers of Woodrow Wilson: War and Peace*, eds. Ray Stannard Baker and William E. Dodd (New York, 1927), 1: 621;

America's mission during the peace conference, he expected his fellow citizens to support the League. Its Covenant was an integral part of the Versailles Treaty with Germany. Wilson discovered, however, that other Americans might share his belief in the nation's exceptionalism without necessarily embracing his liberal vision of a new world order.

Although the Senate rejected the peace treaty and prevented the United States from joining the League, Wilsonianism persisted. Its tenets continued to influence how Americans understood their national character and global role. Later generations embraced the Wilsonian ideals and institutions of collective security, national self-determination, and Open Door international commerce and finance as key features in U.S. foreign policies. They also continued to believe in America's exceptional place in progressive world history. Wilson's vision of a new world order provided an enduring legacy for the United States throughout the twentieth and into the twenty-first century.

A SECOND CHANCE FOR A NEW WORLD ORDER

Peacemaking after World War II gave the United States a second chance to achieve what Wilson had failed to accomplish after World War I. It also helped restore his reputation. Franklin D. Roosevelt's Office of War Information enlisted Darryl F. Zanuck to make a brief documentary on Wilson. Zanuck decided that the project merited a full-length feature film. Twentieth Century Fox provided the resources for *Wilson*. Released in 1944, the film depicted Wilson's life from Princeton to the White House and climaxed with his fight for the League of Nations. It glorified his leadership, which succeeded at each stage of his career until the film's villain, Republican senator Henry Cabot Lodge, defeated the League and prevented Wilson from fulfilling his vision. The film made the former president the personification of world peace. With millions of viewers, *Wilson*, more than anything else, revived his reputation.[9]

With the founding of the United Nations, the world seemed to join the United States in grasping the second chance to fulfill Wilson's liberal vision of peace through collective security. Truman paid tribute to the former president in his address to the closing session of the United Nations Conference in San Francisco on June 26, 1945. "By this Charter,"

Woodrow Wilson, *The Papers of Woodrow Wilson*, ed. Arthur S. Link (Princeton, NJ, 1990), 63: 43–51.
[9] Robert A. Divine, *Second Chance: The Triumph of Internationalism in America During World War II* (New York, 1967), 169–71.

he told the delegates who approved the replacement for the Covenant of the League of Nations, "you have given reality to the ideal of that great statesman of a generation ago – Woodrow Wilson." Truman said that FDR too, as the "gallant leader" during the war, had given his life to reach this goal. "The new structure of peace is rising upon strong foundations," Truman avowed. "Let us not fail to grasp this supreme chance to establish a world-wide rule of reason – to create an enduring peace under the guidance of God."[10] Wilson had failed, but after a generation and another war, world history had presumably progressed to the advent of his far-sighted vision.

Roosevelt had expanded Wilson's legacy at home and abroad. Both presidents promoted progressive internationalism and reformed capitalism. The New Freedom laid the foundation for the New Deal during the Great Depression and its global extension during World War II. Emphasizing this continuity, historian Emily S. Rosenberg observed "how FDR built upon, but updated, Wilson's notion of a reformed capitalist order." "Throughout his administration," she explained, "Wilson worked energetically to expand the nation's commercial and financial networks, yet he stood opposed to businesses that violated his notion of progress toward an open, liberal, and democratic world." A generation later the Roosevelt administration epitomized "the formula of Wilsonian progressivism." FDR too wanted the state to regulate capitalism by determining the ground rules for the international economic order and also to "help responsible businesses expand their trade and investments into the world." Rosenberg concluded, "Wilson and Roosevelt both sought to establish checks on the excesses of capitalists to save the world for capitalism."[11] Thus Wilson's New Freedom anticipated a New Deal for the world.

FDR's New Deal went beyond Wilson's New Freedom to reform the political economy and transform America and its international relations. The Democratic coalition that supported the reforms of the 1930s included corporate executives from capital-intensive firms and from new investment banks that funded them. They welcomed the separation between commercial and investment banking in the Glass-Steagall Act of

---

[10] Harry S. Truman, "Address in San Francisco at the Closing Session of the United Nations Conference," June 26, 1945, *Public Papers of the Presidents*, by Gerhard Peters and John T. Woolley, The American Presidency Project, <www.presidency.ucsb.edu/ws/?pid=12188>.

[11] Emily S. Rosenberg, "Progressive Internationalism and Reformed Capitalism: New Freedom to New Deal," *Reconsidering Woodrow Wilson*, 253–77.

1933. As advocates of multinational liberalism, they favored the reciprocal trade treaties, which Secretary of State Cordell Hull championed, to expand world trade. Rather than deal with costly strikes, they preferred the federal government's involvement in labor disputes, and thus supported the National Labor Relations Act of 1935. These corporate executives also approved the state's new role in providing old-age pensions and other benefits with the Social Security Act of 1935. They joined the eclectic constituency in the fragile New Deal political coalition to help resolve the so-called labor question with collective bargaining and the welfare state. As Roosevelt built on Wilson's progressive legacy, the federal government took greater responsibility to ensure widespread benefits for Americans as producers and consumers. Although embracing some aspects of social democracy, the New Deal mostly sought to save capitalism by making liberal reforms. Wartime mobilization, which finally overcame the Great Depression, expanded the dominance of American corporations in the marketplace and ensured their centrality in the global economy. FDR's policies endured in the nation's liberal politics and the world's new international institutions after World War II.[12]

Roosevelt sought to avoid Wilson's mistakes as he planned for peace. As historian Elizabeth Borgwardt noted in *A New Deal for the World* (2005), FDR's peacemaking offered a more comprehensive but less idealistic vision of a new multilateral order. He integrated collective security through the United Nations with economic recovery and stability through the World Bank and International Monetary Fund. The Bretton Woods Conference in July 1944 adopted charters for these two postwar financial institutions. Roosevelt hoped these institutions would fulfill the goals of his Four Freedoms and the Atlantic Charter. He had announced the "four essential human freedoms" in his annual message to Congress on January 6, 1941. Eight months later, on August 12, he joined British prime minister Winston Churchill to sign the Atlantic Charter. Along with plans for the future Nuremberg trials of German war criminals, these documents proclaimed what Borgwardt called "America's vision for human rights." These were FDR's equivalents of Wilson's Fourteen Points. "The core idea in international diplomacy to emerge from World War II for American policy planners was the conviction that security was indivisible: political, legal, and economic developments supported (or

[12] Thomas Ferguson, "Industrial Conflict and the Coming of the New Deal: The Triumph of Multinational Liberalism in America," Steve Fraser, "The 'Labor Question'," Alan Brinkley, "The New Deal and the Idea of the State," *The Rise and Fall of the New Deal, 1930–1980*, eds. Steve Fraser and Gary Gerstle (Princeton, NJ, 1989), 3–31, 55–121.

undermined) one another in myriad direct and indirect ways." The Four
Freedoms and Atlantic Charter "internationalized this New Deal sensibility by explicitly embedding it in the inspirational rhetoric of Allied war
aims." Thus, Borgwardt concluded, "It transformed the domestic New
Deal into an Allied fighting faith."[13]

Roosevelt largely avoided the Manichaean worldview that Wilson had
proclaimed in his wartime crusade against Imperial Germany. He combined
realism with liberalism. Historian Michaela Hoenicke Moore emphasized
this important difference between the two presidents. FDR thought that
Wilson and the Allies should have required unconditional surrender by
Germany instead of negotiating an armistice in 1918, and that they should
have given a more lenient peace settlement to the new German republic,
which would have enabled Germany to reenter the international order
sooner. Both harsher and more generous, this kind of peace would have
combined realistic and liberal features. In his own plans for postwar peace,
Roosevelt incorporated these lessons by affirming both the liberal democratic ideals of the Atlantic Charter and the demands for Germany's unconditional surrender and elimination of Nazism.[14]

Roosevelt added realism to the Wilsonian legacy of liberalism in the
peacemaking after World War II. As political scientist G. John Ikenberry
emphasized, Wilson's pursuit of a new world order lacked a realistic assessment of the existing balance of power. He had denounced the
very idea of a balance of power and of military alliances to sustain it.
Hoping to keep from entangling the United States in Europe's traditional
diplomacy and wars, while seeking to reform international relations, he
had refused to make firm U.S. commitments to deter Germany or other
potential aggressors. The Covenant of the League offered no such guarantee, yet promised collective security. Wilsonian peacemaking was not
durable. Because peacemaking in 1815, 1945, and 1989 incorporated the
aspects of realism that were absent in 1919, the international orders that
emerged in those years were far more lasting than the Versailles peace
settlement.[15]

[13] Elizabeth Borgwardt, *A New Deal for the World: America's Vision for Human Rights* (Cambridge, MA, 2005), 14–45, 280–81.
[14] Michaela Hoenicke Moore, *Know Your Enemy: The American Debate on Nazism, 1933–1945* (Cambridge, 2010).
[15] G. John Ikenberry, *After Victory: Institutions, Strategic Restraint, and the Rebuilding of Order after Major Wars.* (Princeton, NJ, 2001); Lloyd E. Ambrosius, *Woodrow Wilson and the American Diplomatic Tradition: The Treaty Fight in Perspective* (Cambridge, 1987); Norman A. Graebner and Edward M. Bennett, *The Versailles Treaty and Its Legacy: The Failure of the Wilsonian Vision* (Cambridge, 2011).

New Deal liberalism guided the United States not only during the war but throughout the twentieth century and beyond. As historian David Ekbladh observed, Roosevelt's updated version of Wilson's legacy defined "the great American mission." From World War I onward, as Americans increasingly engaged in foreign relations, they believed their own liberal style of "modernization" or "development" would benefit others. Their own national history presumably offered the best guidance for progressive world history. Wilson had heralded this vision and FDR expanded it. The Tennessee Valley Authority (TVA), a major New Deal project, epitomized the kind of development that other countries should embrace to facilitate their own modernization. "What is important," Ekbladh perceived, "is that a historically specific variant of international development that took its cues and justification from the experience of the United States had a clear strategic rationale within a new American globalism." The New Deal's TVA served as the model for the world throughout the remainder of the so-called American Century.[16]

COLD WAR LIBERALISM

The postwar consensus of Cold War liberalism affirmed the legacies of Wilson and Roosevelt; it also defined limits. Democratic and Republican presidents believed that the federal government should promote economic growth, affirming Keynesian economics. They hoped the expanding consumer economy would benefit all Americans, workers as well as producers. They accepted labor unions and corporations as legitimate interest groups on the condition that unions did not disrupt the capitalist order by strikes or challenge it by advocating radical reforms. Republicans in the 80th Congress adopted the Taft-Hartley Act of 1947 to restrict labor unions. Truman and other Democrats denounced the law but never repealed it. Cold War liberals rejected socialism, which they conflated with communism as an easy way to discredit it. When unions tried to organize both black and white workers in the South, white southerners prevented it by using race and accusations of communist influence to divide them. These limits in Cold War liberalism followed the traditions of Wilson and FDR, who had not championed the civil rights of African Americans. So too did the postwar restrictions on women, who were expected to stay at home and participate as consumers but not

[16] David Ekbladh, *The Great American Mission: Modernization and the Construction of an American World Order* (Princeton, NJ, 2010), 69.

as workers in the economy. Although women voted, they were largely excluded from public affairs. America's democracy and capitalism did not guarantee equal freedom for women and people of color.[17]

The 1960s witnessed further changes, which altered and eventually destroyed the postwar liberal consensus. Kennedy's New Frontier and Johnson's Great Society broadened the definition of liberalism beyond the scope of Wilson's and FDR's legacies. With the emergence of the civil rights movement, African Americans and other people of color demanded greater equality. So too did white women. In response, Kennedy and Johnson expanded the nation's liberal agenda. They won congressional approval of several major reforms. The Civil Rights Acts of 1964 and 1965 gave greater powers to the federal government to ensure equality under the law for people of color and also for women. Kennedy and Johnson also launched the War on Poverty, which promised to open the benefits of capitalist prosperity for poor people. They sought to enable poor Americans to move up the social ladder in the growing national economy. They championed only equality of opportunity, not equality of results. Their new programs, such as Medicare, expanded the welfare state within the framework of democratic capitalism. Nevertheless, these reforms challenged the existing gender, race, and class divisions in the American nation. Critics often identified the anti-poverty programs with black Americans, although there were more white Americans living in poverty. The political base of Cold War liberalism began to erode as the term "liberalism" was identified with people of color and feminists. Some liberals, who had been comfortable in Wilson's and Roosevelt's tradition, identified themselves with a new "conservatism" and left the Democratic Party. The expansion of the state's role in social welfare and race relations during the 1960s generated a backlash that destroyed the New Deal political coalition. Cold War liberalism gave way by the 1980s to the new conservatism of Ronald Reagan and the Republican Party.[18] Yet the fall of the New Deal order only altered but did not destroy the legacies of Wilson and FDR. Reagan, like many other conservatives, had once supported Roosevelt and admired his style of presidential leadership. He also operated within the liberal institutions that FDR and Truman had founded and he continued to champion the tenets of Wilsonianism.

---

[17] Nelson Lichtenstein, "From Corporatism to Collective Bargaining: Organized Labor and the Eclipse of Social Democracy in the Postwar Era," *The Rise and Fall of the New Deal*, 122–81.

[18] Ira Katznelson, "Was the Great Society a Lost Opportunity?," *The Rise and Fall of the New Deal*, 185–211.

Cold War presidents identified themselves with Wilson's liberal ideals, but they sought to avoid his mistakes by focusing on power relationships in global politics. As journalist Martin Walker noted, "They have almost universally seen Wilson as a highly useful embodiment of a higher American purpose in the country's engagement with other countries and as a standing symbol of an America that seeks a just and fairer world." Yet they used more realistic means to achieve his liberal goals. Walker made a persuasive argument that the goals of Wilson's Fourteen Points guided U.S. foreign policies and found expression in major liberal international institutions throughout the Cold War. The means, however, were often different from what he had heralded. Walker observed that one might offer either "a Wilsonian history" or "a realistic history" of the Cold War, depending on which features were stressed in the international relations of that era. Nevertheless, he concluded, "The end of the Cold War, and the end of the Soviet Union, brought a measure of vindication to the scholar-president Woodrow Wilson, one of those rare prophets who found at least posthumous honor in his own land."[19]

Adding realism to Wilsonian liberalism in the American planning for peace after World War II laid the foundation for the new international order in the West during the Cold War and its expansion into former communist countries after 1989. In *Liberal Leviathan* (2011), G. John Ikenberry analyzed the enduring features of this America-led liberal international order, which affirmed a broad and integrated definition of America's role as global hegemon in the tradition of the New Deal for the world. "Defined in terms of the provision of security, wealth creation, and social advancement, this liberal hegemonic order has been, arguably at least, the most successful order in world history." Wilson's legacy, expanded by FDR, provided the conceptual framework for this liberal American system of international relations. Ikenberry explained, "The building of American postwar order went through several stages. In the first, the Roosevelt administration sought to build on and update the Wilsonian vision. Like Wilson's version, it would be a one-world system in which the major powers would cooperate to enforce the peace." Although it affirmed universal ideals, it assigned the dominant role to the great powers, including the United States. As he prepared for a postwar order to fulfill the goals of the Four Freedoms and the Atlantic Charter, FDR updated Wilson's vision with a more hierarchical

[19] Martin Walker, "Woodrow Wilson and the Cold War: 'Tear Down This Wall, Mr. Gorbachev'," *Reconsidering Woodrow Wilson*, 279–98.

system of international institutions to manage economic and political interdependence. In turn, Ikenberry argued,

This updated Wilsonian vision of liberal order gave way to a more far-reaching and complex set of arrangements. The ultimate outcome was more Western-centered, multilayered, and deeply institutionalized than originally anticipated, and it brought the United States into direct political and economic managements of the system. The weakness of Europe, the looming Soviet threat, and the practical requirements of establishing institutions and making them work transformed the tasks of order building. The updated Wilsonian vision of liberal order turned into true liberal hegemonic order.[20]

Redefined by FDR and revised during and after the Cold War, Wilsonianism endured into the twenty-first century.

HUMAN RIGHTS AND THE COLOR LINE

Both affirming universal human rights and drawing the global color line characterized Wilson's liberalism and his legacy. During the Cold War, U.S. presidents extolled human rights as a way to condemn the Soviet Union and other communist countries for denying freedom. As champions of liberal democracy and capitalism, they affirmed Wilson's liberal ideals, which they identified with the United States and its allies. Historians and political scientists as well saw the former president as the foremost prophet of a new world order based on modern liberalism. Identifying him with liberal values, they often found it difficult to recognize his illiberal flaws. Although they knew he held racist views of African Americans and restricted civil liberties during World War I, they tended to downplay those negative features of his character and presidency. Wilson's record on human rights did not fit well into the dominant liberal narrative that interpreted his New Freedom and Wilsonianism as the apogee of American progressivism. Even after the civil rights and feminist movements expanded the definition of "liberalism" to include race and gender equality, liberal scholars still placed him in the progressive tradition of universal human rights going back to the American Declaration of Independence and forward to the triumph of liberal internationalism after World War II. In this framework, Wilson and his legacy epitomized America's liberalism and its global mission. Yet as president, he had drawn the global color line and denied civil liberties. Some scholarship

[20] G. John Ikenberry, *Liberal Leviathan: The Origins, Crisis, and Transformation of the American World Order* (Princeton, NJ, 2011), xi, 165–66; Paul Kennedy, *The Parliament of Man: The Past, Present, and Future of the United Nations* (New York, 2006).

has recognized this discrepancy between the real Wilson and his liberal reputation, and thus acknowledged his mixed legacy.

More clearly than most scholars, historian Paul Gordon Lauren understood Wilson's prominence in both advocating human rights and drawing the color line. Noting that the U.S. president and his Bolshevik rival, Vladimir I. Lenin, proclaimed alternative visions of human rights, Lauren wrote: "Perhaps the most ultimately influential statements about the meaning of rights in this world of war and revolution emerged from the political leaders of those two countries destined to greatly shape global affairs during the rest of the twentieth century: the United States and Russia." Wilson championed individual civil and political rights, while Lenin preferred group or class-based social and economic rights. At the beginning of the Great War, Lauren observed, Wilson had asserted "that his country 'puts human rights above all other rights' and that 'her flag is the flag not only of America, but of humanity.' " He later affirmed this vision of America's mission when he called for making the world safe for democracy and proclaimed the Fourteen Points. At the Paris Peace Conference he endeavored to guarantee human rights not only in the Versailles Treaty with Germany but also in the Minority Treaties with new nation-states in Central and Eastern Europe. These treaties, which sought to protect racial, religious, and linguistic minorities, assigned to the new League of Nations the responsibility for supervising their rights. But Wilson also placed strict limits on the League's role. In collaboration with the British Empire's delegates, he rejected Japan's amendment to the Covenant, which would have affirmed racial or national equality. British and American leaders in Paris drew the global color line. They prohibited the League, moreover, from intervening in the internal affairs of nation-states to protect minority rights unless its Council approved. This limit on the League's future action effectively gave both the United Kingdom and the United States the right to veto international interference in their empires. Thus the British successfully thwarted potential challenges to imperial restrictions on immigration by people of color, while Wilson prevented the League from challenging the Jim Crow system of racial segregation in the United States. They affirmed the sovereignty of nation-states as a higher priority than the human rights of individuals or minorities. With British support, the president drew the global color line, while advocating ostensibly universal human rights.[21]

[21] Paul Gordon Lauren, *The Evolution of International Human Rights: Visions Seen* (Philadelphia, PA, 1998), 91; Paul Gordon Lauren, *Power and Prejudice: The Politics and Diplomacy of Racial Discrimination* (Boulder, CO, 1988), 50–107; Carole Fink,

Wilson's mixed legacy continued after World War II. The United States emerged as the champion of human rights in the United Nations, yet still practiced racial segregation at home. During the drafting of the UN Charter and the 1948 Universal Declaration of Human Rights, African Americans claimed these rights for themselves. Like Wilson earlier, Truman resisted. Preserving the global color line, he limited America's liberal promise in practice. "In short," historian Carol Anderson concluded, "America's position as the Jim Crow leader of the 'free world' posed a constant, nagging stumbling block to the full implementation of U.S. foreign policy." Because of the South's political influence on the Truman administration, she added, "America's human rights policy could only be sung in the key of white supremacy and Jim Crow."[22] Wilson's legacy persisted.

During the Cold War, the inconsistency between America's affirmation of universal human rights and its preservation of the global color line became increasingly obvious and unsustainable. The emergence of anticolonial nationalism in Africa and Asia combined with the civil rights movement in the United States to challenge white supremacy over people of color. By the 1960s, the Kennedy and Johnson administrations accommodated these mutually reinforcing developments by redefining the meaning of liberalism. They extended civil rights to African Americans and other minorities at home. In the Cold War competition with the Soviet Union, the United States also adopted a new orientation toward the so-called Third World. It recognized the new nations that emancipated themselves from European empires and welcomed their diplomats in Washington, DC, and at the United Nations in New York City. The Cold War rivalry thus helped erase the global color line.[23]

Defending the Rights of Others: The Great Powers, the Jews, and International Minority Protection, 1878–1938 (Cambridge, 2004); Micheline R. Ishay, *The History of Human Rights: From Ancient Times to the Globalization Era* (Berkeley and Los Angeles, CA, 2004), 173–243; Lloyd E. Ambrosius, "Woodrow Wilson and *The Birth of a Nation*: American Democracy and International Relations," *Diplomacy and Statecraft* 18 (2007): 689–718; Marilyn Lake and Henry Reynolds, *Drawing the Global Colour Line: White Men's Countries and the International Challenge of Racial Equality* (Cambridge, 2008).

[22] Carol Anderson, *Eyes Off the Prize: The United Nations and the African American Struggle for Human Rights, 1944–1955* (Cambridge, 2003), 106, 131; Thomas Borstelmann, *Apartheid's Reluctant Uncle: The United States and Southern Africa in the Early Cold War* (New York, 1993).

[23] Mary L. Dudziak, *Cold War Civil Rights: Race and Image of American Democracy* (Princeton, NJ, 2000); Thomas Borstelmann, *The Cold War and the Color Line* (Cambridge, MA, 2001); Jonathan Rosenberg, *How Far the Promised Land? World*

A redefinition of "liberalism" removed white supremacy from the Wilsonian legacy and contributed to a new world order that the former president would never have approved. During World War I, some civil rights leaders had used his ostensibly universal liberal rhetoric to legitimize their own vision of racial democracy. The real Wilson, however, had disappointed not only African Americans, who hoped that making the world safe for democracy would include them, but also anti-colonial nationalists in other countries who expected his support at the Paris Peace Conference. Because of his racism, he was not ready for what historian Erez Manela called "the Wilsonian moment."[24] Nevertheless, from the perspective of a progressive interpretation of history, Wilson appeared to later generations as America's foremost liberal champion of human rights. Some Americans continued to focus on his words rather than his actions. The emphasis on continuity in this progressive framework obscured the radical change in race relations in the United States and around the world during the Cold War. This positive view of Wilson and his legacy conflated his liberalism with the revised "liberalism" of the 1960s. Even some scholars found it difficult to acknowledge fully his illiberal flaws that resulted from his dedication to the global color line. Yet, contrary to this interpretation, the later "liberalism" that affirmed racial equality at home and abroad departed substantially from Wilson's own liberalism, which was less universal in practice than his rhetoric suggested. Political scientist David P. Forsythe recognized that Wilson did not live up to the image of him that political scientists in the twenty-first century still identified with "Wilsonian liberalism." Nor had Roosevelt, who also advocated human rights but adopted illiberal policies such as the internment of Japanese Americans during World War II. Forsythe observed: "Actually not just FDR, but Woodrow Wilson himself, was not a consistent Wilsonian liberal in international relations."[25]

Not only did Wilson draw the global color line; he also repressed civil liberties during World War I. Soon after the United States declared war against Imperial Germany, he asked Congress to adopt a new law to prohibit dissent. The Espionage Act of 1917, although weaker than he wanted, gave extensive powers to the federal government to stifle criticism

Affairs and the American Civil Rights Movement from the First World War to Vietnam (Princeton, NJ, 2006).

[24] Erez Manela, *The Wilsonian Moment: Self-Determination and the International Origins of Anticolonial Nationalism* (New York, 2007).

[25] David P. Forsythe, *The Politics of Prisoner Abuse: The United States and Enemy Prisoners after 9/11* (Cambridge, 2011), 34–35.

of wartime mobilization. The Justice Department quickly began to use this authority. So too did the Post Office Department, which prevented the distribution of so-called disloyal publications. Adding the Sedition Act of 1918, the Wilson administration strengthened its powers to limit the First Amendment's guarantee of free speech. It continued to suppress dissent throughout the war and during the postwar Red Scare, and did so with the approval of the Supreme Court that refused to protect civil liberties. Law professor Geoffrey R. Stone observed, "President Wilson laid the foundation for an era of repression. Wilson did not use the loyalty issue in a cynical effort to destroy his political opponents. Rather, his goal was to squelch disharmony that might impede his mission of making 'the world safe for democracy.' But his emotional invocation of disloyalty fed the natural fears of a nation under stress." Later U.S. presidents in wartime followed Wilson's legacy by attempting to stifle dissent. Not only FDR during World War II but also his successors during the Cold War, notably Richard M. Nixon during the Vietnam War, sought to restrict civil liberties in the name of freedom and patriotism. Wilson's record also served as a precedent for George W. Bush's administration, which won congressional approval after 9/11 for the USA PATRIOT Act in its global war on terrorism. As Stone noted, Wilson was not the first president to attack free speech in wartime, nor was he the last to limit civil liberties in the name of protecting freedom and promoting universal human rights.[26]

WILSONIANISM AFTER THE COLD WAR AND 9/11

After the Cold War, Wilsonianism flourished as the ideological framework for U.S. foreign policies. President George H. W. Bush reaffirmed its tenets in his vision of a new world order, and so did President Bill Clinton.[27] Republicans and Democrats identified with Wilson's legacy to celebrate the victory of liberal democracy and capitalism over communism. Scholars as well as presidents, whether liberal or conservative, acclaimed this global transformation. Neoconservatives, whose intellectual roots were embedded in modern liberalism, also affirmed this consensus. Political scientist Francis Fukuyama rejoiced over "the end of history." Another Wilsonian moment had apparently arrived. He acknowledged that democratization

---

[26] Geoffrey R. Stone, *Perilous Times: Free Speech in Wartime* (New York, 2004); Geoffrey R. Stone, "Mr. Wilson's First Amendment," *Reconsidering Woodrow Wilson*, 189–224.

[27] Lloyd E. Ambrosius, "War and Peace in the Global Community, 1989–2001," *A Companion to International History, 1900–2001*, ed. Gordon Martel (Malden, MA, 2007), 394–407.

and market economies might suffer temporary setbacks in some countries but asserted that the larger progressive pattern in world history pointed toward the eventual triumph of modern liberalism and the failure of alternatives. He avowed that "the only form of government that has survived intact to the end of the twentieth century has been liberal democracy."[28] Former secretary of state Henry Kissinger agreed that Wilsonianism had become the triumphal ideology after the Cold War. "For three generations," he conceded, "critics have savaged Wilson's analysis and conclusions; and yet, in all this time, Wilson's principles have remained the bedrock of American foreign-policy thinking." Despite his political failure after World War I, "Wilson's intellectual victory proved more seminal than any political triumph could have been. For, whenever America has faced the task of constructing a new world order, it has returned in one way or another to Woodrow Wilson's precepts."[29]

Liberals, conservatives, and neoconservatives alike celebrated the global triumph of Wilsonianism. Although realists such as Kissinger added a note of caution, their voices were largely ignored in the 1990s. Historian Akira Iriye believed that the "ideological offensive led by President Wilson" during World War I was the defining moment for the United States in the twentieth century and that "'democracy' was a key guiding principle precisely in such a context, for it stood for a new political order at home and, therefore, abroad." Although some "realists" had criticized Wilson, his legacy prevailed. "Because the globalizing of America has been a major event of the century," Iriye concluded, "Wilsonianism should be seen not as a transient phenomenon, a reflection of some abstract idealism, but as a potent definer of contemporary history."[30] Political scientist Tony Smith also applauded the resurgence of liberal democracy after the Cold War. "Since Wilson's time," he noted, "the most consistent tradition in American foreign policy with respect to global change has been the belief that the nation's security is best protected by the expansion of democracy worldwide." That vision had become reality. "Certainly the new global enthusiasm for democracy is the closest the United States had ever come to seeing its own traditional foreign policy agenda reflected on an international scale."[31]

[28] Francis Fukuyama, *The End of History and the Last Man* (New York, 1992), 45.
[29] Henry Kissinger, *Diplomacy* (New York, 1994), 52, 54.
[30] Akira Iriye, *The Cambridge History of American Foreign Relations*, Volume III: *The Globalizing of America, 1913–1945* (Cambridge, 1993), 45, 71–72.
[31] Tony Smith, *America's Mission: The United States and the Worldwide Struggle for Democracy in the Twentieth Century* (Princeton, NJ, 1994), 6, 9.

This dominant post–Cold War interpretation of international relations, with its dualistic framework of progressive history, placed Wilson's contribution to building a world community and establishing international institutions in the vanguard of global modernity, while his critics still appeared as reactionaries. Political scientist John Gerard Ruggie affirmed this viewpoint, seeing Wilson's advocacy of the League of Nations as the harbinger of the kind of multilateral diplomacy that Ruggie urged for "winning the peace."[32] Former defense secretary Robert S. McNamara and political scientist James G. Blight also emphasized Wilsonianism. They thought "Wilson's ghost" – like Jacob Marley's in Charles Dickens's *A Christmas Carol* – was calling out to them with a message for reducing the risk of conflict, killing, and catastrophe in the twenty-first century. "The message of Wilson's ghost is this," McNamara and Blight claimed: "Beware of the blindness and folly that led Europe's leaders into the First World War, a disaster theretofore without compare in world history; and beware of the temptation to believe that sustainable peace will be maintained simply by plotting to achieve an alleged 'balance of power' without a strong international organization to enforce it."[33] Wilson's legacy of multilateralism, they all agreed, provided the best means for peacemaking and peacekeeping in the post–Cold War era. They neglected, however, his equally strong commitment to unilateralism. The League of Nations, as Wilson conceived it, combined both internationalist and nationalist approaches to world affairs, but they identified him only with a global order based on liberal internationalism. The framework of American exceptionalism prevented them, like him, from recognizing that his worldview was not as multilateral or universal as they thought.

Neoconservatives shared with other conservatives and liberals a dedication to Wilsonian ideals, which had guided U.S. foreign relations throughout the twentieth century. Political scientist Amos Perlmutter saw Wilsonianism as the alternative to communism and fascism, and welcomed its final triumph. Yet he emphasized that ideology alone had not won America's victories over Nazi Germany and the Soviet Union. He also credited military force. "Under the banner of progressive internationalism and the ideal of democracy lies a nationalist concept," he stressed. Moreover, the United States needed to continue its role as the global

---

[32] John Gerard Ruggie, *Winning the Peace: America and World Order in the New Era* (New York, 1996).

[33] Robert C. McNamara, and James G. Blight, *Wilson's Ghost: Reducing the Risk of Conflict, Killing, and Catastrophe in the Twenty-first Century* (New York, 2003), 3.

hegemon. Peace required enforcement by great powers. While recognizing that "the Wilsonian legacy of democracy and self-determination cast a long shadow over U.S. foreign policy concepts, and to some extent still does in the Clinton era," Perlmutter warned Americans not to place false confidence in this liberal promise. "A great misconception on the part of President Wilson was that the evolution of democratic regimes would lead to a peaceful international order. No such evidence has been seen in this century."[34] Historian Frank Ninkovich, however, emphasized the crucial role of Wilsonian idealism in the defeat of totalitarianism. "For the United States," he contended, "ideology worked." It gave real power to the United States to vanquish its fascist and communist enemies during "the Wilsonian century."[35] Political scientist Michael Mandelbaum agreed that liberal democracy and capitalism now prevailed in the world and provided the foundation for peace. He believed that Wilson's legacy of peace, democracy, and free markets had furnished "the ideas that conquered the world."[36]

With the collapse of the Soviet Union and communism, a new world order had emerged that seemed to fulfill Wilson's vision. The old strategic balance no longer existed in this era of globalization and modernization, which opened new opportunities for humanitarian intervention to promote democracy and human rights. The United States, now the world's unipolar power, could promote its ideals without the risk of war that had characterized the Cold War. In this age of global governance, political scientist Anne-Marie Slaughter avowed in *A New World Order* (2004), transnational as well as domestic networks empowered people and resulted in "a new conception of democracy, of what self-government actually means. It is a horizontal conception of government, resting on the empirical fact of mushrooming private governance regimes in which individuals, groups, and corporate entities in domestic and transnational society generate the rules, norms, and principles they are prepared to live by ... without relying on a higher authority."[37] This complex form of multilateralism had presumably made the world safe for liberal democracy and capitalism.

---

[34] Amos Perlmutter, *Making the World Safe for Democracy: A Century of Wilsonianism and Its Totalitarian Challengers* (Chapel Hill, NC, 1997), 35, 134, 165–66.

[35] Frank Ninkovich, *The Wilsonian Century: U.S. Foreign Policy Since 1900* (Chicago, 1999), 5.

[36] Michael Mandelbaum, *The Ideas that Conquered the World: Peace, Democracy, and Free Markets in the Twenty-first Century* (New York, 2002).

[37] Anne-Marie Slaughter, *A New World Order* (Princeton, NJ, 2004), 194–95.

George W. Bush's global war on terrorism, however, generated new controversy over the relevance and meaning of Wilsonianism in the twenty-first century. To justify his war of choice against Iraq, not just Afghanistan for its role in 9/11, he appealed to Wilsonian ideals. Liberal advocates of democracy promotion and humanitarian intervention, such as Slaughter and journalist-scholar Samantha Power, were intellectually unequipped to question Bush's rationale for war when he used rhetoric so similar to theirs. In contrast, realists among political scientists and historians, such as Ronald Steel, Michael Howard, Walter A. McDougall, John J. Mearsheimer, and Norman A. Graebner, refused to join Bush's crusade or endorse his doctrine of preemptive war. They were concerned about the means he used, not just the ends he promised. Realists understood the costs of war and the likelihood of unintended consequences. Recognizing the limits of American power, they did not expect world history – perhaps guided by Divine Providence – to end with the universal triumph of modern liberalism.[38] Some liberals recoiled as they recognized how Bush had used the Wilsonian legacy. Journalist John B. Judis criticized him for repeating the mistakes of America's imperial experience a century earlier. Theodore Roosevelt and Wilson had come to understand "the folly of empire," but Bush failed to learn this lesson.[39] Tony Smith viewed Washington's bid for world supremacy as the betrayal of the American promise. He now regretted that liberal proponents of worldwide democracy promotion had given intellectual credibility to Bush's wars. They had, unfortunately, made "a pact with the Devil."[40] Even some neoconservatives had second thoughts after witnessing the results of Bush's global war on terrorism. Fukuyama still criticized realists for not sharing the post–Cold War consensus in favor of intervening in other countries to promote freedom and democracy. Yet he understood their point about overlooking means while focusing on Wilsonian ideals. "What we need, in other words," he attempted to explain, "is a more realistic Wilsonianism that better matches means to ends in dealing with other societies."[41]

---

[38] Lloyd E. Ambrosius, "Woodrow Wilson and George W. Bush: Historical Comparisons of Ends and Means in Their Foreign Policies," *Diplomatic History* 30 (2006): 509–43; Stephen Wertheim, "A Solution from Hell: The United States and the Rise of Humanitarian Interventionism, 1991–2003," *Journal of Genocide Research* 12 (2010): 149–72.

[39] John B. Judis, *The Folly of Empire: What George W. Bush Could Learn from Theodore Roosevelt and Woodrow Wilson* (New York, 2004).

[40] Tony Smith, *A Pact with the Devil: Washington's Bid for World Supremacy and the Betrayal of the American Promise* (New York, 2007).

[41] Francis Fukuyama, *America at the Crossroads: Democracy, Power, and the Neoconservative Legacy* (New Haven, CT, 2006), 9.

CONTESTED LEGACY AND DISPUTED REPUTATION

Controversy over the meaning and relevance of Wilsonianism in the twenty-first century coincided with the crisis of American foreign policy in the wake of Bush's wars. While devaluing the Wilsonian legacy of the New Deal for the world, he touted Wilsonian ideals.[42] "The survival of liberty in our land increasingly depends on the success of liberty in other lands," he proclaimed on January 20, 2005. "The best hope for peace in our world is the expansion of freedom in all the world.... So it is the policy of the United States to seek and support the growth of democratic movements and institutions in every nation and culture, with the ultimate goal of ending tyranny in our world."[43] Bush ignored the destructive potential of American exceptionalism, which realists had warned against. "As a blueprint for world order," historian Walter A. McDougall had admonished, "Wilsonianism has always been a chimera, but as an ideological weapon against 'every arbitrary power anywhere,' it has proved mighty indeed. And that, in the end, is how Wilson did truly imitate Jesus. He brought not peace but a sword."[44] In view of Bush's use (or misuse) of the Wilsonian legacy, some liberals, such as Tony Smith, lamented their role in giving legitimacy to the global war on terrorism. Others did not. Anne-Marie Slaughter lambasted Smith for losing faith in the progressive Wilsonian values that had made America and should guide it in the dangerous world. Still others, such as historian Thomas J. Knock, denied that Wilson would have endorsed Bush's policies, thereby reaffirming Wilson's legacy and reputation.[45] Frank Ninkovich exonerated Wilson in a different way. He argued that Wilsonianism was dead. It was no longer relevant, paradoxically, because it had succeeded in creating a new world order during "the Wilsonian century."[46]

---

[42] Philippe Sands, *Lawless World: America and the Making and Breaking of Global Rules from FDR's Atlantic Charter to George W. Bush's Illegal War* (New York, 2005).

[43] George W. Bush, "Inaugural Address," January 20, 2005, by Gerhard Peters and John T. Woolley, The American Presidency Project, <www.presidency.ucsb.edu/ws/?pid=58745>.

[44] Walter A. McDougall, *Promised Land, Crusader State: The American Encounter with the World Since 1776* (Boston, 1997), 146.

[45] G. John Ikenberry, Thomas J. Knock, Anne-Marie Slaughter, and Tony Smith, *The Crisis of American Foreign Policy: Wilsonianism in the Twenty-first Century* (Princeton, NJ, 2009); Anne-Marie Slaughter, *The Idea That Is America: Keeping Faith with Our Values in a Dangerous World* (New York, 2007); Anne-Marie Slaughter, "Afterward: Making Democracy Safe for the World," *Reconsidering Woodrow Wilson*, 327–35.

[46] Frank Ninkovich, "Wilsonianism after the Cold War: 'Words, Words, Mere Words,'" *Reconsidering Woodrow Wilson*, 299–325.

Profound disagreements characterized the debate among scholars. Historian Joan Hoff criticized America's use of illiberal means in pursuit of its high ideals, which had produced "a Faustian foreign policy from Woodrow Wilson to George W. Bush."[47] Journalist-scholar Peter Beinart agreed that hubris characterized these and other U.S. presidents who, suffering "the Icarus syndrome," promised a new world order but produced tragedy. He had supported Bush's wars but later recanted and came to appreciate the wisdom of realists.[48] John Cooper rejected any such critical interpretation of Wilson as "a secular messiah or a naïve, woolly-headed idealist" with dreams of perfectibility, arguing that he was instead "one of the most careful, hardheaded, and sophisticated idealists of his time."[49] As during his presidency, Wilson remained controversial in the twenty-first century. He left a contested legacy and disputed reputation.

[47] Joan Hoff, *A Faustian Foreign Policy from Woodrow Wilson to George W. Bush: Dreams of Perfectibility* (Cambridge, 2008).
[48] Peter Beinart, *The Icarus Syndrome: A History of American Hubris* (New York, 2010).
[49] John Milton Cooper, Jr., *Woodrow Wilson: A Biography* (New York, 2009), 5.

Conclusion

During World War I, Woodrow Wilson offered his vision of a new world order based on his understanding of American and world history. He drew on his Americanism to define a new internationalism, known as Wilsonianism. Other Americans, such as Theodore Roosevelt and Henry Cabot Lodge, advocated alternative concepts of internationalism and different views of America's place in the world. Americans were not alone in reconciling their nationalism with various forms of internationalism. On both sides of the Great War, the Allies and the Central Powers also identified their national and imperial interests with their global war aims. Anticolonial nationalists, who wanted independence from the empires of the great powers, identified their national interests with the Wilsonian promise of a new world order. So too did leaders of the new nations that emerged from the collapse of the Russian, Austro-Hungarian, German, and Ottoman empires. All these competing claims made it impossible for Wilson and the Allies in 1919 to negotiate a peace settlement that reconciled the differences in a deeply divided world.

In this era of both nationalism and internationalism, Wilsonianism was only one of many alternatives. With the Bolshevik seizure of power during the Russian Revolution, Vladimir I. Lenin offered his Marxist vision of international communism, which rivaled Wilsonianism throughout most of the twentieth century. All too frequently historians have interpreted World War I and its legacy from a single national or ideological perspective, overlooking the rich diversity of peoples and cultures in the modern world. While recognizing that globalization was connecting the world and making it increasingly interdependent, they often failed to appreciate its continuing pluralism. Like Wilson or Lenin, they assumed that world history was progressing in a single direction and that, sooner or later, it would culminate in the triumph of a particular vision. When Lenin's promise of international communism obviously failed with the collapse of the Soviet Union, it appeared that the Wilsonian alternative of liberal democracy and capitalism had finally triumphed. But the terrorist attacks on 9/11 shattered that illusion, or at least should have. After World War I, Wilson had not succeeded in creating an international community based on Western civilization, as he understood it from a particular American perspective. Nor did subsequent American and other Western advocates of his legacy of liberal internationalism establish such a worldwide community of nations later in the twentieth century. Nor did any alternative vision of a global society or civilization become universally accepted. Pluralism still existed in the modern world.

To understand America's place in the world, historians need to recognize its diversity as well as its interconnectedness. For better or worse, the modern world has both come together and fallen apart. This pattern, which World War I vividly demonstrated, has continued to shape international relations ever since. The contemporary historiographical trends that have produced the emerging field of world history and the internationalizing of American history have pointed in the right direction toward understanding the United States in a global context. This book on Woodrow Wilson and American internationalism, hopefully, has also done so for its readers.

Index